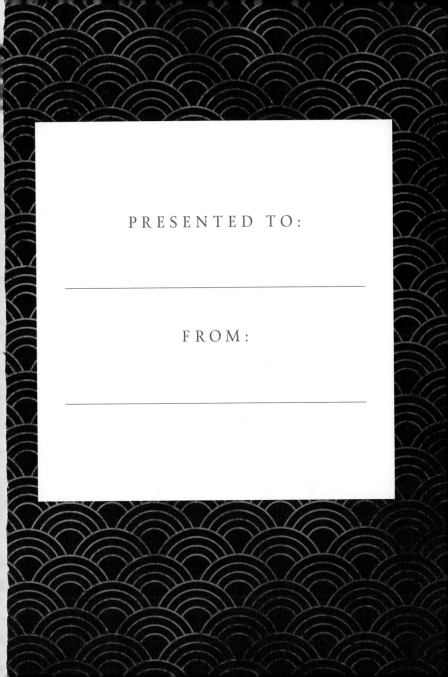

PRESENTED TO:

_____

FROM:

_____

In MOMENTS *Like These*

DAVID JEREMIAH

with Dr. David Jeremiah

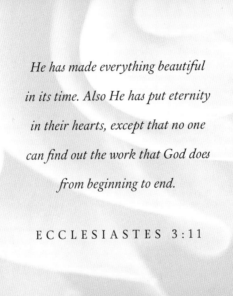

He has made everything beautiful

in its time. Also He has put eternity

in their hearts, except that no one

can find out the work that God does

from beginning to end.

ECCLESIASTES 3:11

INTRODUCTION

Our lives are filled with many moments—
times of joy over the birth of a child, times
of sorrow over the death of a loved one, and
then there are moments when we are confused about what direction to take or even
where to live and work. The joy of being a
Christian is that whatever "moment" we find
ourselves in, God is there with us. What a
precious promise that He will never leave us
or forsake us (Hebrews 13:5). That knowledge
makes the happy times even more joyful, and
the sad times bearable—for He is with us!

To keep attuned to God, we need to stay
in contact with Him through His Word. He
speaks to us through His Word, He gives
direction through His Word—the Word
has the answers to our questions. That is the

purpose for planning a time each day to read His Word, to pray, and seek His face—to keep our line of communication open with our Heavenly Father. Our hope is that this devotional will encourage you in your walk and enrich your time with the Lord.

As you begin your daily journey into Bible study in the coming year, thank God for the moments we have to live for Him and learn more about His amazing love for us. Take the time to read the Scripture daily and pray that God will open your eyes of understanding as you read. Apply the truths found in each devotional and Scripture for that day to your life. Having the Word of God in your heart and mind will give you a renewed sense of His presence as you go throughout your day. You will discover even more opportunities to worship Him and to rejoice in what He provided for you—*In Moments Like These*.

JANUARY

JANUARY 1
Begin With God

But seek first the kingdom of God and His righteousness.
MATTHEW 6:33

There are many vocations focused on problem-solving: consultants, psychologists, psychiatrists, counselors, practitioners, advisors, life coaches, mentors, and more. Some may be biblically focused, but most use secular approaches to solving problems.

Because Christians live in the world, it is hard not to be influenced by how the world approaches life—which is generally not from a biblical perspective. We need to constantly remember that no one knows as much about our life, our circumstances, and the solutions we need than God. While we may end up getting helpful advice from a consultant of some sort, our first counselor should be God: *Lord, You know my situation and my need. I begin with You, asking for You to be involved in this with me. Give me Your wisdom; help me choose the right path; show me Your purposes; reveal to me any error on my part. If You want me to get help from others, please show me who to talk to.*

If you need wisdom or guidance today, begin with God. Start by asking Him to direct your thoughts and your steps.

JANUARY 2
Patterns for Prayer

Be anxious for nothing, but in everything by prayer and supplication, with thanksgiving, let your requests be made known to God.
PHILIPPIANS 4:6

If someone suggests praying according to ACTS, they may mean to follow this pattern: Adoration, Confession, Thanksgiving, Supplication. Or you could use the PRAISE pattern: Praise, Repentance, Ask, Intercede, Speak the Word, and Enjoy His presence. Those and other acronyms serve as good patterns for prayer—ways to keep prayers purposeful.

The prayer Jesus gave His disciples is also helpful. We know it as the Lord's Prayer, though it could be called the Disciple's Prayer (Matthew 6:9-13). It begins with praise (verse 9), a desire for God's kingdom (verse 10), a petition for provision (verse 11), a desire to be forgiving and forgiven (verse 12), a prayer for spiritual protection (verse 13), and concludes with a confession of God's sovereignty (verse 13). Such an outline has served Christians well for twenty centuries.

First, pray! Second, develop a pattern of prayer that incorporates themes of praise, thanksgiving, confession, meditation, intercession, petition, and more. Such patterns can serve as a guide for the time you spend alone with God.

JANUARY 3
The Weight of the World

The Lord is my light and my salvation; whom shall I fear?
The Lord is the strength of my life; of whom shall I be afraid?
PSALM 27:1

When it comes to lifting weights, there is a tremendous gap between professionals and beginners. Professionals have trained and know how to lift heavy weights without injuring themselves, while beginners are prone to injury.

When David faced unceasing persecution from King Saul, the weight of his circumstances and responsibilities crushed his soul. Fear and depression began to dictate his reality and choices. He fled to the land of the Philistines for safety and lived deceitfully under the rule of King Achish.

When it comes to difficulty, we will always be beginners. Certain situations use up all the strength we have: emotional, physical, and even spiritual strength. When we feel the weight of the world on our shoulders, we can carry it on our own or we can look to God. Our burdens are light to Him. As we meditate on His promises amidst the storms of life and listen for His guidance, He will remind us that this situation is not the end of our story. He is the God of possibilities and hope. We have a future.

For Jesus, With Jesus

*Though He was a Son, yet He learned obedience
by the things which He suffered.*
HEBREWS 5:8

In the classic board game Monopoly®, one of the most coveted cards to draw is the orange "Get Out of Jail Free" card. Every player eventually winds up in jail—you land on the policeman in the corner or you draw the "Go Directly to Jail" card. But if you have the "Get Out of Jail Free" card … no problem! You can go to jail and get out of jail in the same turn!

That's fun because it's a game. Unfortunately, life doesn't work that way. Sometimes we end up in the jail of suffering, calamity, sickness, trouble, or pain—and there is no orange card to set us free. New Christians sometimes think following Jesus means no more troubles. Then they learn that Jesus suffered during all three years of His earthly ministry. And His disciples, later as apostles, suffered as well, even as they walked in God's will. Here's what we must remember: Suffering *for* Jesus is to suffer *with* Jesus. He promised to be with us until the end (Matthew 28:20), never leaving or forsaking us (Hebrews 13:5).

Following Jesus, whether through blessings or burdens, has the same result: being conformed to His image (Romans 8:28-29).

JANUARY 5
To a God Who Loves Me

*Moreover David said, "The Lord, who delivered me
from the paw of the lion and from the paw of the bear,
He will deliver me from the hand of this Philistine."*
1 SAMUEL 17:37

There is a common denominator when people give a shout-out
to a friend, teammate, coworker, or other significant person:
Shout-outs occur in public. No one sits alone in a room and
gives a shout-out to someone. It's always for the benefit of
others—out loud, for specific reasons, to praise or thank
another person.

The Bible is full of people giving a shout-out to God for a
multitude of reasons. Young David is a good example. When
he was about to face the Philistine giant, Goliath, he praised
God—out loud and for specific reasons. First, he praised
God for His deliverance in the past from wild animals. This
was a clear message to Goliath to beware of God's power. But
then David did something else: He gave God a shout-out for
something that hadn't even happened yet. He thanked God that
he would be delivered "from the hand of this Philistine." David
knew the promise of God's love was as certain for the future as
for the past.

When was the last time you praised God—out loud, in
public—for His love and provision for you?

Your Neighbor

But a certain Samaritan, as he journeyed, came where
he was. And when he saw him, he had compassion.
LUKE 10:33

Context is so important when reading the Bible! Take the story of the Good Samaritan for instance (Luke 10:25-37). Everyone knows the story: a man being kind to a stranger. But there is more to the story. Jesus told it in response to a question from a lawyer: "Who is my neighbor?" (verse 29) That is, since the Law says "love your neighbor" (Leviticus 19:18), who is my neighbor? Who am I bound to love?

Jesus answered the question with a story: A Jew was set upon by robbers who stole his goods and left him for dead. Two Jewish religious leaders passed by and ignored the man's plight. But when a cultural enemy of the man came by—a Samaritan—he stopped to help the injured man. The Samaritan "had compassion" on the man. He bound the man's wounds, took him to an inn, and paid for his care. The Samaritan used what resources he had with him—oil, wine, money—to meet the injured stranger's needs. Jesus' point: Compassion is based not on wealth or party lines; it is based on a willingness to help with whatever we have.

Who is your neighbor? On whom can you have compassion today? If your resources match another's need, do what you can.

JANUARY 7
Profitable

Blessed are You, O Lord! Teach me your statutes.
PSALM 119:12

Most of us develop proficiency in some area of life. School-teachers master their subjects. Investors grasp the ins and outs of the stock market. Mechanics learn their way around engines. Baristas learn to make the perfect caramel macchiato.

Christians should become proficient with God's Word, for the moment we trust Christ as Savior, we enter the school of Scripture. We hear it being taught and preached; we read books about it; but most of all, we spend time reading it line by line, precept upon precept, word upon word. The Bible may seem confusing at first, but the more we study it, the clearer it becomes.

As we read the Bible as seen in 2 Timothy 3:16, we learn more about God's Truth (doctrine). We learn what we're doing wrong (reproof). We often read a passage about how we can live better (correction). And much of the Bible simply helps us grow to be more like Christ (instruction in righteousness).

Perhaps we should trade in some television or social media time for serious Bible study. It's more profitable!

JANUARY 8
Glory Where Glory Is Due

But thanks be to God, who gives us the victory through our Lord Jesus Christ.
1 CORINTHIANS 15:57

Most Protestant Christians are familiar with what is referred to as the Common Doxology which begins, "Praise God, from whom all blessings flow: praise Him, all creatures here below." It was composed in 1674 as the final verse of two hymns used in morning and evening worship at England's Winchester College. There is a world of theology and counsel bound up in the phrase, "from whom all blessings flow."

And there is a world of danger in forgetting that God is the source of all we have: victory, strength, blessing, success—it all comes from Him. The danger is that we might accumulate credit unto ourselves for our victories and successes instead of giving credit and glory to Him. That is, we put ourselves in the place of God as the source of all that is good. Everything can be traced back to God. Yes, we may use our intelligence and skill in daily life—but where does intelligence and skill come from? As the Doxology says, we "praise God from whom all blessings flow." Some blessings come directly and some indirectly. But He is the source of them all.

Make sure to give credit, glory, and thanks to God for what He enables you to accomplish in life.

JANUARY 9
Abundant Life

I am the vine, you are the branches. He who abides in Me, and I in him,
bears much fruit; for without Me you can do nothing.
JOHN 15:5

What if our life had a single purpose and we kept it at the forefront of our minds every moment of the day—to stay connected to Christ. It's easy to make our connection to Christ complicated by a long to-do list: pray more, go to church, read the Bible, serve others, practice patience …. It's easy to get lost in tasks instead of remembering the Creator. This leads to shame over tasks forgotten or under-performed. We forget that Jesus is "the author and finisher of our faith" (Hebrews 12:2).

When we focus fully on connecting and less on performing, spiritual practices become stepping stones to Him. Spiritual practices without love are empty, but when they are practiced with the single desire of drawing close to God and hearing His voice, our faith is strengthened.

Abundant life comes from God's work in and through us. As we use spiritual practices to express our love for Christ and experience His love, our hearts and desires become entwined with His. Everything we seek is found in God's powerful and eternal presence. Which stepping stone will you choose to draw close to Him today?

JANUARY 10
Bumping Into Isaiah

The Lord said to Isaiah, "Go out now to meet Ahaz … and say to him: 'Take heed, and be quiet; do not fear or be fainthearted.'"
ISAIAH 7:3-4

Imagine you are in a distressing place in life, say, at a hospital as a loved one languishes. Or in a courthouse before the verdict is rendered. Or in an office building before the financial reports are issued. You're tense, uneasy, and discouraged. But imagine walking down the corridor, turning the corner, and bumping into an olive-skinned young man, robe-clad, with a short black beard. Imagine it was Isaiah the prophet, and he pulled you aside. He had a message from God for you: "Take heed, and be quiet; do not fear or be fainthearted."

That's what happened to Ahaz, and it happens to us whenever we open the Bible. Almighty God sent Isaiah, Moses, Luke, Paul, and all the other biblical writers with an infallible message, and, by interpreting the verses correctly, we can put our names in them and apply their truths to our situations.

Personal Bible study yields a myriad of outcomes, including inner peace, moral clarity, and good works.

Those who live according to the flesh set their minds on the things of the flesh, but those who live according to the Spirit, the things of the Spirit.
ROMANS 8:5

Sexual harassment cases have ruined a "who's who" of reputations in recent years, and much of the blame falls on our pornographic culture. Writing in the *Los Angeles Times*, Zac Crippen points out that behind the harassment problem is a pornography crisis, which has fostered a sexually aggressive society. "Nobody is talking about what could be one of the most effective ways to attack the problem: Recognizing that pornography consumption is a public health crisis," Crippen said.

Like most addictions, pornographic habits are difficult to control, and it requires great effort to keep one's mind and habits free from immorality. But we possess a powerful weapon in God's Word—the sword of the Spirit. Scripture offers protection against the lust of the flesh. We must set our minds on the things of the Spirit, and nothing helps more than Bible study and Scripture memorization.

Do you need a healing verse to memorize today? Try Romans 8:6: "The mind governed by the flesh is death, but the mind governed by the Spirit is life and peace" (NIV).

JANUARY 12
Love Like God Loves

He who does not love does not know God, for God is love.
1 JOHN 4:8

You have no doubt learned to expect certain traits to be evident in certain friends when you meet with them. Perhaps one is consistently encouraging, another is always humorous or winsome, still another is caring and kind. While those who met Jesus face-to-face would have encountered many godly traits, they could all be incorporated into this: "God is *love*" (1 John 4:8, 16). Because Jesus is God, He also is love. Jesus never failed to show love in what He did and said.

Jesus said to His disciples, "By this all will know that you are My disciples, if you have love for one another" (John 13:35). Why? Because He knew the Holy Spirit would soon come to indwell His followers and manifest His (Christ's) life in them. If God is love and Jesus is God, and if the Holy Spirit is God in us, then love will always be present in and through us—provided we allow the Spirit of God unhindered lordship in our life. Paul conveys that by describing the fruit of the Spirit, the first of which is love (Galatians 5:22-23).

Live your life "filled with the Spirit" (Ephesians 5:18) and manifest the love of God to all you meet. Let them learn to expect love whenever they meet you.

JANUARY 13
A Blessed By-Product

Blessed is the one who trusts in the Lord.
PSALM 40:4, NIV

When a giant oak, cedar, walnut, or pine tree is ripped into planks at a sawmill, lumber is the product. But there are by-products, too. In the case of sawmills sawing lumber, there are two by-products: bark and sawdust. And they have huge value. Bark is turned into mulch for our yards, sawdust is made into particleboard, briquettes for wood stoves, and pulp for making paper.

There are "by-products" in the spiritual life as well, being blessed is one the Bible identifies clearly. An oft-used phrase in Scripture is, "Blessed is the man who." In fact, Jesus' Beatitudes are based on the by-product premise (Matthew 5:1-12). What does this mean? It means the person who does something or other will be happy, or blessed. Happiness is a by-product of doing something specific. In the case of Psalm 40:4, happiness is a result of trusting in the Lord. In Psalm 1:1-2, happiness comes from delighting in God's Word. Our modern culture seeks happiness as an end-game, a quest that is rarely rewarded. True happiness is not a product but a by-product of knowing God.

Are you happy today? Continue to put your trust in God and His Word and watch as happiness rises in your heart.

JANUARY 14
Children of the Day

You are all sons of light and sons of the day.
We are not of the night nor of darkness.
1 THESSALONIANS 5:5

When evangelist Vance Havner was advanced in age, his wife died. His grief and loneliness overwhelmed him, but he determined to persevere in his work with an increased longing for heaven. He wrote, "I once read of a man who lived beside a river but had little interest in the people on the other side until his daughter moved over there to live. I have lived beside the river many years, but this past year has heightened a thousand-fold my concern about the other side."[1]

Every passing day brings us closer to heaven and closer to our loved ones who have preceded us, and one day soon we'll have the reunion of the ages to enjoy. But until then, we must press on with cheerful faithfulness, walking and working as children of the day.

In these dark times, we must spread the light and patiently persevere for Christ's return.

[1] Vance Havner, *Hope Thou in God* (Old Tappan, NJ: Fleming H. Revell Co., 1977), 107-108, 126.

If My people who are called by My name will humble themselves, and pray and seek My face, and turn from their wicked ways, then I will hear from heaven, and will forgive their sin and heal their land.

2 CHRONICLES 7:14

The ebb and flow of mankind's connection to God is woven throughout the Bible. In the beginning, there was a strong and intimate connection of trust. When the serpent deceived Adam and Eve, their relationship with God was broken. Instead of remembering the goodness of God in giving them life and abundantly providing for them, they believed they could attain more on their own.

The struggle between prideful self-sufficiency and trust in a kind and generous God continues today. The ministry of Jesus was an open invitation to a restored connection with God. When He taught His disciples to pray, He was inviting them back into a relationship with God as "our Father." Jesus paid the ultimate price so that nothing could ever separate us from God's love. Just as a father does not despise his children's weaknesses or ignore their need for help, God provided the perfection of Christ so that everyone could be welcomed in. Will you call out to Him today and trust Him with your life and challenges?

Spiritual Journaling

*Treasure my commands within you .... Write
them on the tablet of your heart.*
PROVERBS 7:1, 3

When writing God's Word on the tablet of your heart, it's sometimes helpful to also use pen and ink to record it on a piece of paper at your desk. From early Christian history, believers have practiced journaling as an aid to spiritual growth.

How to start? First, use whatever technique works best for you. Some people use applications on their phones or laptops, others use a paper journal, a calendar with enough space for notes, or a wide-margined Bible.

Second, jot down whatever is helpful to you. You might choose to write a short paragraph about your day to keep track of the events of your life. Otherwise, simply record the passage you're coming to in your daily Bible reading along with insights from the verses. If you want to take your journal to church, it's a good place to record sermon notes.

Third, connect journaling to your daily time of Bible study and prayer. Add a thanksgiving list or a prayer list if you like. Keep it simple, but do it consistently. As you make your walk with God a priority, journaling is a great way to establish consistency in your steps.

JANUARY 17
The Only Way

When He had by Himself purged our sins, [He] sat down at the right hand of the Majesty on high.

HEBREWS 1:3

In an age of tolerance and compromise, the idea that there is only one way to do something is roundly rejected. "One way" is considered narrow-minded, intolerant, inconsiderate, and even disrespectful. So it's not surprising that the New Testament's message of forgiveness through Jesus alone is not received by many.

The writer of the letter to the Hebrews was not hesitant to make a "narrow" point about Jesus. He spent the first ten chapters of his epistle pointing out that Jesus did what no one else in Israel's history had been able to do: provide salvation from sin, once and for all. The writer points out that Jesus was superior to the angels, to Moses, to the thousands of Aaronic priests, and to the sacrifices of those priests. "By Himself [Jesus] purged our sins [and] sat down at the right hand" of God—something no one else could have done. Peter confirmed that narrow point of view by saying there is salvation in no one else besides Jesus (Acts 4:12).

Are you willing to embrace the Bible's presentation of Jesus as the only Savior of mankind? It may not be popular, but it is true.

The Living Book

For the word of God is living and powerful, and sharper than any two-edged sword, piercing even to the division of soul and spirit, and of joints and marrow, and is a discerner of the thoughts and intents of the heart.
HEBREWS 4:12

Amazon.com has more than 3 million book titles for sale. In spite of the claims those books make, none makes a claim like the Bible makes about itself: that it is alive.

What does that mean? It means the Bible is not just words. The words are inspired by God's Spirit (see 2 Timothy 3:16). And because the words are alive, they can find their way into the lives of those who read them, right down to the division between soul and spirit, joints and marrow—down into the inner parts of our life. God's Word can even cause us to see the true intention of our thoughts and desires. And, like all living things, the Word of God can produce new life. As Peter wrote, we are "born again ... through the living and enduring word of God" (1 Peter 1:23, NIV).

Be forewarned: Reading the Bible is not like reading any other book. It has the power to change your life!

JANUARY 19
View From the Summit

Then he said, "O Lord God of my master Abraham,
please give me success this day."
GENESIS 24:12

In Genesis 24, the patriarch Abraham sent his servant on a mission to find a bride for Isaac, and all along the way the servant pleaded with God for success, knowing the only true success we experience in life comes from prayer and perseverance. God gave the servant success, and Isaac received his bride.

In her book *Reach for the Summit*, former Tennessee basketball coach Pat Summitt wrote, "There are different kinds of success. There is fame and fortune, which … is a pretty flimsy, short-lived kind of success. Then there is the more gratifying kind of success that comes from doing something you love, and doing it well. Still another kind of success results from committing to one person and raising a child with them. Yet another is finding a sustained faith in your church. But notice something about all the various forms of success. They are *open-ended*. They aren't tasks that you finish. Success is a project that's always under construction."[2]

God wants to give us success as He defines it—the fulfilling of His perfect will for our lives. That's a lifelong process that unfolds as we follow Him daily.

[2] Pat Summitt, *Reach for the Summit* (NY: Broadway Books, 1998), chapter 12.

A Life Worth Living

The following day Jesus wanted to go to Galilee, and
He found Philip and said to him, "Follow Me."
JOHN 1:43

Dr. Martin Luther King Jr. is credited with observing that life is not worth living until you find something worth dying for. When Jesus called His first disciples in the region of Galilee, they followed Him without knowing very much about Him. But they would all die for Him eventually. Between their calling and their death, they discovered that Jesus was worth living *and* dying for.

The Christian life begins with a profession of faith, a willingness to follow Jesus. The longer we follow Him, the more we leave our old self behind. We "put off the old man with his deeds" (Colossians 3:9) and "put on the new man which was created according to God, in true righteousness and holiness" (Ephesians 4:24). When we see the old man fading in our memory and the new man becoming the reality of our lives, we realize what following Christ has done. Following Christ changes our lives.

Are you following Christ? If so, is your life changing? Look for markers today that the old is being replaced by the new.

JANUARY 21
Children of the Father

Jesus said to them, "If you were Abraham's children, you would do the works of Abraham. ... You do the deeds of your father."

JOHN 8:39, 41

The phrase "chip of the same block" dates back at least to a 1621 sermon: "Am not I a child of the same Adam ... a chip of the same block, with him?" (English bishop Robert Sanderson's *Sermons*.) Later, it became "chip *off* the old block," referring to a parent (the block) and a child (the chip). We all know what it means: Children are often much like their parents.

Jesus affirmed this point when talking with religious leaders who were proud of their Abrahamic lineage but were also seeking to kill Him. Because of that disconnect, Jesus said they were not children of Abraham but were children of the devil (John 8:34-47). Jesus said He did what He learned from His Father and they did what they had learned from theirs (verse 38). That is a strong indictment, but full of theology. The whole purpose of the new birth (John 3:3) is to be transferred from one family to another (from Satan's family to God's—Colossians 1:13).

Ask the Father to reveal the family likeness in you by the fruit of the Spirit in your life (Galatians 5:22-23).

JANUARY 22
Cocoon of Light

Your word is a lamp to my feet and a light to my path.
PSALM 119:105

Just as a caterpillar enters the safety and security of a cocoon to be transformed into a butterfly, Christians enter God's Word to be transformed. Even though we may wish our lives were linear and steady, our days are marked by change and the unexpected. When we are faced with a dilemma or challenge, it can feel as though we are facing a locked door or wandering lost in a dark forest.

God's Word is His vessel of divine guidance, wisdom, and assurance. When we neglect God's Word, we neglect the transformation He offers. In His Word we are reminded that we do not need to worry about our lives: He is the God who protects, provides, and pursues us. It is often through His Word that we find the answer to a lingering question, and a new path forward appears.

God does not simply reveal existing paths, He creates new paths where there were none before—through water, through fire, and even through death. Satan provides many excuses and lies to keep us from meditating on God's Truth because our transformation has a powerful effect on those around us.

The Overseer of Your Soul

*For you were like sheep going astray, but have now returned
to the Shepherd and Overseer of your souls.*
1 PETER 2:25

Sometimes an employee is offered a promotion and he or she says, "Thank you, but I'm good." There could be many reasons for such a response, one of which is not wanting the burden of increased responsibility. Supervision and leadership come with a price. Perhaps not everyone wants to pay that price when the opportunity arises. No problem—it's a matter of priorities and preferences.

What might Jesus' response have been when offered the responsibility of becoming "Shepherd and Overseer" of all the human beings who willingly turned to God in repentance and faith? Fortunately, He said "Yes." He paid the ultimate price to accomplish the Father's will and become Overseer of our soul. And what does it mean for us? It means that Jesus Christ is both Shepherd and Overseer of *your* life—all of it. There is no aspect of your life to which He is not attentive. A human overseer—elder, pastor, boss, supervisor—may disappoint, but Jesus will not.

Put your faith in the One who willingly has said, "I will watch out for his soul; I will oversee her life."

JANUARY 24
Shortly

And the Lord God of the holy prophets sent His angel to show His servants the things which must shortly take place.
REVELATION 22:6

Sir Isaac Newton, the father of physics, was an ardent student of Scripture who maintained a lifelong interest in prophecy. He felt too many people were setting dates for the end of the world, but he said the end would not come until wicked nations are in ruins and the Jews are back in their ancient homeland. Based on his study of the Bible, Newton foresaw the world in crisis and the reestablishment of the state of Israel. But even Newton couldn't stop himself from setting a date. According to a recently discovered letter, he estimated the end of the world would occur in 2060.

It's tempting to speculate when Christ will return, but we do not know the day or year. We simply know His coming is "shortly." Romans 16:20 says, "The God of peace will crush Satan under your feet shortly." Revelation 1:1 says these things "must shortly take place."

People tend to ignore the ever-present warnings about the Last Days, but for the believer they represent our ever-present hope.

I have fought the good fight, I have finished the race, I have kept the faith.
2 TIMOTHY 4:7

When a baby is born, there are tears, laughter, hugs, pictures, relief, joy—it is one of life's most meaningful events. But birth is not the ultimate goal. Rather, birth is the beginning of a life of promise, hope, and redemption through submission to the plan of God for human life on earth.

Birth is the perfect metaphor for beginning the Christian life. No wonder Jesus told Nicodemus, "You must be born again" (John 3:7). There is often drama and excitement around spiritual birth just as with physical birth. But it is a mistake to believe that conversion to Christ by faith is the end of the Christian experience. Rather, it is just the beginning! Just as a baby grows slowly into mature adulthood, so born-again Christians are to begin the process of growth toward conformity to Christ (Romans 8:29). The New Testament uses the metaphor of growth from infancy to maturity to describe the Christian life (1 Corinthians 3:1-3; 14:20; 1 Peter 2:2).

Are you growing spiritually? Don't confuse the beginning of the Christian life with the goal. Take steps today and every day to allow the Spirit of God to move you steadily toward maturity in Christ.

JANUARY 26
A Rebellious Spirit

Therefore whoever resists the authority resists the ordinance of God, and those who resist will bring judgment on themselves.

ROMANS 13:2

A popular mindset in our culture is to rebel against authority. We love feeling autonomous, independent, stubborn, and in control. We dislike anyone telling us what to do. But remember what Samuel told King Saul: "Rebellion is as the sin of witchcraft" (1 Samuel 15:23).

According to the Bible, God ordained authority to maintain order in the world, the nation, and the home. That's why Romans 13 tells us to obey those in authority over us. Being ready to carry out the will of God sometimes means being ready to carry out the will of someone over us—like a child wisely obeying a parent. The exception comes when the authority tells us to do something contrary to the will of God, and then we must say, like Peter, "We ought to obey God rather than men" (Acts 5:29).

Has someone in authority over you—a parent, a boss, a public official—told you to act in a certain way? Wisdom listens, submits, and seeks God's will with humility. Don't let a rebellious spirit overtake your heart.

JANUARY 27
Whatever You Do

Therefore, whether you eat or drink, or whatever
you do, do all to the glory of God.
1 CORINTHIANS 10:31

When we think of giving praise to God, we usually think of it in terms of our words: "My lips shall utter praise" (Psalm 119:171). Does that mean if a person is unable to speak, he or she is unable to give praise to the Lord? Not at all. The Bible suggests that our whole life should be a testimony of praise to Him.

For example, the apostle Paul was called on to clarify some issues among the Christians in Corinth: Are there rules to follow regarding what foods are acceptable for eating (1 Corinthians 10)? Is it acceptable to eat meat from the market that is left over from pagan sacrifices? Paul went on to give guidelines about that subject and about taking other peoples' convictions into account. He summarized by saying, "Therefore, whether you eat or drink, *or whatever you do*, do all to the glory of God" (emphasis added). In other words, eating and drinking are just small parts of a whole life that is lived in praise to God. If our whole life is lived in praise to Him, then our eating and drinking will be as well.

Speak His praises today when you can, and live His praises at every moment of the day—*whatever you do.*

Blessed are the pure in heart, for they shall see God.

MATTHEW 5:8

Everyone remembers the epidemic of the Ebola virus in West Africa from 2013 to 2016. Some of the most memorable images are of the medical workers dressed in their protective gear from head to toe. They were so tightly sealed inside their suits that they could only work for short periods of time because of the stifling heat. But when fighting a virus like Ebola, good intentions are not enough. You can't *want* to protect yourself; you *have* to protect yourself. It's a matter of life and death.

Which is more powerful—a deadly virus or sin? Since deadly viruses are usually contained and sin is still rampant, it looks like sin is more powerful. So how much more careful should we be to avoid infection? Yes, Christ has delivered us from the penalty of sin, but He also made provision for protection from the power of sin. Yet resisting the power of sin is a daily battle. Jesus didn't commend those who hunger for holiness; He commended those who *are* holy—who willingly choose a life of purity. Those are the ones who will ultimately see God (Psalm 51:7; Isaiah 6:5; Revelation 22:4).

Live your life clothed with the armor of God (Ephesians 6:10-18)—your first line of defense against the power of sin.

*You are My friends if you do whatever I command you. No longer do
I call you servants, for a servant does not know what his master is
doing; but I have called you friends, for all things that I heard
from My Father I have made known to you.*

JOHN 15:14-15

Everyone has a circle of friends that gets more intimate as
the circle gets smaller. Jesus had 120 in His largest circle after
His ascension (Acts 1:15). Then there were seventy that were
trained disciples (Luke 10:1), and then twelve who were with
Him for three years (Matthew 26:20). Within that group were
His three closest friends—Peter, James, and John (Mark 9:2),
among whom John seems to have been the closest (John 13:23;
20:2).

In John 15:14, Jesus drew the lines of friendship a different
way: Anyone who keeps His commandments can be considered
His friend. By "friend" Jesus meant someone with whom He
would communicate and co-labor, someone He could trust to
carry out His will when He left earth and returned to heaven.
The question for today's believer is: Am I the kind of disciple
that Jesus would see as a friend? Am I committed to obeying
His commands? Can He count on me to fulfill His mission in
His absence?

Those who would be friends of Jesus may have to forsake
some earthly friends. It's one thing to be the friend of man,
another to be the friend of God.

Casting

There is no fear in love; but perfect love casts out fear.
1 JOHN 4:18

Most fishermen know all about casting, but some take it very seriously. In 1881, the first casting championships took place in the outskirts of London. This event led, over time, to the founding of the International Casting Sport Federation. Today, the Federation organizes championships around the world for all ages. Casters are judged by distance and accuracy.

Christ-followers know a lot about casting too. Psalm 55:22 says, "Cast your burden on the Lord, and He shall sustain you." Proverbs 22:10 says, "Cast out the scoffer, and contention will leave." Ecclesiastes 11:1 says, "Cast your bread upon the waters, for you will find it after many days." Ezekiel tells us to cast away our transgressions (Ezekiel 18:31). Jesus told His disciples to cast out their nets for a catch (John 21:6); Paul told us to cast out "the works of darkness" (Romans 13:12); and Peter told us to cast all our care on Him, for He cares for us (1 Peter 5:7).

The apostle John, who was, after all, a fisherman, added a special word in 1 John 4:18. We should remember how much God loves us, and be reminded that "There is no fear in love; but perfect love casts out fear."

He who sows sparingly will also reap sparingly, and he who sows bountifully will also reap bountifully. So let each one give.

2 CORINTHIANS 9:6-7

John Chapman, known as Johnny Appleseed, traveled throughout the Midwest, planting seeds for 45 years. It's estimated he spread more than twenty bushels of seeds, and each bushel contained an estimated 300,000 seeds. During Prohibition, the government cut down most of his trees to curtail hard cider. But one tree survives to this day. It's in the courtyard of the Johnny Appleseed Museum in Urbana, Ohio. It's old, but several branches have been grafted onto other trees, so the harvest continues.

Chapman knew the relationship between sowing and reaping. We always reap more than we sow. That is the harvest principle, which works with the concept of giving. When Paul mentioned sowing and reaping in 2 Corinthians 9, he had in mind the sowing of our financial gifts.

This doesn't mean we'll come into lots of money if we give to the Lord's work. As many people have experienced, wealth can be fleeting, but if we faithfully sow into His kingdom, we will reap blessings in both time and eternity far beyond our original gifts. Choose an investment that is reliable, is guaranteed to never fail, and yields great rewards. Invest in the kingdom of God.

FEBRUARY

FEBRUARY 1
Paradigm Shift

Now when [Jesus] had said these things, He cried
with a loud voice, "Lazarus, come forth!"
JOHN 11:43

A paradigm shift happens when a long-held pattern, model, or worldview is changed—something new happens that alters the way we look at life. A paradigm shift occurred in the three years of Jesus' ministry on earth. Prior to Jesus, the pattern was that dead people remain dead. But three times in three years, Jesus brought dead people back to life. They were raised to life, not resurrected; that is, they ultimately died again. But Jesus established a new model for viewing life: Death is not an unconquerable enemy (Hebrews 2:15).

We talk the most about Jesus' Resurrection, but we should not miss the significance of these three individuals who were raised to life by the Savior. Imagine what people of that day must have thought: dead people coming back to life! It was a signal that the kingdom of heaven Jesus was preaching about was a kingdom of power and compassion. It was a signal that death, life's greatest threat, is subject to the power of the Son of God.

We live in the age of the new paradigm—life in Christ is not ruled by death. The new life we have in Christ can be canceled by nothing (Romans 8:35-39).

FEBRUARY 2
God's Love

The Lord your God in your midst, the Mighty One, will save;
He will rejoice over you with gladness, He will quiet you
with His love, He will rejoice over you with singing.
ZEPHANIAH 3:17

Since 1908, the Gideons International has been placing Bibles
in motel and hotel rooms in the United States and distributing
Scripture around the world. Unique to the hotel Bibles is the
presentation of John 3:16 in many languages. Why this verse?
Because it epitomizes God's love for mankind: "God so loved
the world that He gave His only begotten Son."

In modern English-speaking cultures, *love* has been
mischaracterized and misspelled as *luv*—a warm and fuzzy
feeling. But love is not a feeling; love is an action. Just as God
gave the life of His Son to the world, Jesus said that the greatest
demonstration of love is to give one's life for another (John
15:13). Love gives many things: help, money, food, shelter,
advice, comfort, understanding, and more. Besides being an
action verb, love is also a noun, a thing. When we give love, it
is manifested as a selfless, sacrificial gift intended to bless and
make better the experience of the beloved.

Our model for giving is God Himself. He gave so that we
might be blessed. Imitate Him today by loving others through
giving.

FEBRUARY 3
Reading for Change

*Trust in the Lord with all your heart, and lean not
on your own understanding; in all your ways acknowledge
Him, and He shall direct your paths.*

PROVERBS 3:5-6

Successful writers agree on a principle for how to become
an accomplished writer: by *reading* great writing. Why does
reading great writing make one a better writer? Because your
mind becomes trained in the nuances of grammar, syntax, style,
punctuation, and flow. You begin to think like a better writer,
and as a result you become a better writer.

That principle could be applied to almost any field of
endeavor—training the mind to recognize and reproduce
the very best. And it is certainly true in terms of spiritual
development. When we spend consistent hours reading,
meditating on, and memorizing the Bible, it becomes the
guiding light for our pathway. We begin to understand "what
is that good and acceptable and perfect will of God" (Romans
12:2). The ways, means, values, and priorities of the world
are replaced with those of the kingdom of God. Our lives are
transformed.

Don't read your Bible as a requirement or obligation. Read
it to become a different, more Christ-like you.

He laid His right hand on me, saying to me, "Do
not be afraid; I am the First and the Last."

REVELATION 1:17

In 2017, *The New York Times Magazine* ran an article titled, "Why Are More American Teenagers Than Ever Suffering From Severe Anxiety?" The article told of a North Carolina teenager named Jake who was likable, hard-working, and athletic. But the pressures and fears of school and life bore into him, and one day he simply refused to go to school, curled up in the fetal position on the floor, and screamed, "I just can't take it! You just don't understand!"

Jake got the help he needed, but he's indicative of young people everywhere. "In its annual survey of students, the American College Health Association found a significant increase—to 62 percent in 2016 from 50 percent in 2011—of undergraduates reporting 'overwhelming anxiety.'"[3]

Sometimes we need professional help with fear and anxiety; but most of all we need the reassurance of Him who is the First and the Last, who said, "I ... was dead, and behold, I am alive forevermore. Amen. And I have the keys of Hades and of Death" (Revelation 1:18).

When we fear Him in reverence, we have nothing else to fear in life.

[3] www.nytimes.com/2017/10/11/magazine/why-are-more-american-teenagers-than-ever-suffering-from-severe-anxiety.html

The Gateway of the Eye

I have made a covenant with my eyes; why then
should I look upon a young woman?
JOB 31:1

To break a covenant in the ancient Near East was serious business, resulting in shame or judgment (Joshua 9). That's why Job's act was so extraordinary: He made a covenant with his eyes. He couldn't cast his eyes lustfully upon a young woman; to do so would break his covenant of purity with his eyes (Matthew 5:28).

Why did Job make a covenant with his eyes instead of his tongue, hands, or feet? Surely, he wanted to keep those body parts pure. Perhaps he viewed sight—his eyes—as a gateway for temptation. The tongue, hands, and feet only put in motion what the mind has conceived. And often the mind depends on visual information for its ideas. And perhaps he knew that sight was the gateway for mankind's original sin: "When [Eve] *saw* that the tree was good for food ... she took of its fruit and ate" (Genesis 3:6, emphasis added). Those details are of lesser importance—the point of Job's action is that he took willful steps to live a pure life before God. And he chose a covenant with his eyes as a way to express his commitment.

Are there any steps you can take to decrease the likelihood of yielding to the temptation to sin? Job's example may be a good place to begin.

So Peter went out and wept bitterly.
LUKE 22:62

Expungement is a legal term that means "to remove from general review." It means that an offense against the law is sealed in a court record and therefore not viewable in the future. In short, the record of the offense is removed from a person's legal record. For practical purposes, expungement erases the record of legal offense—except for one thing: the consequences of the act. Removing the guilt and punishment of an offense is one thing; removing the consequences is another.

Such is the case with our sins before God. The guilt and punishment for our sins has been removed; Christ has taken upon Himself our sins; Christ has died in our place. But the consequences of our sins remain. Once something is said, heard, or done, it cannot be undone. That happened in the case of David's sin of adultery. A loyal soldier lost his life, a woman and a king lost their honor, and they both lost their child. All were consequences of David's sin. God forgave David of his legal record of sin—by cancelling the debt [sin]—but it did not take away the consequences (Psalm 51).

Instead of hoping you can choose to sin and then ask for forgiveness, it is far better to avoid the sin and its lasting consequences.

FEBRUARY 7
Words From Above

He who has an ear, let him hear what the Spirit says.

REVELATION 2:7

North Korea is arguably the most closed nation in the world, yet the Bible is floating through the clouds and landing in its towns and villages. Hundreds of helium-filled balloons are sent up nightly from South Korea—balloons carrying the Word of God in Korean and flash drives with the text of the New Testament.

God has sent down His message to all of us with wisdom from above, and most of us are blessed to have it readily available without peril or persecution. It brings light to darkened hearts and benighted lands. How we need to read it—all of it—from Genesis to Revelation! God didn't include prophecy in the Bible to confuse us but to enlighten us. It's important for our ears to hear it, for our mouths to proclaim it, and for the world to hear it, even if we must use balloons to deliver the message.

Seven times the book of Revelation says, "He who has an ear, let him hear." Let's listen and learn and spread the message abroad.

Finally, all of you be of one mind, having compassion for one another; love as brothers, be tenderhearted, be courteous.

1 PETER 3:8

Sometimes one word just won't do. In New Testament Greek, when the writers wanted to encourage people to act kindly and affectionately toward one another, they wrote "have *eusplagchnon*"—two words combined into one: *eu* meant "good" and *splagchnon* meant "the internal organs"—heart, liver, bowels. It meant to pull up good feelings and affections from deep within yourself and display those toward others.

When it came to translating *eusplagchnon* into English, again, one word wasn't sufficient. We combined *com* "with" with *passion* "heartfelt emotion" to create *compassion*. *Compassion* is the English version of Greek "good affections from deep within." Both are good words, strong words, that evoke images of what it means to identify with the pain and needs of others. *Com* means compassion is with or toward others; compassion is not a solo act or emotion. Compassion has a human object. And *passion*—well, passion is passion. We know it even when we can't define it.

Compassion cares. Have compassion for someone in your world today. Pull up from deep within the love that will let them know you care.

For our light affliction, which is but for a moment, is working for us a far more exceeding and eternal weight of glory.

2 CORINTHIANS 4:17

The apostle Paul never wrote his autobiography, but he came close in 2 Corinthians. Some in Corinth had bitterly criticized him, and the church was divided. Paul had conflicts on the outside and fears within (2 Corinthians 7:5). In writing 2 Corinthians, he opened his heart, shared his struggles, and sought to win the support of the church. In the process, he showed us how to manage our own struggles, writing: "Though outwardly we are wasting away, yet inwardly we are being renewed day by day. For our light and momentary troubles are achieving for us an eternal glory that far outweighs them all" (2 Corinthians 4:16-17, NIV).

Our problems seem huge to us. They can overwhelm our emotions and violate our peace. But from God's perspective— these are biblical words—they are "light and momentary" when compared to all God is doing for us now and will do for us in the future.

Your problems are temporary, but God's promises are eternal. His promises will outlive your problems and carry you to heaven, where there are no problems, no pain, no death, no tears.

FEBRUARY 10
Love *and* Like

He who says he abides in [God] ought himself
also to walk just as [Christ] walked.
1 JOHN 2:6

In marital counseling sessions, a spouse might say to a counselor, "I know [my spouse] loves me; I'm just not sure [my spouse] likes me." To a troubled spouse, it might mean that a partner goes through all the motions of provision, protection, and parenting—willful choices of love—but might do so without a genuine sense of passion and joy. Life might be conducted at a surface level instead of at a spiritual level.

Those same two dimensions are present in our spiritual life as well. There is love for and from God, then there is intimacy and openness with God—what the Bible means by fellowship. The core meaning of fellowship is not coffee and cookies in the fellowship hall after church. Fellowship means oneness or commonality. It means enjoying a common set of values: honesty, love, sacrifice, openness, integrity, and more. That is what God offers us in His love; it is also what God expects from us in return if we claim to walk with Him.

Jesus lived in total oneness with the Father. That is the way we should live as well. When we are not honest with God, our intimacy with Him is interrupted (1 John 1:9).

If God is for us, who can be against us?

ROMANS 8:31

Some days we awaken to sunny skies. Other days are darker, and we're gripped by pain. Whether the pain is physical or emotional, it can make us question God's love and care for us.

But God counters our questions with some of His own— rhetorical questions—to remind us of His active involvement in our care. We find glorious sets of questions at the end of Job, in Isaiah 40, and scattered throughout the Lord's ministry. But few passages exceed the interrogation of Romans 8, as Paul draws to a close in his theological instruction about justification by grace through faith.

What then shall we say to these things? If God is for us, who can be against us? ... How shall He not with Him also freely give us all things? Who shall bring a charge against God's elect ... Who is he who condemns? ... Who shall separate us from the love of Christ?

If your spirits are low today, answer the questions God sets forth. Who can be against you? No one! What can separate you from His love? Nothing!

God's burning questions have glowing answers that bring heavenly sunshine.

But deliver us from the evil one.
MATTHEW 6:13

The defining act of God in the history of the Jews is the Exodus. God *delivered* the descendants of Jacob from the oppression of the Egyptian Pharaoh: "Our fathers trusted in You; they trusted, and You delivered them" (Psalm 22:4). The word *deliverance* became a defining biblical idea for God's saving acts of His people in both the Old and the New Testament.

Just as God delivered the Jews from Pharaoh's kingdom, so God delivers those who trust in Jesus from the kingdom of Satan to the kingdom of God (Colossians 1:13-14). When Jesus taught His disciples to pray, "but deliver us from the evil one," He was likely speaking against the backdrop of God being the deliverer of His people. In the New Testament, that idea is affirmed by the apostles in terms of eternal security: Satan will do what he can to prevent us from reaching God's eternal kingdom but God "will deliver [us] from every evil work and preserve [us] for His heavenly kingdom" (2 Timothy 4:18).

In Christ you are protected from every temporal and eternal desire of "the evil one" to harm you: "The Lord is my rock and my fortress and my deliverer" (2 Samuel 22:2).

FEBRUARY 13
The Divine Connection

By this all will know that you are My disciples,
if you have love for one another.
JOHN 13:35

Two aspects of the spiritual life have resonated throughout biblical history and to the present day: faith and works. Different groups of Christians have emphasized one aspect more than the other at different times in Church history. But the biblical view is that they are both important. Take the dimension of faith called love. Throughout Scripture, love is validated by works.

For example, Paul's famous words about love in 1 Corinthians 13 are all about the actions of love: patience, kindness, protection, trust, perseverance, and more. Likewise, the absence of love is revealed by the opposite of loving actions. The Bible's most well-known verse—John 3:16—connects God's love to God's action: He loved us and sent His Son to provide a way for us to be forgiven and have eternal life. And the apostle John wrote, "In this the love of God was manifested toward us, that God has sent His only begotten Son into the world" (1 John 4:9). Jesus said that His followers' loving actions would be the way to point the world to Him (John 13:35).

Love (faith) and actions are a divine connection. We are to be toward others as God in Christ has been toward us (Ephesians 4:32).

Love Waits!

Love suffers long.
1 CORINTHIANS 13:4

Most adults are generally patient with infants or people with physical or mental limitations. That is, people who "just can't help it." And we should be. Patience is a godly virtue that the more capable can reasonably be expected to exercise toward the less capable.

But those folks make up a small minority of the people in our lives. Most of the people in our lives are just like us—relatively fit and capable. And it is those people with whom we find ourselves being impatient. We think, "They should know better; they're taking advantage of our good nature"—all of which could be true. But instead of justifying our impatience, we should follow the apostle Paul's words: "Be patient with all" (1 Thessalonians 5:14). He mentions three kinds of people before that exhortation: the unruly, the fainthearted, and the weak. Then he sums up by essentially saying, "Be patient with all"—the old, young, fit, disabled, responsible, irresponsible. Patience is required toward all.

Think of those in your life who consistently try your patience. Ask God for the fruit of His Spirit of love to be manifested in patience toward all.

The Lord will guide you continually, and satisfy your soul in drought, and strengthen your bones; you shall be like a watered garden, and like a spring of water, whose waters do not fail.

ISAIAH 58:11

In his autobiography, Warren Wiersbe described his struggles with getting older. "There are times when I feel like a dinosaur," he wrote. He described one drizzly day when his arthritis was acting up. "I asked the Lord in my morning devotional time to give me a promise that would sustain me for the 'declining' years to come. (No sense fooling myself!) In the course of my regular Bible reading I came to Isaiah 58:11; and I said, 'That's it! Thank you, Lord!'"

It's a promise for us all. Whether we're young or old, we face pain, problems, and unknown possibilities for the future. Sometimes we feel beat up. But God's grace is sufficient, and He uses difficulties to cultivate us like a well-watered garden. Obedience to Him provides the opportunity, through trials, to learn that our only hope is His sufficiency, not our own.

FEBRUARY 16
Learning From Disappointments

I know, O Lord, that Your judgments are right,
and that in faithfulness You have afflicted me.
PSALM 119:75

British inventor James Dyson spent 15 years making 5,126 prototypes of a revolutionary kind of vacuum cleaner—all of them failures. The 5,127th version was a success.[4]

James Dyson learned about the mechanics of design from each failure, but *learn* is the key word. That is the benefit of disappointment or failure in life—the opportunity to learn. There are many things to learn, of course. Jesus learned obedience (Hebrews 5:8), which is another way of saying He learned about trusting His Father, God. We have the opportunity to learn about God as well, with every disappointment. The psalmist wrote that his afflictions reminded him of the faithfulness of God. There is an infinite number of ways to learn about God from life's disappointments.

If you are disappointed today, use it as an opportunity to learn more about God and His love for you. Don't view disappointments as obstacles, but rather as gateways to learning.

[4] Olivia Fox Cabana and Judah Pollack, *The Net and the Butterfly: The Art and Practice of Breakthrough Thinking* (New York: Portfolio/Penguin, 2017), 123.

FEBRUARY 17
Versed for Life

Be strong and of good courage; do not be afraid, nor be dismayed,
for the Lord your God is with you wherever you go.
JOSHUA 1:9

What happens when you're stricken with cancer at age four-teen? Carson Leslie responded by turning to Joshua 1:9. He claimed it not as his cancer verse but his life verse. "No matter how long I live, I want this verse on my tombstone," he wrote in *Carry Me*. "And when people visit my grave, I want them to read the verse and think about how it got me through my struggles in life, and I hope others will see that this verse can offer them the same kind of comfort it gives me."

Carson passed away at age seventeen, but the foundation and medical ministries established in his honor have touched thousands.

Carson's story reminds us that Scripture has the power to bring us through hard times. No matter what comes, God has a verse, a promise, or a passage in the Bible to help us. His Word gives us the tools to defeat our enemies. Find a verse for yourself today, make it your go-to Scripture, and draw courage as you look to God's Word for strength each day.

Sowing and Waiting

Who then is Paul, and who is Apollos, but ministers through whom you believed, as the Lord gave to each one? I planted, Apollos watered, but God gave the increase.

1 CORINTHIANS 3:5-6

When a seed is planted, there is a season where nothing is visible from the surface. Although the seed's roots are beginning to sprout and dig into the soil, there is no life above the ground. In Matthew 13, Jesus explains that there are multiple responses to God's Word. The sower sows generously, but only some of the seeds take root and flourish.

Root work takes time and is aided by continual watering and nurturing. When we share God's Word with others, it is easy to become discouraged when we see little or no fruit. We may struggle with wondering whether our efforts are effective. While we want to develop and increase our skill in sharing God's salvation, we must remember that all new life and growth comes from God. Each type of seed has a unique gestational period. When we surrender our efforts to God, we can battle the discouragement that comes from listeners who do not appear to accept the Word of God offered to them.

*Righteousness will go before Him, and shall
make His footsteps our pathway.*
PSALM 85:13

The Appalachian Trail is approximately 2,200 miles long,
winding up and down and through rugged mountains from
Georgia to Maine. It takes thru-hikers an average of 165
rigorous days to make the trip, and it requires about 5,500
calories a day to sustain their strength. That's equivalent to
nearly 10 Big Macs daily. Hiking the entire Appalachian Trail in
one summer is grueling, but it simply requires putting one foot
in front of the other—about 5 million times.

The Bible often compares our Christian life to a walk—but
it's no easy stroll. It's an arduous hike requiring perseverance.
When we begin our walk with God, we're like infants taking
their first steps—we are filled with glee—but we don't know
quite what we are doing. But as we mature, this should change
and our footsteps should become more stable, firm, and
determined.

If you're tired on the trail, don't give up. Psalm 85:13
says He has gone before us, and we're simply walking in His
footsteps. And Psalm 86:11 offers us a prayer: "Teach me Your
way, O Lord; I will walk in Your truth; unite my heart to fear
Your name."

*I am the door. If anyone enters by Me, he will be saved,
and will go in and out and find pasture.*
JOHN 10:9

If you struggle with being certain about heaven, arm yourself
with assurance by using the acronym ARM:

- A—Ask yourself: Have I asked Jesus Christ to forgive my
  sins? Have I received Him as my personal Savior and Lord?
  If not, it's important to do so today, for "now is the day of
  salvation" (2 Corinthians 6:2).

- R—Realize that once you've received Christ as Savior and
  Lord, doubting your salvation is questioning Jesus' ability
  to keep the promise He made in John 10. Repent of this,
  and tell God you're sorry for doubting His integrity. Ask
  Him to strengthen your faith.

- M—Memorize John 10:27-28. Meditate on these verses
  when you're tempted to fret or fear. Rest in the promises of
  God's Word.

Nothing can separate us from His love. No one can snatch
us from His hand. God has given us eternal life and this life
is in His Son. "He who has the Son has life" (1 John 5:11-12).
Because of this, you can live well beyond reasonable doubt that
you have life through Him.

*Why have you [David] despised the commandment of the Lord,
to do evil in His sight? You have killed Uriah the Hittite with the
sword; you have taken his wife to be your wife, and have killed
him with the sword of the people of Ammon.*

2 SAMUEL 12:9

Christian literature is filled with stories of people appearing
to help a Christian in need, then never being seen again. Are
such beings real people? Are they angels? Both are documented
in Scripture—people and angels sent by the Lord to render
guidance, aid, correction, or any other necessity to those in
need.

King David had sinned grievously but had not confessed
his sin to God. That is, not until God sent Nathan, a prophet,
to call the king to account. Ultimately, David received Nathan's
rebuke and confessed his sin. The question is, Would we? If
God sends someone into our lives, or some circumstances, our
first response should be, "What are You saying to me, Lord?"
Perhaps God is saying nothing in that instance, but perhaps He
is. Our attention should be immediately drawn to Him and to
His purposes.

Walk soberly today. Be aware of what God may be saying
to you through people and events. Let your attention always be
drawn to Him and His purposes.

FEBRUARY 22
Let in the Cleansing Wind

And suddenly there came a sound from heaven, as of a rushing mighty wind,
and it filled the whole house where they were sitting.

ACTS 2:2

There was a day when homes weren't equipped with vacuum cleaners, central air and heat, and multi-pane windows that seal the home from outside impurities. That meant that a regular part of spring cleaning was flinging open the windows to let fresh air in and hanging rugs on a clothesline and beating the dust out of them.

While those practices are no longer routine, the notion of using fresh air as a cleanser is very biblical. In both the Old and New Testaments, the words in the original language for *spirit* were also the words for *wind* or *breath*. It is no wonder that Paul admonished believers to be "filled with the Spirit" on an ongoing basis (Ephesians 5:18). Like the wind, the Spirit of God blows where He will (John 3:8). And He is always willing to come into your life afresh for new power, fruit, gifts, and guidance.

Purpose today to invite the Spirit to fill you with kingdom breath, kingdom wind—to air out the house of your heart with the wind of the Spirit.

And be kind to one another, tenderhearted, forgiving
one another, even as God in Christ forgave you.
EPHESIANS 4:32

Sometimes parents face the awkward dilemma of being caught in an act of hypocrisy. The parent corrects a child's use of language or behavior and the child responds, "Well, you do that!" The parent is then tempted to say, "Do as I say, not as I do!" There may be times when adult and child behavior can diverge, but not often. When it comes to modeling behavior, actions always speak louder than words.

When it came to forgiveness, the apostle Paul gave the church at Ephesus both a command and an example to follow: Forgive each other, just as God in Christ forgave you. It is never a case of God saying to us, "Do as I say, not as I do." What God expects of us is no more than what He Himself has done. We are forgiven completely and unconditionally by God through faith in Jesus Christ. That forgiveness is the model for how our love for others should be expressed by forgiveness.

If you are called to forgive someone today, ask yourself not what Jesus would do, but consider what God has already done and do likewise.

But be doers of the word, and not hearers only, deceiving yourselves.
JAMES 1:22

"It's important to me to take care of my body." The words are easy to say, but if our day-to-day life and actions do not align with our words, the words become empty. Observation is the key to discover what people value. Each area of our lives reveals deep truths about us. The way we treat every area of life—food, work, faith, and family—reveals what we believe and value.

Repetitive thoughts become our deep-seated beliefs, and these are lived out in our actions. It's easy to *say* the right things: "I believe in being connected to God." But if we never have time for His Word or people, our words are meaningless. Although it is easy to deceive ourselves, God has given each of us a mirror in our actions. As we look at our actions and where our time is going, we discover our beliefs and values. Although it is never a good idea to nitpick at others, reflecting on our own lives is a powerful tool to discover growth areas and then invite God into them.

Author Elisabeth Elliot put it this way: *If you believe in a God who controls the big things, you have to believe in a God who controls the little things. It is we, of course, to whom things look "little" or "big."*

FEBRUARY 25
The Duty of Honor

Render therefore to all their due: taxes to whom taxes are due, customs to whom customs, fear to whom fear, honor to whom honor.
ROMANS 13:7

Sadly, it is no longer uncommon for speakers or writers to refer to the President of the United States (or anyone in a position of leadership) in a dishonoring or disrespectful manner. Gone are the days of decorum when courtesy, honor, and propriety took precedence over personal desires. Honor always has a place—a place that should be preserved.

King Saul of Israel was a king who failed in his responsibilities as king. It would have been easy for his successor, David, to point out Saul's flaws after he died in battle. But David wrote a eulogy for Saul (2 Samuel 1:17-27) in which he pointed out Saul's strengths: his bravery in battle and his esteem among his subjects. In other words, David looked for ways to honor God's anointed. Just as God put Saul in place in Israel, He puts civil rulers in place as well (Romans 13:1-7). Regardless of what we think of God's appointees, we honor them because we honor Him.

If there is someone in whom you have lost confidence or by whom you have been hurt, look for ways to honor that person as a way to honor God. Bearing the image of God makes everyone worthy of honor.

FEBRUARY 26
God in Our Troubles

And [Job] took for himself a potsherd with which to scrape
himself while he sat in the midst of the ashes.

JOB 2:8

Job's story is universally known. He endured a series of catastrophes in his personal life until he ended up sitting, *alone*, on an ash heap scraping his boils with a scrap of pottery. How can it come to that? The truth is, we don't have to go through Job's dreadful experiences (Job 1–2) to feel we have landed in a similar place: afflicted and alone.

If we are going to identify with the beginning of Job's story, we must also identify with the middle and the end. Throughout his quest to understand God's reasons for his afflictions, Job never lost confidence in God. And in the end his spiritual eyes were opened to see God in a way he had never seen Him before: sovereign, omnipotent, and gracious. Job's life was restored; he was wiser and deeper than he otherwise would have been. Trouble did in Job's life what it will do in our life if we will give God the benefit of the doubt. If we will but believe that God is with us and working out His perfect will, we will never doubt His presence in spite of our circumstances.

Don't let circumstances determine how you see God. Conform your circumstances to God, not God to your circumstances.

But lay up for yourselves treasures in heaven, where neither moth
nor rust destroys and where thieves do not break in and steal.
For where your treasure is, there your heart will be also.
MATTHEW 6:20-21

The association that tracks state-run lotteries says that Americans spent more than $70 billion on lotteries in 2014. That represents $300 for each adult in the 43 states hosting lotteries. People spend that money on the fantasy that they might be the one to hit the jackpot—as if God appeared and said, "Ask Me for whatever you want."

God did say that to Solomon when he became king of Israel: "Ask! What shall I give you?" (1 Kings 3:5) Solomon's answer would surprise many modern lottery players. Instead of great wealth and power, Solomon asked for wisdom: "Therefore give to Your servant an understanding heart to judge Your people" (verse 9). And God did. Solomon became the wisest king on earth. Because Solomon recognized that true wealth is found in the wisdom to advance God's kingdom on earth, God rewarded Solomon later with great wealth and stature. Centuries later, Jesus said we should seek God's kingdom first, after which God will add everything else we need.

How do you measure wealth today? Lay up your treasures in heaven, Jesus said, where they will be safe for eternity.

But who do you say that I am?

MARK 8:29

There is a turning point in the ministry of Jesus in Mark's Gospel. Prior to chapter 8, our Lord's main emphasis was in His identity. Through His teachings, conversations, parables, and miracles, He wanted His disciples to comprehend His personhood, that He was the Messiah. In Mark 8, He took the disciples to the remote areas of Caesarea Philippi and quizzed them. "Who do men say that I am?" He asked (verse 27). They had various answers—John the Baptist, Elijah, or one of the prophets. Then Jesus said, "But who do you say that I am?" Peter answered, "You are the Christ."

Jesus abruptly changed subjects and began teaching them about His work—what He had come to do. Mark 8:31 says, "And He began to teach them that the Son of Man must suffer many things ... and be killed, and after three days rise again." In the next chapter, He repeated the lesson (Mark 9:31). In then in the next chapter, He explained it again (Mark 10:32-34).

These are the two foundational questions we must understand—the person and the work of Christ. Who is Jesus? What did He do?

The answers to those questions provide the basis for our entire walk of faith.

MARCH

But Samuel said to Saul, "I will not return with you, for you have rejected the word of the Lord, and the Lord has rejected you from being king over Israel."

1 SAMUEL 15:26

Sir Isaac Newton was the most brilliant mathematician and physicist of his day. His *Mathematical Principles of Natural Philosophy*, published in 1687, gave expression to immutable laws of force in the universe—like the law of equal and opposite reaction. Put in a spiritual way, actions have consequences—we reap what we sow (Galatians 6:7).

All of our actions in life move us in one of two directions: toward God or away from God. Our actions either result in God's blessing or God's discipline. While there are many examples of this in Scripture, Israel's King Saul is a good illustration. As Israel's first king, he was given an assignment by God to subdue the neighboring Amalekites. Because he didn't obey God's directive completely, he was removed from being king. Saul thought God's judgment was an overreaction; Samuel stressed that it was a matter of obedience. Only obedience leads to His blessing.

Think about the actions of your life today and the spiritual laws at work. Choose actions that will move you closer to God and His blessing.

MARCH 2
Filled to Overflowing

The Holy Spirit, whom He poured out on us abundantly
through Jesus Christ our Savior.
TITUS 3:5-6

The concept of pouring something out has a strong biblical basis. In the Old Testament sacrifices, containers of ashes (Leviticus 4:12) and blood (Deuteronomy 12:27) were poured out. Job (Job 30:16) and Hannah (1 Samuel 1:15) poured out their souls before the Lord. God poured out His wrath on rebellious Israel (2 Chronicles 34:21). Indeed, the Old Testament's use of the image of pouring is frequently connected to wrath.

It is no surprise that, oftentimes in the New Testament, the use of pouring out is the opposite of wrath: It is God pouring out His Spirit (Acts 2:33; 10:45) and His love (Romans 5:5; Titus 3:3-7). In the Old Testament, God poured out His wrath upon sin and sinners; in the New Testament He pours out His love. What does the image suggest? We have been filled to overflowing with God's Spirit and love—love being a manifestation of the presence of the Spirit (Galatians 5:22). He poured out His wrath on Jesus and His love on those for whom Jesus died.

God has filled you with His love so you can share it with others. Pour out your overflow of God's love to someone today.

Contradicting and blaspheming, they opposed the things spoken by Paul.

ACTS 13:45

Corrie ten Boom came up with a powerful definition of anxiety. "Worry," she said, "is a cycle of inefficient thoughts whirling around a center of fear." The old hymnist, John Newton, author of "Amazing Grace," suggested an alternative to anxiety—faith. He wrote, "If the Lord be with us, we have no cause of fear. His eye is upon us, His arm over us, His ear open to our prayer— His grace sufficient, His promise unchangeable."

Many Christians around the world are under the pressure of persecution, and even in the Western world, there is growing anti-Christian sentiment. We live in a world trying to intimidate us. Our blasphemous culture contradicts and opposes our message of Christian hope and love. When we suffer as a follower of Christ, it is not insignificant to us nor to God. He sees and understands and cares. He is with us, and we must always remember that His eye is on us, His arm over us, His ear is open to our prayer, His grace is sufficient, and His promises are unshakable and unchangeable.

Our hope is in Him!

Needing Strength

But those who wait on the Lord shall renew their strength.

ISAIAH 40:31

The church in Philadelphia was doing its best to take advantage of the open door God provided for its ministries. They were keeping His Word and not denying His Name. They had kept the Lord's command to persevere, but sometimes they felt they needed more strength.

Do you ever feel that way?

Turn to the Bible's great verses about strength and claim them. Remember the prayer in Ephesians 3:16, that God "would grant you, according to the riches of His glory, to be strengthened with might through His Spirit in the inner man." Remember the promise Moses made in Deuteronomy 33:25: "As your days, so shall your strength be."

As we are faithful to the Lord—as individuals and as churches—He will always give us the strength we need to bear the burdens He allows and fulfill the tasks He assigns. As we wait upon Him, He renews our strength like that of an eagle.

Ask the Lord today for the strength you need.

But immediately, when Jesus perceived in His spirit that they reasoned thus within themselves, He said to them, "Why do you reason about these things in your hearts?"

MARK 2:8

When children are very small, they develop a predictable short list of answers to some of their parents' routine questions: "Did you eat the cookies?" "No." "Will you go and pick up your toys?" "I'm too tired." "Please come and help me set the table for supper." "Okay—in just a minute." Parents understand these responses because they are childish versions of their own (occasional) responses to their own responsibilities.

Sanctification involves learning to think and act honestly and righteously before God. And one of the primary motivations for righteous acts and thoughts is that God knows what we think, and what we think about doing, all the time. We have no secrets before God. When a group of men brought their friend to be healed by Jesus, a group of Pharisees took exception—silently—to Jesus' compassion on the man. Jesus called them out on their self-centered and non-compassionate thoughts (Mark 2:1-12).

Jesus knows the human heart like parents know their child's heart. Rather than be called out, it is far better to have thoughts we are willing for God and man to know.

MARCH 6
Finish the Race!

Do you not know that those who run in a race all run, but one receives the prize? Run in such a way that you may obtain it.

1 CORINTHIANS 9:24

We often see the grimacing image of a long-distance runner struggling to cross the finish line. Perhaps they pulled a muscle or had a cramp or got dehydrated. It happens at every level of the sport—from high school to the Olympics. The commitment of crossing the finish line is so ingrained in these athletes that they *will not quit*. They hobble, crawl, or walk—sometimes aided by a fellow athlete or a family member from the stands—until they finish the race. There is no disgrace. Finishing the race is even more important than winning the race.

Paul used the metaphor of a race to illustrate the responsibility of running the Christian life until we cross the finish line. He never entertained the possibility of slacking off because of old age or infirmity. We run until our time on earth is finished or until Jesus comes again. Yes, younger and stronger may win the speed race. But faithfulness wins the race of commitment to Christ and kingdom.

Prepare now to run the *whole* race. Commit yourself to finishing strong with whatever strength and abilities you have—until your last breath or your first sight of Jesus.

*And about the ninth hour Jesus cried out with a loud voice,
saying, "Eli, Eli, lama sabachthani?" that is, "My God,
My God, why have You forsaken Me?"*

MATTHEW 27:46

A mysterious passage in the Bible has Jesus feeling forsaken by God the Father. It is mysterious because we think of the Godhead as being united in love and purpose. And it is. But in the moment that Jesus Christ hung on the cross, He was bearing the sins of the world. He had become sin for us (2 Corinthians 5:21). Because holy God cannot dwell in the presence of sin, He turned away from His Son who had become sin in our place. Could there be any lonelier cry in history than these words of Jesus?

Yes, Jesus felt abandoned. But just as He knew David's "forsaken" lament from Psalm 22:1, He also knew David's hope of resurrection in Psalm 16. He knew that God's forsaking was only for a season. On the third day He was alive again! There may be times of discipline in our life in which God's actions may be "painful" (Hebrews 12:11). But He has not forsaken us; He is not punishing us. He is teaching us to share in His holiness (Hebrews 12:10).

God does not leave nor forsake us (Hebrews 13:5). We must walk by faith and not by sight (2 Corinthians 5:7).

Three Spiritual Rs

I marvel that you are turning away so soon from Him who called you in the grace of Christ, to a different gospel.
GALATIANS 1:6

On a hike in the mountains, you come to a fork in the trail and choose what you think is the right path. But after a couple miles, you realize you should have taken the other path. Venturing off the trail farther along, you realize that a very steep ravine now separates you from the other trail. You realize you will have to hike back to the fork and take the other trail to reach your destination.

That is what is meant by repentance: Change your mind and direction; return and take the path of righteousness. That was the message of Christ to the first-century church at Ephesus. They had "left their first love"—their love for Christ (Revelation 2:4). His words to them were, "Remember therefore from where you have fallen; repent and do the first works" (Revelation 2:5). Remember and repent in order to be restored. Remembering produces the goal; repenting gets you back to the goal; restoration is the fruit of remembering and repenting.

If you need to repent of anything in your life, remember the goal and go back to it. There is no other way to be restored.

MARCH 9
Opening Doors

In His hand are the deep places of the earth;
the heights of the hills are His also.

PSALM 95:4

Have you ever felt lost or unsure? Even the disciples, who spoke to Jesus face to face, felt confusion, fear, and uncertainty from time to time. When Jesus asked them to feed the crowd of thousands, they lacked the resources to complete the task until someone found a young boy with a lunch. When a storm's waves shuddered their boat, they lacked the power to save themselves until Christ stepped out to calm the sea.

Thankfully our feelings, abilities, and resources are not an indicator of God's power, or of our usefulness to the kingdom. Even in the Old Testament, some people questioned God's calling: Moses wondered how he would lead the Israelites to freedom, Saul hid among the equipment when he was about to be declared king, and Jonah walked in the opposite direction of God's call.

The solution and key to the challenges being faced lies not in our power or abilities, but in God. He is the source of truth, wisdom, power, guidance, and ability. Nothing can thwart His purpose or deter His calling on a person's life. When we stop looking at our circumstances and begin looking to Him, everything changes. Whatever challenge or opportunity you are facing today, turn your eyes toward Jesus—He has the power to open the door and He will walk through it with you!

Renew Your Mind

*And do not be conformed to this world, but be transformed by the
renewing of your mind, that you may prove what is that good
and acceptable and perfect will of God.*

ROMANS 12:2

One of the best benefits of spring cleaning is finding lost or
forgotten treasures—keepsakes, tools, pictures, books, CDs,
mementos, and more that you haven't seen in years. When that
happens, the memories come flooding back. Your memory is
renewed; you recapture a long-lost pleasure or benefit.

For the Christian, the renewing of memories comes not
from finding lost objects but from rediscovering lost truths.
Perhaps you read a passage of Scripture that had a certain
relevance to you in the past. Maybe you read a passage in your
journal or diary and recall how God blessed you or saw you
through a very difficult trial. Maybe the truth of worship is
renewed by finding a favorite CD of praise music that takes you
back to a time when more of your heart belonged to God than
it does today.

The best place to start renewing your mind is in the Word
(Truth) of God. Use this spring season of renewal and cleansing
as a time to open your mind afresh to God.

Therefore I say to you, do not worry about your life, what you will eat or what you will drink; nor about your body, what you will put on. Is not life more than food and the body more than clothing?

MATTHEW 6:25

Think of all the different kinds of "daily bread" that can be here today and gone tomorrow: money, house, cars, possessions, jobs, health, and more. In fact, every tangible thing in our life is something we have no ultimate control over. And those are the things Jesus said we should never spend time and energy worrying about—which makes perfect sense. Why worry about those things over which we have no control?

The one thing that cannot be taken away is the only thing we need going forward into the future: our faith and the intangible values (perseverance, hope, and the like) that arise from our faith. The apostle Paul confirmed the necessity of faith: "Moreover it is required in stewards that one be found faithful" (1 Corinthians 4:2). We are stewards (slaves) of the God who has bought us for Himself. Our provision is His "worry," not ours. He has promised to meet the needs of those who love Him.

Don't worry about tomorrow, Jesus said. Trust your Heavenly Father with the faith you can never lose.

He who is unmarried cares for the things of the
Lord—how he may please the Lord.
1 CORINTHIANS 7:32

More than thirty years ago, a storm swept the sand from a beach on the Irish island of Achill, leaving nothing but rock pools. Hotels closed as tourists stopped coming. Last year, record tides caused the sand to reappear. Suddenly the beach was back again for the first time since 1984. Tourists are returning.

In life, the tide goes out and comes in. Sometimes our world is filled with friends, family, and fellowship; other seasons are lonelier. But even when we tread among rocks, there's a charm and beauty to life. Loneliness leads to reflection; when we reflect on the goodness and nearness of God, we find comfort.

In 1 Corinthians 7, Paul listed the advantages of those who are unmarried. They don't have to concern themselves with caring for a spouse; they can devote themselves fully to pleasing the Lord.

If you feel alone in some way, think of the Lord as your closest friend, your constant companion, and your abiding comfort. He will never leave or forsake you; as we follow Him faithfully, He always turns the tide in our direction.

No longer do I call you servants, for a servant does not know what his master is doing; but I have called you friends.
JOHN 15:15

You've seen them—lists of reasons why dogs are man's best friend. Dogs love unconditionally, are always there for you, are always glad to see you, are ready to forgive, love going places with you, will protect you from danger, and on and on. We would be fortunate to have a human friend who is as faithful as a canine friend!

Actually, we do have such a Friend—and this Friend adds a trait of which not even our four-legged friends can boast. That friend is Jesus and He understands everything we go through in our life. Jesus can "sympathize with our weaknesses" since He was "in all points tempted as we are, yet without sin" (Hebrews 4:15). Besides faithfulness, empathy may be a friend's most desirable trait. The concept of friendship was clear in the Old Testament—it was a covenant idea, as in Abraham being friends with God (2 Chronicles 20:7). When Jesus instituted the new covenant with His disciples, He told them that He was now their friend—loyal, sacrificial, loving, and empathetic.

Human friends may disappoint us, but Jesus never will. He is a friend that "sticks closer than a brother" (Proverbs 18:24).

*And if anyone sins, we have an Advocate with the
Father, Jesus Christ the righteous.*
1 JOHN 2:1

The English language has words that can be used as both nouns
and verbs: *walk, mail, park, play, milk, light, whistle, scare,* and
more. *Advocate* is one of those words: An advocate is someone
who advocates for others—from the Latin word *advocare,*
meaning "to call to one's aid." *Advocate* in English has come
to be primarily a legal term—"defender or representative in
court."

Jesus is described as the Christian's Advocate in 1 John 2:1.
On the basis of His role as the Christian's Mediator (1 Timothy
2:5) and Intercessor (Hebrews 7:25), we get a picture of a
heavenly courtroom with four participants: the Christian,
the Judge (God the Father), the Defender-Advocate (Jesus
Christ), and the "accuser of [the] brethren" (Satan—Revelation
12:10). When we sin and Satan comes to accuse us before the
Father, "we have an Advocate with the Father, Jesus Christ the
righteous." (Recall how Satan came to accuse Job before the
Father—Job 1–2.)

Why does Christ defend you against Satan? Because there
is "no condemnation to those who are in Christ Jesus" (Romans
8:1). Give thanks today for your Heavenly Advocate.

MARCH 15
Food for the Race

My soul melts from heaviness; strengthen me according to Your word.
PSALM 119:28

Extreme athletes—marathoners, triathletes, distance runners, road bikers—know that nutrition can be a secret to success. Carbohydrates and protein before an event; more carbs, electrolytes, and liquids during; and within a critical half-hour window after extreme exertion, more carbs, liquids, and electrolytes. Strength depends not just on conditioning but on nutrition, too.

And the same is true in the race of the Christian life. Paul used the analogy of extreme sports—runners in the Greek games—to illustrate the endurance needed for the Christian life (1 Corinthians 9:24; 2 Timothy 4:7), as did the writer to the Hebrews (Hebrews 12:1). What, then, is the nutrition needed for finishing the race? Prayer is certainly critical as Jesus demonstrated (Matthew 26:36). But alongside prayer, nothing is as sustaining as the truth of God's Word: "Revive me, O Lord, according to Your word" (Psalm 119:107). Why? Because it is living and active (Hebrews 4:12); it tells us the truth about the past, present, and future; it affirms the promises God has made to us (2 Peter 1:4).

Are you weak or strong today? To maintain your strength for the race, take in daily portions of nutrition from God's Word.

MARCH 16
My Sheep Hear My Voice

*My sheep hear My voice, and I know them, and they follow Me. And I give
them eternal life, and they shall never perish.*
JOHN 10:27-28

If you live in an urban environment with a dog, you probably
let your pooch frolic with other canine pals at a dog park. Then
(depending on how well-trained your dog is), when it's time
to go you call your pet's name. Out of the several dozen dogs
playing in the park, yours is the only one who stops and turns
to look at you. Even if there is another dog in the park with the
same name as your pet, only your dog stops and looks because
he or she not only knows its name, it *knows your voice.*

Modern science is only now confirming what ancient
shepherds knew—that sheep can recognize their shepherd's
voice. And that was important. Whenever flocks got mingled
together, in a pasture or a market, the shepherd could call his
flock out and they would follow him. It's not hard to see why
Jesus used this as a spiritual metaphor. Jesus' followers know
He has called them and they follow Him. In the cacophony of
modern, multicultural voices, Jesus' sheep can hear His voice in
His Word.

The more you pay attention to Jesus' voice in Scripture, the
more you will recognize His voice in His Spirit's leading.

MARCH 17
To Love Is to Obey

Now by this we know that we know Him, if we keep His commandments.
1 JOHN 2:3

Every parent experiences the disconnect between a child's words when being put to bed at night—"I love you, Mommy"—and a willful act of disobedience the next morning. That disconnect between profession and practice illustrates the intimate connection between love and devotion (or obedience).

To be sure, a child is immature and not to be held to adult standards of understanding and practice. But the illustration serves its purpose in a way that is instructive for us as adults. When we say we love God but do not obey His commands and desires, we make ourselves out to be liars (1 John 2:4). "But whoever keeps His word, truly the love of God is perfected in him" (1 John 2:5). So obedience to God is a kind of barometer, a measure, of our love for God. Just as small children learn to combine love and obedience in their relationship with their parents, so we grow in the same understanding in our relationship with God. The relationship between love (faith) and obedience (good works) is a key theme in the letter written by James (James 2:14-26).

Give thought today as to how your obedience to God reflects your profession of love for God.

For we are God's handiwork, created in Christ Jesus to do good works, which God prepared in advance for us to do.
EPHESIANS 2:10, NIV

Think of a tall tree covered in green leaves with birds nesting in its branches. If we cut off a branch, it withers and dies. The only branches that thrive are connected to the flourishing tree. Sunlight is received by the leaves and water is drawn up through the roots.

When we are connected to Christ, opportunities and blessings we cannot imagine in our own strength become available to us. Instead of being limited by our own capacity and strength, we have His strength and power available to us. Each person called by God is equipped by God. We can rely on God, just as Moses and Joshua did.

God's power is like a towering tree. We can let go of our expectations and self-sufficiency. The life He has for us is beyond what we can imagine or achieve on our own. The best part, He is with us and we can remain connected to Him through every season and in every moment of our lives. It is in our best interest to stay fixed on God. He is life.

MARCH 19
Why Do We Give?

*But do not forget to do good and to share, for with
such sacrifices God is well pleased.*
HEBREWS 13:16

Texas and Louisiana were hit hard by Hurricane Harvey in late
August 2017, and Hurricane Irma roared through Florida and
the southeastern states in early September. Both hurricanes did
extensive damage in the Caribbean and the United States. News
reports showed gymnasiums and other large structures stacked
high with relief supplies donated for the survivors: clothing,
blankets, food, water, medical supplies. In those situations,
donors aren't seeking credit for their gifts. They are giving to
meet urgent needs; they are giving out of love and compassion
for the displaced.

The same thing happened in the early Jerusalem church.
As the church grew, persecution increased; many new believers
suffered as a result. So, the believers began bringing whatever
they could to give to those in need. They weren't seeking credit,
they were demonstrating compassion. They weren't after
recognition, they were providing relief.

May our giving be as selfless as the early Christians. God
sees and will bless our gifts all in His time—maybe in this life,
maybe in eternity (1 Corinthians 3:11-15).

Lord, I Believe!

Lord, I believe; help my unbelief!
MARK 9:24

If you like Downton Abbey, you'd enjoy Lydney Park Estate in the English countryside west of London. The magnificent manor house was built by the family Wintour, then acquired by Benjamin Bathurst in 1719. Bathurst's descendants still own the estate and conduct tours. To Christians, the Bathurst name is best known for his spiritual legacy of deeply meaningful hymns like this one: "O, for a faith that will not shrink, though pressed by many a foe, / That will not tremble on the brink of poverty or woe! / A faith that shines more bright and clear when tempests rage without; / That when in danger knows no fear; in darkness feels no doubt."

If your faith is wavering, try offering that prayer, for it expresses our need for a stronger faith. Or adopt a prayer like the one in Mark 9:24: "Lord, I believe; help my unbelief!"

Our confidence must firmly remain in God's ability to do as He has said. If you're facing a challenge today, take your stand on God's promises and ask for a faith that will not shrink.

MARCH 21
A Clean Heart

Create in me a clean heart, O God, and renew a steadfast spirit within me.
PSALM 51:10

Is there a particular room in your house you keep cleaner than the rest? When it comes to weekly house cleanings—or spring cleaning—where do you start? Maybe it's wherever you consider the nerve center of your life, the room which, if it is dirty or disorganized, keeps you off balance until it's back in order. Maybe it's the kitchen? The den or family room? Your bedroom and clothes closet? Or maybe for commuters it's their car—interior and exterior.

Wherever the center of your physical life is, the center of your spiritual life is what the Bible calls the "heart." Not the physical organ in your chest, but the place where the mind, will, and emotions merge to create your true spiritual life. And when the heart is dirty or disorganized, everything else is, too. After King David sinned against Bathsheba and Uriah, her husband, David lived with an unclean heart for many months—until he finally confessed his sins to God and asked for a clean heart.

Does your heart need spring cleaning today? God is ready to hear your prayer if only you will talk to Him (1 John 1:9).

I know that You are a gracious and merciful God, slow to anger and abundant in lovingkindness, One who relents from doing harm.
JONAH 4:2

When theologians talk about the attributes of God, they refer to His characteristics, qualities, and features. As we study the vastness of creation, we discover what God is like. He is infinite, without beginning or ending in time. He is omnipresent—always present in every place. He is holy, without a trace of evil or deception about Him. He is a loving God. He is powerful.

Some people compile lists or studies on the attributes of God to study Him more carefully. Pondering God is the highest and happiest pursuit of the human mind. We can do this through prayer. When we pray, it's vital to focus on the wonderful qualities of God. Prayer isn't simply a matter of bringing our needs to the Lord; it's a matter of getting to know the God to whom we bring our needs. For every problem we face, there's an attribute of God to help us.

Are you concerned about a loved one far from home? God is there, too. Are you worried about the future? God already knows what tomorrow holds. Are you distressed about world events? God is powerful, sovereign, and in control of all things. Try praying the attributes of God and your prayers will gain a new focus.

Fruitful Families

You wife shall be like a fruitful vine in the very heart of your house, your children like olive plants all around your table.

PSALM 128:3

Many modern families have instituted strict policies for mealtimes: NO ELECTRONIC DEVICES AT THE TABLE! Smartphones, tablets, music players and headphones—all are banned from mealtimes. Why? It's hard enough getting families—especially those with busy teenagers—together for meals. But when everyone is eating with one hand and holding a phone or tablet with the other, well ... let's just say the possibility of meaningful interaction and closeness is significantly reduced.

Scripture places a premium on family. After all, it is a central building block in the propagation and stability of God's economy: first marriage, then family, then church, then righteously-run governments, and so on. The psalmist pictured the family who fears the Lord like fruitful vines and plants in the house and around the table (Psalm 128:1-3). Fruit is a symbol of growth, health, nurture, and abundance of blessing (Psalm 1:3). But fruit doesn't happen automatically or accidentally. It is the result of choices, of priorities, of saying "Yes" and "No" according to biblical standards.

There are no perfect families, but there are families moving purposefully toward the high calling of life in Christ Jesus. Take stock of your family's fruit-bearing. What changes would make family moments together more memorable?

MARCH 24
Decide Today

But Peter and the other apostles answered and said:
"We ought to obey God rather than men."
ACTS 5:29

The Toleration Act of 1689 was an act of the English Parliament giving permission to non-Church of England Protestant Christians to worship according to their conscience. These Christians—Baptists, Congregationalists, Puritans—disagreed with the Church of England on various doctrinal issues and had been persecuted for their lack of allegiance, their nonconformity.

This clash of views has happened countless times in Church history—beginning in the first century in Jerusalem. There, followers of Jesus were prohibited by the prevailing (Jewish) religious institution from preaching publicly about Jesus. But Peter and the other apostles did not let this intolerance stop them. Quite simply, they declared that they were obliged to obey God and not man. And they paid a price for standing firm in their convictions. Throughout history, followers of Christ have lived in intolerant societies and paid a price for their faithfulness.

When someone says "No" to your faith, that is not the time to examine your convictions. The time to decide is before you encounter intolerance. Decide today that you will stand for your Savior no matter the cost.

Seven times a day I praise You.
PSALM 119:164

One day when missionary physician Harold Adolph was walking through his house, he saw a verse on the wall of his daughter's room. It was Proverbs 17:22: "A cheerful heart is good medicine" (NIV). Adolph thought, "If only I could harness the secret of that cheerfulness and share it with my patients, a great deal of physical and spiritual suffering could be avoided." Another verse came to mind—Psalm 119:164: "Seven times a day I praise You." That verse, he thought, was like a prescription off a medicine bottle.

Most patients resist taking a medicine seven times a day, which is why pharmaceutical companies develop pills to be taken only once or twice daily. But Dr. Adolph suggests we try the remedy exactly as God prescribed it. You might set your phone alarm to remind yourself to praise God seven times throughout this day. The goal isn't legalism, but to learn to praise God continuously and to keep our hearts cheerful all day long.

Life is a good gift from God and we must treasure it.

From Bottom to Top

*Yet it shall not be so among you; but whoever desires to
become great among you shall be your servant.*

MARK 10:43

Something in us inspires us to reach for the top. On our best days, call it the desire for excellence. But on our worst days, it amounts to a quest for place, prestige, and the power that comes with life at the top. There's a fine line between one and the other. And because it is part of the human condition, that line can be crossed even when serving the Lord.

The disciples learned that lesson the hard way. Two of them, the brothers James and John, asked Jesus to appoint them to positions sitting at His right and left when He came into His glory. That is, they wanted positions of ruling in God's kingdom—co-prime ministers, if you will. When the other ten disciples heard about the brothers' request, they were indignant. (Were they upset at the brothers' quest for power, or upset that the brothers had the idea first? There's the thin line again.) Jesus denied their request, telling them there was a prerequisite to greatness called service: "Whoever desires to become great among you shall be your servant" (Mark 10:43). That was true of Jesus (Philippians 2:5-8) and it would be true of His disciples.

Jesus taught that the most important place in life is at the bottom (Luke 14:7-11).

MARCH 27
Secret Ingredient

The thief does not come except to steal, and to kill, and to destroy. I have come that they may have life, and that they may have it more abundantly.
JOHN 10:10

Restaurants and chefs often guard their best recipes. They work hard to create the perfect entrée and don't want others taking advantage of their labor to create something unique and precious. Thankfully, God is not stingy with His best. He freely gave His Son, Jesus. Throughout the Gospels, Jesus encountered sickness, death, and confusion, and brought light and healing.

From the miracle at the Cana wedding to His ascension to heaven, Jesus entered situations and made them better. Because Jesus is deeply connected to God, unaffected by pride and self-absorption, He sees below the surface and knows how to bring the missing insight, healing, and hope to those who feel hopeless and lost.

We can invite God into each area of our lives. He has promised His Spirit and strength. Regardless of how or when our prayers are answered, Jesus is life. As we grow in our trust of Him, we realize that nothing is beyond His reach. We can invite Him into the darkest seasons and spaces of our lives and trust that He will bring light.

Don't Play Games

That which we have seen and heard we declare to you …. And
these things we write to you that your joy may be full.
1 JOHN 1:3-4

Have you ever seen a book on the joy of the Pharisees? That's
not to say the subject has never been explored. But where
would a writer begin? There is nothing in the Gospels to
suggest that the legalistic religious leaders of Jesus' day were
overflowing with joy. Instead, there is plenty to suggest that
they spent a good deal of time nurturing their religious
outward appearance to conceal a barren inner spiritual life.

Hypocrisy—that's what Jesus called it (Matthew 23:13,
15, 23, 25, 27-29). His most vivid illustration of the Pharisees'
spiritual life was calling them "whitewashed tombs," beautiful
on the outside but filled with "dead men's bones and all
uncleanness." How can anyone cultivate joy when their
attention is focused on being right about religious rules and
living a double-standard life? The apostle John raised the same
issue in 1 John. Joy is found in fellowship with God and others
(1 John 1:3-4). We can't live a hypocritical life and walk in that
fellowship.

As we transition from spiritual darkness to light, we are
tempted to play spiritual games. Stay true; stay joyful; stay in
fellowship with God.

*Therefore, having been justified by faith, we have peace
with God through our Lord Jesus Christ.*
ROMANS 5:1

The world is fragmented and many nations are at war. The United States and its allies are never far from being drawn into escalating conflicts. One influential leader told reporters, "The world is in a state of war in bits and pieces .... The world is at war because it has lost peace."

The fundamental war—and the one that spawns all the others—is humanity's war against God. Without Jesus Christ, we're in a state of war with our Creator. We are estranged from Him, and that spills over into all the other conflicts.

Jesus Christ came to be the Mediator, to be the peacemaker, and to reconcile us to God so we can have peace with God through our Lord Jesus Christ—and then peace with others. When we're at peace with God through Christ, we have continual, constant, unbroken, enduring access to His grace, all the time. We have access into God's presence. We have access to prayer, to the throne of grace. We have access to all His promises in the Bible. We become people of peace.

Peace with God is something only the believer in Jesus Christ can claim, and that's why our message is called the "gospel of peace" (Ephesians 6:15).

But what things were gain to me, these I have counted loss for Christ.

PHILIPPIANS 3:7

Dinner party games often include this one: "A raging wildfire is forcing the sudden evacuation of your neighborhood. What three things do you grab before leaving home?" The answers are varied, but often include family photos, a keepsake heirloom, the baby's supplies, legal and financial papers, a note-filled Bible. What we would take says something about what we value and what our priorities are.

If the apostle Paul were to have played that game, he might have said something like, "First and foremost, I would take my relationship with Jesus Christ." Well, that's cheating a bit, since a relationship is not a tangible thing one can put in a suitcase. But it's easy, after reading Philippians 3:4-11, to sense what Paul meant. In that passage we find a stark comparison between Paul's priorities before meeting Christ and after meeting Christ. Before his conversion, Paul was all about Paul—his Jewish pedigree, his advancement as a Pharisaic scholar, and his zeal for persecuting Christians. After meeting Christ, things changed: "But what things were gain to me, these I have counted loss for Christ." He considered knowing Christ Jesus his Lord the most important thing in his life (Philippians 3:8).

How have your priorities changed since meeting Christ? Is anything in your life more important than Him?

*The heavens declare the glory of God; and the
firmament shows His handiwork.*

PSALM 19:1

When Soviet premier Nikita Khrushchev was promoting anti-religious propaganda among young people, he asked, "Why are you [young people] clinging to God? Here [Soviet cosmonaut Yuri] Gagarin flew into space and didn't see God." In 1963, another Russian cosmonaut, Valery Bykovsky, told reporters that no Soviet cosmonauts believed in God and had seen nothing in space to change their minds.

For the Christian, 2 Corinthians 5:7 comes immediately to mind: "For we walk by faith, not by sight." And John 1:18: "No one has seen God at any time." When we look for the wrong things in life, we miss what is actually there. And what is there in the universe—in all of creation—is evidence of God's presence, His creativity, and His glory. Psalm 19 extols the virtues of God's spoken and written Word, but the psalmist introduces those verses (7-11) by pointing out how God speaks through creation: "There is no speech nor language where their voice is not heard" (verse 3). So clear and articulate is the voice of creation that Paul says those who deny the existence of God are without excuse (Romans 1:19-20).

Don't marvel just at the glories of nature. Marvel at the glory of the One who created what you see. Learn to "read" about God through the words the heavens declare.

APRIL

APRIL 1
Tools for Life

Also day by day, from the first day until the last day,
[Ezra] read from the Book of the Law of God.
NEHEMIAH 8:18

Imagine you've hired a contractor to carry out some major remodeling on your home. You open the door to find a man dressed in casual clothes and no sign of tools or workers. Expressing surprise, you ask him if he is there to begin work and he says, "Yes, I am!" When you ask where his tools and workers are, he says, "Well, I'll figure something out!"

This is a man who is not "thoroughly equipped" for his job (2 Timothy 3:17). And sometimes we find ourselves not equipped for the job of living life. But sometimes we meet people who are—they possess a sense of wisdom, of peace, of contentment, and of purpose that amazes us. When we get to know them, we discover they have spent consistent time, for many years, studying the Word of God. The doctrine, reproof, correction, and instruction they have gained is evident in their lives (2 Timothy 3:16).

Don't show up for the job of life without the tools you need. Let the Word of God thoroughly equip you for life.

Come to Me, all you who labor and are heavy laden, and I will give you rest.
MATTHEW 11:28

When a team begins losing to their opponent, most coaches call for a time-out. Rather than leave their team out on the field facing discouragement and distraction, the time-out serves to remind them of their strengths and refocus them on their strategies.

During times of stress and conflict, God beckons us to take a time-out. To stop. To breathe. To pray. During chaotic seasons, draw close to God and bask in His faithfulness and affection. Our right standing and connection with Him is unaltered by anything or any being. Charles Spurgeon recalled, "You may have no joy in your situation, but you can rejoice in your Savior. You may be encased in shadows, but you can still walk in the light as He is in the light. To rejoice in the Lord means that we rejoice in our unassailable, unchanging relationship with the Sovereign Lord and in His qualities, gifts, promises, and attributes."

Jesus paid the price for us to have a steadfast relationship with God. Whether the stress of a situation remains or is removed, our souls can rest in Him.

APRIL 3
Our High Priest

*[Christ] does not need daily, as those high priests, to offer up
sacrifices, first for His own sins and then for the people's,
for this He did once for all when He offered up Himself.*

HEBREWS 7:27

Several priests in Israel are named in the New Testament.
Zacharias, the father of John the Baptist, was one of hundreds
of priests who rotated through various duties at the temple in
Jerusalem (Luke 1:5). Caiaphas, who participated in the trials of
Jesus, is named as a high priest in the year of Jesus' death (John
11:49). One word can best describe all the priests of Israel:
temporary. Priests—even the high priest—came and went.

The impermanence of these priests is a primary point of
comparison between them and Jesus. Jesus offered Himself
"once for all when He offered up Himself." In that way, He
became a better High Priest than all who preceded Him in
Israel. As the permanent High Priest, Jesus is an Advocate in
heaven for all who He represents (1 John 2:1), always there to
make intercession for us (Romans 8:34; Hebrews 7:25). No
earthly priest could, or can, do that for us.

When you pray today, imagine Jesus as your Advocate,
interceding for you before the Father.

APRIL 4
Always More

But rise and stand on your feet; for I have appeared to you for this purpose, to make you a minister and a witness both of the things which you have seen and of the things which I will yet reveal to you.

ACTS 26:16

When a group of English Puritans decided to seek religious freedom in America, their pastor, John Robinson, exhorted them to follow Christ and His Word in the New World. He said, "I am verily persuaded the Lord hath more truth and light yet to break forth from His holy word."

He meant that the Spirit of God would continually give them new insights and applications from Scripture to apply to their lives in America. It is a similar notion to what Christ told Saul of Tarsus when He commissioned him as the apostle to the Gentiles. Saul (later Paul, the apostle) was to be "a minister and a witness" of not only what he had seen to that point but of what would be revealed to him in the future. The idea that God is continuing to guide us and instruct us from His Word is long-standing: "Open my eyes, that I may see wondrous things from Your law" (Psalm 119:18).

Hopefully, where you are today in your understanding of God and His Word is not where you will be in the future. Expect God to illuminate your path daily as you study His Word.

APRIL 5
What Do You Need?

When Jesus saw him lying there, and knew that he already had been in that condition a long time, He said to him, "Do you want to be made well?"

JOHN 5:6

We know why people stand in line at the post office. We know why the people in the dentist's waiting room are there. In the first century, if you saw scores of people gathered around the Pool of Bethesda in Jerusalem, you would know why they were there. They were there to be healed.

The pool called Bethesda was really twin pools in Jerusalem surrounded on four sides by porches and another porch dividing the two pools. The sick would gather on the porches and wait for a stirring of the waters—supposedly by an angel of heaven—entry into which might result in healing. So those on the porches were there for healing. Yet Jesus approached a man and asked what must have seemed like an obvious question: "Do you want to be made well?"

Much could be said of Jesus' question, but it begs another question: Do we want to be made whole? Forgiven and delivered from sin? Saved for eternity? The God of miracles is waiting for our answer. He wants us to say what we need.

Jesus Christ is the same yesterday, today, and forever.
HEBREWS 13:8

People have always dreamed of telling the future; the devil, leveraging that desire, has enslaved millions of people in astrology, fortune-telling, gambling, and the occult. There are also scholars who study current trends to anticipate tomorrow's world. And science fiction writers use vivid imaginations to create scenes of the future. They all have little success. You can read hundreds of science-fiction books from the first half of the twentieth century, for example, without finding one that envisions the Internet. The writers simply couldn't foresee how modern technology would unfold.

But Jesus Christ knows the future—"yesterday, today, and forever."

He knows your past, every moment of every day since your conception, all you've endured or experienced. He knows what's going on right now in your life—every blessing, every burden, every tear, every fear. He knows what will happen tomorrow, and He has specifically told us not to worry about that (see Matthew 6:34). As we learn from studying biblical prophecy, the Lord has the future well in hand.

He has you well in hand too!

Jesus said to them, "My food is to do the will of Him who sent Me, and to finish His work."
JOHN 4:34

In the hunter-gatherer era there was one primary diet. It was called the "Whatever You Can Find to Eat Diet." Today, you can choose from vegan, vegetarian, whole-food and plant based, keto, low-carb, Mediterranean, standard American, and various diets named after their developers. Food is a primary focus of people in every culture.

Once when Jesus' disciples offered Him food to eat, He told them He already had the food He needed: "My food is to do the will of Him who sent Me, and to finish His work." This was yet another eye-opening lesson for the disciples, not about food but about focus. Jesus was saying, "It is not food that sustains Me. What sustains Me is the will of God for My life." Yes, Jesus ate real food along with everyone else. But His stomach was not His god (Romans 16:18; Philippians 3:19). As He told the devil in the wilderness, "Man shall not live by bread alone, but by every word that proceeds from the mouth of God" (Matthew 4:4). Food may sustain the body, but the Word and will of God sustains the spirit.

Are you getting daily spiritual nourishment from time spent with God? It's the only way to grow in wisdom and stature with God and man (see Luke 2:52).

APRIL 8
Better to Give

And Jesus said to him, "Foxes have holes and birds of the air have nests, but the Son of Man has nowhere to lay His head."
MATTHEW 8:20

In 2018, Americans spent nearly $3 billion on self-storage. In 2015, less than ten percent of U.S. households rented a self-storage unit. In 2017, construction on new self-storage units topped $291 million *per month*.[5] Some of that storage is short-term, of course: people in transition, settling estates, storing business inventories, and so on. But the majority is in use for one reason: We have more stuff than we know what to do with.

There's nothing wrong with having possessions, of course—or storing them outside our homes for various reasons. But the booming personal self-storage industry stands in sharp contrast to the life of Jesus. We have no record of His owning anything except His clothes (Matthew 27:31). He Himself testified to owning nothing in this world (Matthew 8:20). He came into this world to give rather than to receive (Acts 20:35). Even the apostle Paul cited "food and clothing" as being adequate for life in this world (1 Timothy 6:8).

When considering generosity, consider how Christ lived. Imitate Him as the Spirit of God leads. Give as you have been given.

[5] https://www.sparefoot.com/self-storage/news/1432-self-storage-industry-statistics/.

APRIL 9
Be a Fruit Inspector

Therefore bear fruits worthy of repentance.
LUKE 3:8

In biblical days, fruit played a significant role in the diet of the average person. Grapes, figs, pomegranates, olives, melons, dates, berries, stone fruits, and citrus fruits were available. Even in the off-season, people could look at a tree and tell what kind of fruit one might expect to harvest from it. Thus, "bearing fruit" became a spiritual metaphor used by the writers of Scripture.

When John the Baptist began his ministry of announcing the coming of Jesus the Messiah, crowds journeyed from all over Judea to the Jordan River to hear him preach and to be baptized by him. But before baptizing them, John warned them: "You must bear fruit in keeping with your so-called repentance." That is, just saying "I repent" and being baptized were not proof enough of the state of your heart. You, as a spiritual tree, must bring forth fruit in keeping with your profession of repentance and faith. "What kind of fruit?" the crowds asked. "Be generous to the poor," John said. "Tax collectors and soldiers, be honest; don't overcharge people or extort money. Live a life consistent with God's kingdom. Do what God would do in your situation."

The same is true for us. The apostle James wrote that faith without works is no faith at all (James 2:14-17). Fruit must be consistent with the tree. Our walk must match our talk.

APRIL 10
Powerful Promise

If you abide in Me, and My words abide in you, you will
ask what you desire, and it shall be done for you.
JOHN 15:7

In the Old Testament, unconditional covenants were like God's promise to Abraham (Genesis 12:1-3); all the responsibilities were God's. Conditional covenants were like the promises made to Israel: *If* Israel walked in God's ways, *then* they would enjoy God's rich blessing. Both parties had responsibilities.

Jesus made a conditional promise to His disciples: "*If* you abide in Me, and [*if*] My words abide in you, [*then*] you will ask what you desire, and it shall be done for you." Both parties had responsibilities. The disciples were to remain faithful to Jesus and His words and He would meet their needs. Did He promise to give them anything they wanted? No, He promised to provide for them as they followed Him: wisdom, courage, provision, assurance, and the like. His promise was not a blank check to purchase the bells and baubles of this world. Jesus was saying to His disciples what Jonathan said to his covenant brother, David: "Whatever you yourself desire [as Israel's anointed king], I will do it for you" (1 Samuel 20:4).

With such a powerful promise comes great responsibility: to ask in the spirit, and within the bounds, of the promise. When you pray, make sure you are meeting your responsibility of abiding in Jesus and His Word.

APRIL 11
The Damascus Road

*As he journeyed he came near Damascus, and suddenly
a light shone around him from heaven.*

ACTS 9:3

On a journey home from the University of Erfurt, where
21-year-old Martin Luther studied law, a frightening thunderstorm suddenly enveloped him. A lightning bolt flashed and
struck so close that Martin, petrified, cried out, "Saint Anne,
help me! I will become a monk." Shortly thereafter, he entered
an Augustinian monastery and eventually traveled to the little
town of Wittenberg to teach at the university. His mentor,
Johann von Staupitz, assigned him the books of Romans and
Galatians. While studying, Luther's eyes were opened to the
true Gospel message—salvation by grace through faith. This
discovery was a Damascus Road experience for him, and he
devoted his life to advancing the cause of the Gospel.

We're often on the road to life as we design it when God
intervenes with storms, lightning bolts, mentors, and the
Gospel message. Every one of us needs a Damascus Road
experience. It may not be as dramatic as Paul's or Luther's, but
we need a moment in our life when we understand and receive
the Gospel. No one is the same after an encounter with God.
Martin Luther put it this way: *The Bible is alive, it speaks to me; it
has feet, it runs after me; it has hands, it lays hold of me.*

APRIL 12
One in the Spirit

We know that we have passed from death to
life, because we love the brethren.
1 JOHN 3:14

While Peter Scholtes was parish priest at St. Brendan's Church on the South Side of Chicago in the 1960s, he began leading a youth choir in the church basement. America was being torn apart by racial and cultural divisions, and Scholtes wanted to teach his kids about the unifying power of Christian love. When he couldn't find the right song, he wrote one himself, in a single day. It became one of the earliest praise songs of the Jesus Movement: "We are one in the Spirit, we are one in the Lord. And we pray that all unity may one day be restored. And they'll know we are Christians by our love."

According to 1 John, if we are true Christians who have genuinely trusted Christ as our Savior, the evidence will be in our love for others. John wrote, "We know that we have passed from death to life, because we love the brethren. He who does not love his brother abides in death."

When we supernaturally love others, and display a steadfast faith in God, we show evidence of being a child of God. They will know we're Christians by our love.

APRIL 13
So Great!

How shall we escape if we neglect so great a salvation.
HEBREWS 2:3

Why is salvation great? Because we have a *great* need, which burdened the heart of a *great* God, who paid a *great* price by sending a *great* Savior. But there's more. It's also great because it saves us from *great* danger. Dr. Martyn Lloyd-Jones said, "This is so great a salvation because it saves us from a great and a terrible calamity. 'How shall we *escape*, if we neglect so great salvation?' You measure the greatness of the salvation by measuring the greatness of the calamity from which it saves us."[6]

The word *great* occurs more than a thousand times in the Bible, and many of the references speak of the greatness of the deliverance we receive and the blessings God bestows in Christ. Because of that, we should greatly rejoice! Psalm 21:1 says of the godly person: "[He] shall have joy in Your strength, O Lord; and in Your salvation how greatly shall he rejoice!"

Regardless of what else is happening in your life today, you can rejoice in your great Savior!

---

[6] Martyn Lloyd-Jones, *Setting Our Affections Upon Glory* (Wheaton, IL: Crossway, 2013), 93.

He is able to keep what I have committed to Him until that Day.
2 TIMOTHY 1:12

Your God is able! He is able to keep you, bless you, use you, and care for all you entrust to Him.

The three Hebrew children in Daniel 3 said, "Our God whom we serve is able to deliver us" (verse 17). John the Baptist said, "God is able to raise up children to Abraham from these stones" (Luke 3:8). Paul said, "[God] is able to establish you" (Romans 16:25) and "God is able to make all grace abound toward you" (2 Corinthians 9:8) and "[He] is able to do exceedingly abundantly above all that we ask or think" (Ephesians 3:20). According to Hebrews 2:18, "He is able to aid those who are tempted." Jude said, "[He] is able to keep you from stumbling" (Jude 1:24).

The impact we make on the world doesn't depend on our ability, but on His. Our legacy isn't established by our capability but by His capacity. He enables us to live beyond our wildest dreams because when we serve Him faithfully, only eternity can record the results.

Don't be discouraged if you aren't reaching certain goals or if your results don't match your expectations. Give all your work to Him. Give Him your dreams and all your doings. He is able to keep that which we have committed to Him until that day.

Yes, and Amen!

Now hope does not disappoint, because the love of God has been poured out in our hearts by the Holy Spirit who was given to us.

ROMANS 5:5

Think of what we hope for in this life: good health, a bright future for our children, pleasant weather, world peace, a fulfilling vocation, and more. All of these hopes have one thing in common: None of them is certain. Everything we hope for in life holds the potential for disappointment. Except for one thing.

The Bible says that the Christian's hope "does not disappoint." All the things we hope for in the spiritual life— blessings, love, forgiveness, eternal life, and more—are made certain in Christ. How can that be? How can we be certain that God will never disappoint us? "Because the love of God has been poured out in our hearts by the Holy Spirit who was given to us." The inner witness of the Holy Spirit gives us assurance that "all the promises of God in [Christ] are Yes, and in Him Amen, to the glory of God through us" (2 Corinthians 1:20). Because of the bedrock reality of the Resurrection of Christ from the dead, we know that God is true. Without the Resurrection, we would be most disappointed (1 Corinthians 15:14-19).

Temper your hopes with the possibility of disappointment—except for your hope in God. In Christ your hopes are "Yes" and "Amen!"

APRIL 16
The Strength of Weakness

So [Gideon] said to [the Lord], "O my Lord, how can I save Israel? Indeed my clan is the weakest in Manasseh, and I am the least in my father's house."

JUDGES 6:15

How many times have you heard someone say, "I'd like to help, but I wouldn't know where to begin"; "I'm really not qualified to take on a ministry like that"; "I'm a nobody"; "I couldn't expect people to follow my leadership on that project." Those aren't always unreasonable perspectives. After all, an eighty-year-old saint is not likely to be chosen to be an astronaut. So, life does have its limitations.

But for the most part, we are too quick to look at our human stature—age, education, maturity, leadership skills—and disqualify ourselves from serving the Lord or others. That is, we tend to look at *our weaknesses* instead of *Christ's strengths*. The Bible is filled with examples of God using the under-qualified and the weak to accomplish great things—like Gideon, for example. He was the weakest member of the weakest family in one of the smaller tribes of Israel. But God used him to defeat the Midianites (Judges 6–7).

God calls the weak to manifest His strength through them (2 Corinthians 12:9).

But God demonstrates His own love toward us, in that
while we were still sinners, Christ died for us.
ROMANS 5:8

Elizabeth Barrett Browning's poem "How Do I Love Thee?" (Sonnet 43) is a well-known love poem. She begins, "How do I love thee? Let me count the ways," and proceeds to list more than half a dozen ways. We understand the poet's desire to meditate on the many reasons and ways of love. But it raises the question, "Can love be counted?" Quantifying love runs the risk of taking the focus off its beauty.

Biblical love is boundless, unconditional, sacrificial, and generous. God demonstrated His love by giving His Son's life for ours. If our giving to God and others is motivated by love, we will spend less time figuring out how much to keep and more time in the act of giving. When we focus on love and generosity, we will always give more than if we focus on numbers.

That's not to say we shouldn't be careful stewards. But it is to remember that we are giving what God has first given to us. Our concern is less with how much we can keep than how much love we can show.

[Jesus] said to them, "All too well you reject the commandment of God, that you may keep your tradition."

MARK 7:9

As exhaustive as the laws in the Mosaic Covenant were (600+ statutes), they could not cover every single situation in life that might arise. To fill in the gaps, Jewish leaders wrote new statutes that, over time, acquired nearly the same status as the Mosaic laws. These man-made ordinances were referred to by Jesus as traditions—and not in a positive sense. The Jews often used their traditions to avoid compliance with an actual statute of God (as illustrated in Mark 7:9-13). For their hypocrisy, they earned the Lord's rebuke.

This hypocritical use of traditions is not a blanket condemnation of practices learned over time. In fact, Paul wrote to the Thessalonians, "Therefore, brethren, stand fast and hold the traditions which you were taught, whether by word or our epistle" (2 Thessalonians 2:15). Traditions are nothing more than customs or beliefs ratified by practice over time. Traditions can be a help or a hindrance; they can be biblical or man-made. Anytime we say, "But we've always done it that way," we should examine that tradition and its basis. Is it founded on the Word of God or the preferences of man?

When the traditions of man conflict with the traditions (teachings) of God, the choice is clear as to which takes priority.

On the Third Day

*He rose again the third day .... Therefore, my beloved brethren, be
steadfast, immovable, always abounding in the work of the Lord,
knowing that your labor is not in vain in the Lord.*

1 CORINTHIANS 15:4, 58

Easter is why we don't give up. According to the Resurrection
Chapter of the Bible—1 Corinthians 15—Christ arose as the
firstfruits of all who fall asleep in Him (verse 20). He destroyed
our last enemy (verse 26) and provided the power, proof, and
pattern for our own resurrection (verse 49). Because of Easter,
the trumpet will sound and we'll be raised incorruptible (verse
52). Our Lord gives us the victory (verse 57), which is why we
remain immovable and abounding in His will and work.

We don't give up when Satan attacks, when friends turn
against us, when family upsets us, or when the work seems
futile.

History's worst moment occurred on Good Friday, when
the Savior perished and the devil gloated. But everything was
different three days later—so don't give up. Look up. Cheer up.
Your life and labor in the Lord is not in vain. That's His promise
at the end of the Resurrection Chapter.

After that, [Jesus] poured water into a basin and began to wash the disciples'
feet, and to wipe them with the towel with which He was girded.
JOHN 13:5

When you welcome visitors to your home, you take their coats, you offer them a seat by the fire if they're cold, you bring food and drink, inquire as to their health and well-being, and more. One thing you likely don't do is remove their shoes and wash their feet.

In biblical days—beginning in Genesis (18:4; 19:2; 43:24)—washing the feet of guests was a common act of courtesy. It was because people wore sandals, the roads were dusty, and clean feet was a refreshing sign of hospitality. But this act was always accomplished a certain way: *servants* oversaw the foot-washing, not the host (Genesis 43:24). That's why, when Jesus and His disciples gathered for a meal at Passover, it was such a shock for Jesus, the host, to begin washing the disciples' feet. Peter objected, but Jesus insisted (John 13:8). This was obviously an object lesson in the humility of service, something Jesus had stressed in His teachings (Mark 10:43-45; Luke 22:27). He knew the disciples would need humility as the backdrop to their future ministry of the Gospel (James 4:6).

When it comes to service, very few people will volunteer for the menial roles in life. But it's often the little things that validate the bigger things.

He is not here; for He is risen, as He said. Come,
see the place where the Lord lay.
MATTHEW 28:6

After the death and burial of Jesus, His disciples were stunned, even dismayed. They had failed to watch with Jesus in prayer in Gethsemane and fled when soldiers appeared to arrest Him (Matthew 26:36-46, 56). And Peter had denied Him (Matthew 26:69-75). Besides that, they feared the Jews; they were hiding behind locked doors in Jerusalem (John 20:19). They had not yet processed Jesus' own prior words about being resurrected from the dead (John 2:19-22).

But then, in the midst of their dark despair, Jesus appeared to them, alive from the dead, and said, "Peace be with you" (John 20:19). His words meant, "Don't be anxious. Don't worry about what happened before. I am alive from the dead. Everything is new now; it's time to begin again. It's time to continue and complete the work the Father sent Me to do." That's what Easter means for us as well. Because Jesus has been raised from the dead, we can be born again to a new life in Him.

As you contemplate Easter, give thanks for the cleansing work of Christ in your life because He is risen.

APRIL 22
The Absence of Arrogance

By humility and the fear of the Lord are riches and honor and life.
PROVERBS 22:4

One day Dr. Sheila Murray Bethel attended a luncheon in Washington, D.C., hosted by Katharine Graham, the far-famed publisher of *The Washington Post*. Mrs. Graham's parties were legendary, and she rubbed shoulders with the greatest statesmen on earth. "Mrs. Graham," asked Dr. Bethel, "you have hosted all the greatest leaders from around the world. What is the single most important trait of all great leaders?" Mrs. Graham answered without even pausing to think. "The absence of arrogance," she said.

When you think of influential leaders—those whose legacy has grown over time—you think of people with a streak of humility, whose desire for service eclipsed the desire for fame and fortune. Great leaders are those who listen and who pause to speak to others without concern for rank or status. They are individuals who are willing to listen to the concerns of others. Most of all, they seem to possess an absence of arrogance.

We're all leaders in one way or another. To be effective, we should display God's humility, not a false pretense of our own. Let's all develop the quality of being humble, not haughty.

And Ezra blessed the Lord, the great God. Then all the people answered, "Amen, Amen!" while lifting up their hands. And they bowed their heads and worshiped the Lord with their faces to the ground.

NEHEMIAH 8:6

It could happen at the reading of a relative's will, wherein you are named as a beneficiary. It could happen when you are hired or promoted or accepted to college. Maybe it happens when you are the grand-prize winner in a contest. Or when your beloved says "Yes" to your marriage proposal.

Good news can produce excitement, passion, joy, surprise, and even worship. That's right—the revelation of profoundly good news can bring a response of worship. That's what happened to the Jews who had returned from exile in Babylon and were attempting to rebuild Jerusalem when Ezra read to them from God's Word (Nehemiah 8). What good news did they hear? That God's love for them was everlasting, that His blessings were never ending, that His love and protection were theirs if they would give themselves to Him. To which they responded, "Amen, Amen!"

Let the Good News of God's Word move you to worship each time you read God's "great and precious promises" (2 Peter 1:4).

APRIL 24
It Took a Miracle

He ... supplies the Spirit to you and works miracles among you.
GALATIANS 3:5

In the Gospels, the miracles of Jesus were usually prompted by problems. He turned water to wine because the wedding feast had run out. He healed Peter's mother-in-law because of her fever. He raised the widow's son because of the woman's pitiful grief. He calmed the storm because the disciples were panicked. He fed the multitude because of hunger.

Every miracle begins with a problem, and every problem presents an opportunity for Christ to help us in our difficulty.

God can still perform miracles, but they come in all shapes and sizes. Because of the crowning miracle of Scripture—the Resurrection of Christ—all our problems are in the process of resolving for our good. The backdrop of every believer's life is the miraculous curtain of God's grace. He turns curses into blessings for us every day. He protects us when we don't know it. He overrules circumstances when we don't even realize it.

Take your problem to the Lord today and ask Him for a miracle—in His timing, in His way, and for the glory of Him who supplies the Spirit to us and works miracles among us.

Let perseverance finish its work so that you may be
mature and complete, not lacking anything.
JAMES 1:4, NIV

Irving Stone studied the lives of some of the greatest and most interesting characters in history, and he wrote biographical novels about them—people like Vincent van Gogh, Michelangelo, and Abraham Lincoln. After years of research into some of the greatest men and women who ever lived, he concluded these individuals were unique because they had a vision or dream of something that should be accomplished, and then they went to work. Each of them were knocked down, vilified, and appeared to be failing, but every time they were knocked down they got up. They persevered. And at the end of their lives they accomplished a portion of what they set out to do.[7]

Endurance and perseverance are at the heart of character. According to Romans 5:3-4, suffering produces perseverance; perseverance, character; and character, hope.

If you're under attack right now, don't give up. Persevere. Trust in the Lord and let Him provide the strength you need.

[7] Pat Williams and Jim Denney, *Go for the Magic* (Nashville: Thomas Nelson, 1995), 175-176.

> *Our Father in heaven, hallowed be Your name. Your kingdom*
> *come. Your will be done on earth as it is in heaven.*
> MATTHEW 6:9-10

There is a lot of waiting in life. You file your income taxes and then you wait for your refund if one is due. You fill out a loan application to purchase a home, then wait while the bank's legal and financial wheels turn toward your approval. Waiting is a part of life.

Christians are in a waiting mode right now as well. We are waiting for Jesus' prayer to be answered—for God's kingdom to be established on earth as it is in heaven. Everything has been done to make that possible. Jesus' sacrifice for sin has made it possible for any who want to gain entrance to the eternal kingdom of God to do so. Jesus said in Matthew 24:14 that the Gospel would be preached in all the world, to all the nations, "and then the end will come." So, at the moment, we are waiting while we participate in the spread of the Gospel to all the world.

Are you planning to enter God's kingdom when it comes to earth, when Jesus returns? Only through embracing His once-for-all death and Resurrection is that possible.

APRIL 27
The Priority of Scripture

My people are destroyed for lack of knowledge. Because you have rejected knowledge, I also will reject you from being priest for Me.

HOSEA 4:6

Parents sometimes restrict a teenager's use of the family car when the rules for driving the vehicle are broken. Through discipline, the young driver learns that using the car is conditional based upon obedience to the parents' expectations for its use. When the conditions set by the parents are broken, the privilege is rescinded.

Such is the nature of conditional covenants—like the Mosaic Covenant in the Old Testament. Priests in Israel would enjoy God's blessing as long as they were good stewards of the covenant, that is, the Word of God. As long as they taught the people God's laws and statutes, and led them in walking faithfully in those laws and statutes, they would remain as priests. Failure to teach the people the Word of God would mean they would be removed as priests. And that's what happened as recorded by the prophet Hosea. That's how central the Word of God is to the community of God's people.

The responsibility to embrace the Word of God is not only for leaders (2 Timothy 4:2) but for everyone (1 Peter 2:2). Adherence to Scripture is non-negotiable.

APRIL 28
The Peace Maker

*My peace I give to you; not as the world gives do I
give to you. Let not your heart be troubled.*
JOHN 14:27

Frederick Edward Marsh (1858-1931) was a Bible teacher and prolific author who devoted his life to the Word. He listed some of God's blessings for His children, saying we have:

An acceptance that can never be questioned (Ephesians 1:6).
An inheritance that can never be lost (1 Peter 1:3-5).
A deliverance that can never be excelled (2 Corinthians 1:10).
A grace that can never be limited (2 Corinthians 12:9).
A hope that can never be disappointed (Hebrews 6:18-19).
A bounty that can never be withdrawn (1 Corinthians 3:21-23).
A joy that can never be diminished (John 15:11).
A nearness to God that can never be reversed (Ephesians 2:13).
A righteousness that can never be tarnished
(2 Corinthians 5:21).
A salvation that can never be canceled (Hebrews 5:9).
A peace that can never be disturbed (John 14:27).

Peace may not be possible in our world, but it's possible in our hearts because God has given us acceptance, inheritance, deliverance, grace, hope, bounty, joy, nearness, righteousness, and salvation. Hallelujah!

He Ain't Heavy ...

Bear one another's burdens, and so fulfill the law of Christ.
GALATIANS 6:2

James Wells, a leader in the United Free Church of Scotland, wrote a book on the parables of Jesus in 1884. In his book, he told the story of a little girl who was seen carrying a rather big baby boy. When someone asked her if she needed to rest, her reply of surprise came in her Scottish brogue: "He's na heavy. He's mi brither." That phrase has appeared in popular versions ever since, most wide-spread in the late-sixties pop song by the British group The Hollies, "He Ain't Heavy, He's My Brother."

It's a beautiful sentiment; one wonders if the Scot James Wells drew inspiration for his story from Paul's words in Galatians 6:2: "Bear one another's burdens, and so fulfill the law of Christ." Which raises the question, "What is the 'law of Christ' to which Paul refers?" What "law" requires us to bear the burdens of our brothers and sisters? It likely doesn't refer to a specific teaching of Christ, but rather to His whole teaching on love. His "new commandment" requires us to "love one another" (John 13:34), the greatest expression of which is to lay down our life for a friend (John 15:13).

Does someone near you have a burden that you can share? As the saying goes, "A burden shared is a burden halved."

And if Christ is not risen, then our preaching is
empty and your faith is also empty.
1 CORINTHIANS 15:14

A Latin phrase has survived for two millennia: *sine qua non.*
Like many Latin words and phrases, it is rarely translated into
English. Instead, it is used in its Latin form. A literal translation
explains why: "[that] without which not." To paraphrase, *sine
qua non* means "something indispensable or essential," as in
anatomy is a *sine qua non* for a career in medicine.

The Christian faith has its own *sine qua non*—its own
indispensable or essential element: The Resurrection of Jesus
Christ from the dead. To paraphrase the words of the apostle
Paul in 1 Corinthians 15:14, 17, without the miracle of the
resurrection of Christ, faith and the Christian life are futile.
We are still in our sins. Those who say it really doesn't matter
if Christ rose from the dead have it all wrong. Everything
depends on the Resurrection! Christ's being raised from
the dead was God's seal on the work Christ accomplished
on the cross—the work of propitiation, forgiveness, and
reconciliation—the greatest miracle of all.

Good news! The same power and Spirit that raised Jesus
from the dead will also transform us from death to life (Romans
8:11).

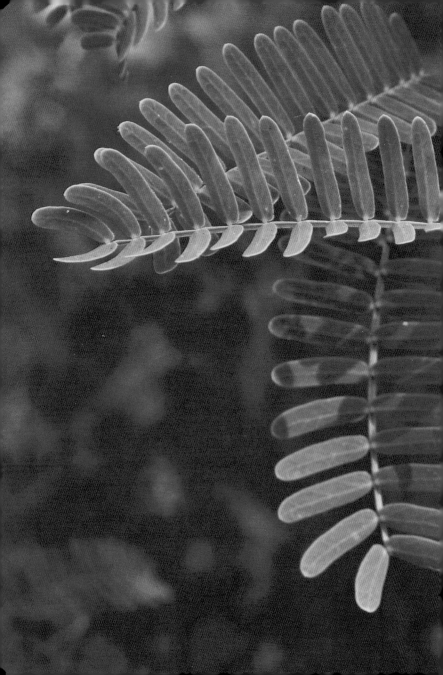

MAY

MAY 1
Key Words

When He, the Spirit of truth, has come, He will guide you into all truth.
JOHN 16:13

In a little book on Bible study published in 1901, Professor James McConaughy of Mount Hermon School in Northfield, Massachusetts, suggested:

"To get [the] most good from your daily reading keep in mind these key-words: (1) *Think*. Keep the mind fixed on the passage. If it is difficult, read aloud .... (2) *Pray*. The heart must be taught as well as the mind. God's Spirit only can do this. (3) *Obey*. God's Word is more than history, more than literature. It is a revelation of His will, a message to the reader... Only those who *do* what is written in it are blessed. (4) *Share*. The gospel is not private property .... The things which have been seen and heard must be spoken ... The privilege of following a course of Bible study brings with it the responsibility of using the results for God."

It's hard to beat those suggestions. We should anticipate Bible study as those seeking light and truth, for His Word "is a lamp to my feet and a light to my path" (Psalm 119:105).

Enoch walked with God.
GENESIS 5:24

What does it mean to walk with God? There's a clue in Hebrews 11:5: "By faith Enoch was taken away so that he did not see death, 'and was not found, because God had taken him'; for before he was taken he had this testimony, that he pleased God."

To walk with God is to please God; we please God by trusting Him with our troubles. Hebrews 11:6 says, "But without faith it is impossible to please Him, for he who comes to God must believe that He is, and that He is a rewarder of those who diligently seek Him."

As we worship this powerful God we know, we should be encouraged in our walk with Him. We should come to know God better—His omnipotence, His holiness, His ever-present nature, His faithfulness and truthfulness, His justice and love. By coming to know Him better, we trust Him more. By trusting Him more, we please Him. By pleasing Him, we walk with Him as Enoch did.

Is there a burden you need to entrust into God's care? Do it now, trust Him fully, and enjoy walking with Him through the ups and downs of life.

*Let us draw near with a true heart in full assurance
of faith, having our hearts sprinkled from an evil conscience
and our bodies washed with pure water.*
HEBREWS 10:22

Much of what happened literally in the Old Testament fore-shadowed something that would happen figuratively in the New Testament. In the Old Testament, the blood of sacrificial animals was sprinkled on the altar and on the Ark of the Covenant. That sprinkling of blood was a literal picture of the washing away of sin. In the New Testament, the same image is conveyed: Our heart is sprinkled figuratively with the blood of Christ's perfect sacrifice, cleansing us "from an evil conscience" and the stain of sin.

In the Old Testament, such sprinkling was performed intimately—literally, the length of an arm was the distance from the blood to the object it covered. Just so, in the New Testament we must "draw near" to God "with a true heart in full assurance of faith." Drawing near to God in faith avails us of the benefits of Christ's blood cleansing us from sin.

Draw near to God today with a true heart in full assurance of faith. And be assured of your cleansing.

MAY 4
Like Sheep

All we like sheep have gone astray; we have turned,
every one, to his own way.
ISAIAH 53:6

In the ancient world, if there were sheep there was also a shepherd. Together, they are mentioned close to 500 times in Scripture. Literal sheep and shepherds became a metaphor for spiritual sheep and shepherds because we manifest similar behaviors. Most troublesome is a sheep's tendency to wander away and become lost, injured, or attacked by predators. And the same thing happens with us.

Our tendency to act like sheep—to wander away from God—prompted the words of Isaiah the prophet when describing the coming Messiah: "All we like sheep have gone astray; we have turned, every one, to his own way." That reflects the actions of Adam and Eve—choosing their way instead of God's—and it reflects our actions, too. Thankfully, God sent His Son to be the Good Shepherd who will lead, protect, and provide for His sheep. We must guard against our human tendency to wander by staying close to the Good Shepherd, Jesus Christ.

If you have wandered away from God—maybe a little, maybe a lot—let today be the day you return to God's Good Shepherd.

But you shall receive power when the Holy Spirit has come upon you; and you shall be witnesses to Me in Jerusalem, and in all Judea and Samaria, and to the end of the earth.

ACTS 1:8

The late founder of Campus Crusade for Christ (now known as Cru), William R. "Bill" Bright, was a gifted evangelist. When people said to him, "We can never be as effective at evangelism as you," Dr. Bright would remind them of the biblical definition of evangelism: "To share Christ in the power of the Holy Spirit and leaving the results to God."

What is a witness? In a court of law, a witness is called upon to do one thing: tell what they saw and heard. That fits the biblical definition of a witness as well. Saul of Tarsus was told why he had been called by Christ: "For you will be His witness to all men of what you have seen and heard" (Acts 22:15). The apostle John wrote his epistles declaring "that which we have seen and heard" (1 John 1:3). And just before Jesus left this earth He commissioned His apostles to be "witnesses to Me … to the end of the earth" (Acts 1:8).

You have "seen and heard" the words and works of Jesus through Scripture. You know what He has done in your own life. Share that with others and you will be His witness.

MAY 6
The Answer to "Why?"

My brethren, count it all joy when you fall into various trials.
JAMES 1:2

The most frequently heard word by parents is often the word "Why?" It might come in a question like, "Why is the sky blue?" But more often it comes after an instruction: "Susie, I need for you not to do that." "Why, Mommy?" We've heard it—and said it.

That question could easily be asked about some exhortations in Scripture like James 1:2: "Count it all joy when you fall into various trials." We're not always given the explicit answer to the "Why?" question, but in this case we are: Because trials produce patience and patience leads to maturity and completeness as God works in our life (James 1:3-4). Nobody would wish for trials in life, but we all wish for maturity. So just as parents can give a good reason when their children ask "Why?" God does as well. And when we know that trials lead to maturity, we understand how it is possible to maintain our joy in the midst of them. Trials are just another means God uses to conform us to the image of Christ (Romans 8:29). After all, Jesus Himself suffered trials and learned patient obedience through them (Hebrews 5:8).

Trials can hurt, for sure. But if we keep our focus on the maturity that comes through the trial, it will change our perspective.

MAY 7
Fragrance of Christ

*For we are to God the fragrance of Christ among those who
are being saved and among those who are perishing.*
2 CORINTHIANS 2:15

Global Industry Analysts, Inc., predicted that the global
fragrance and perfume market would exceed $45 billion in
2018. There are more than 1,160 women's fragrances sold in the
United States alone. From ancient to modern times, fragrances
have been sought and valued.

The Song of Songs mentions fragrances frequently (1:3, 12;
4:11; 7:8); a perfume was also used to anoint the feet of Jesus
(John 12:3). Those were literal oils and perfumes, but the apostle Paul wrote of a metaphorical fragrance spread by those who
know Christ. It is the "fragrance of Christ" that is recognized
both by those "being saved" and those "who are perishing."
To the former, Christ in us releases a fragrance of life; to the
latter, it is a fragrance of death. And what is the fragrance? It
refers to a Roman victory procession, a victorious commander
returning from battle, and the crowds who burned incense and
spices in honor of the victory. Christ is our victor who "leads us
in triumph" into His kingdom (2 Corinthians 2:14). Our lives
release the fragrance of His love, the perfume of His victory on
our behalf.

As we yield our lives to Christ who lives in us, He becomes
the fragrance of love and salvation to all who will embrace
Him.

Harassed or Blessed?

Blessed are those who are persecuted for righteousness' sake,
for theirs is the kingdom of heaven.
MATTHEW 5:10

Anyone who has had their car damaged by an uninsured motorist knows the feeling of being unfairly wronged. It is troubling and upsetting and costly, but it is not what today's verse refers to. "Persecution for righteousness' sake" occurs when we take a stand for our Lord and Savior and we experience anything from irritation to intimidation to injury because of it.

How do we respond to those who are unfair, deceitful, and unkind to us because we belong to Christ? His example to us is "when He was reviled, [He] did not revile in return; when He suffered, He did not threaten" (1 Peter 2:23). The world is watching our response to the people and circumstances around us. Anger or forgiveness or compassion is up to us. We can bear injustice, unfairness, or persecution, Jesus said, because we are part of a greater kingdom. When we are being persecuted for His sake, then God is on our side and will defend us His way. Suffering is only for a season for "Christ also suffered for us, leaving us an example, that you should follow His steps" (1 Peter 2:21).

Let your response to persecution, injustice, or unfairness be like Christ—the kingdom of heaven is our future.

*For as the sufferings of Christ abound in us, so our
consolation also abounds through Christ.*
2 CORINTHIANS 1:5

Job's fortunes were destroyed in a very short time. And the
same can happen to us. One day we feel fine, the next day we
feel finished—at least that's how it can seem. In a matter of a
few months' time, the same thing happened to the apostle Paul.
His perspective can teach us how to think about suffering.

Paul wrote two letters to the church at Corinth—they were
both written around A.D. 55. In 1 Corinthians, Paul is at his
apostolic best, exhorting and guiding the church in spiritual,
doctrinal, and practical matters. But something happened to
Paul after he wrote 1 Corinthians; 2 Corinthians came from
the pen of a man who was "burdened beyond measure, above
strength, so that [he] despaired even of life" (2 Corinthians
1:8). It seems he had come under attack from false apostles
(2 Corinthians 11:13-15). The whole letter is a *description* of his
suffering and a *defense* of his apostleship. More importantly
for us, he pointed to the comfort he received from God
(2 Corinthians 1:3-7; 4:7-12). He told the Corinthians that the
comfort we receive from God is the comfort we can extend to
others.

Learn from trouble; let suffering be a teacher. As God
comforts you, offer that same comfort to those who are
suffering around you.

MAY 10
Love in Spite Of

But God demonstrates His own love toward us, in that while
we were still sinners, Christ died for us.
ROMANS 5:8

Relief comes in many ways. Perhaps it's arriving home on Friday evening after a challenging work week. Maybe it's finishing a five-mile run or fifteen-mile bike ride. For a student, maybe it's an "A" on an exam grade, or a college acceptance letter. But no relief is as strong as the experience of unconditional love— knowing we are loved in spite of our sin and failures.

Unconditional love is the theme of the New Testament. It was a new kind of love, scarcely considered in the Greek or Roman worlds. But the introduction of the Greek word *agape* into the New Testament conversation defined God's love for the world. It's the word used in the New Testament's best-known verse, John 3:16—"For God so loved the world that He gave." Whereas John named "the world" at large as the recipient of God's love, Paul got more specific (Romans 5:8): "sinners" are the recipients of God's unconditional love. We know we have sinned; we know we are guilty. But the Bible tells us that, in spite of our sin and guilt, God loves us.

Have you experienced the relief that comes with knowing you are loved by God unconditionally? It's a proven love—God gave Christ to die in spite of our sins.

MAY 11
Drifting

Therefore we must give the more earnest heed to
the things we have heard, lest we drift away.
HEBREWS 2:1

When parents take their little children to a park they will often say, "I want you to stay where I can see you." Of course, that's another way of a parent saying, "I'm not going to let you out of my sight!" And when inexperienced sailors take their boats into the ocean, even if they are equipped with GPS, they feel more secure when they stay in sight of land. Whether it's young children playing, or boaters enjoying the sea, there is a similar danger: drifting away.

There is also a danger of drifting away from biblical truth, and therefore sound moral and spiritual practice, if we don't keep familiar landmarks in sight and mind. And what are the landmarks? The writer to the Hebrews called them "the things we have heard"—that is, the truth and doctrine they had been taught by the apostles in person and through letters. The father in Proverbs called them "sound judgment and discretion," warning his son, "do not let wisdom and understanding out of your sight" (Proverbs 3:21, NIV). And Paul wrote to the Colossians about staying deeply rooted in Christ, as they had been taught (Colossians 2:6-7).

Drifting brings on fear, confusion, disorientation—but it's easy to correct. Get back in sight of the truth, principles, promises, and doctrines of the Word of God.

The Joyful Mom

And Mary said: "My soul magnifies the Lord, and
my spirit has rejoiced in God my Savior."
LUKE 1:46-47

When it comes to happy nations, Denmark is near the top. The Danes explain their joyful attitude in one word: *hygge* (pronounced hue-gah). It's an art of creating warm, inviting, and cozy environments, especially through the use of candles and lamps. One Danish author, Poul Henningsen, said, "When, in the evening, from the top of a tram car, you look into all the homes on the first floor, you shudder at how dismal people's homes are … [because of] the positioning of the lighting." He and others taught the Danes how to better create pools of light using candles and lamps, thus creating hygge in the home.

We need spiritual light far more. Psalm 34:5 says, "They looked to Him and were radiant." A joyful mother brightens the home, for she reflects the radiance of the Lord. One of the reasons the Lord chose Mary as the mother of Christ was undoubtedly because she knew how to rejoice in God her Savior.

Thank God for joyful moms like her who brighten the lives of others!

MAY 13
Powerful Prayers

*Now this is the confidence that we have in Him, that if we
ask anything according to His will, He hears us.*

1 JOHN 5:14

Arlene Blanchard grew up in a violent Cleveland, Ohio,
housing project, and her life was hard from the very beginning.
She was often hungry, and she sometimes wished she'd never
been born. She dreamed of being a lethal weapon and even
considered becoming an assassin. Joining the army, she was
stationed in Italy and Alaska, and spent much of her time
drinking and carousing. One morning when she saw herself
in the mirror, she felt horrified at the person she had become.
That's when she remembered how her mother prayed for her. "I
soon learned that no matter how hard I ran, I couldn't outrun
her prayers." Shortly thereafter, she gave her heart to Christ in
a small Alaskan church.[8]

A mother's prayers convey long-distance and long-term
power. But there is One who intercedes for us with even greater
might—Jesus Christ, our Advocate, our Great High Priest. If
anyone is going to intercede for us, we want someone who is
appointed, approved, and accredited. In the spiritual realm,
there is only One who can serve in that role—Jesus Himself.

If you don't like the person you're becoming, remember
Who is interceding for you and place your trust in Him.

[8] William and Randy Petersen, *100 Amazing Answers to Prayer* (Grand Rapids: Revell, 2003), 17-18.

MAY 14
Put on Your Armor

*Put on the whole armor of God, that you may be able
to stand against the wiles of the devil.*
EPHESIANS 6:11

For most of recorded history, records exist of soldiers wearing some sort of defensive body armor for protection. We are most familiar with suits of armor worn in the Middle Ages—with shaped plates, often highly decorated—covering the soldier from head to toe and often his horse as well. The apostle Paul was familiar with Roman armor but introduced a new kind based on the new type of warfare Christians would face.

Paul wrote to the Corinthians that Christians "do not war according to the flesh" (2 Corinthians 10:3). "The weapons we fight with are not the weapons of the world" (verse 4, NIV). The world's battles are fought in the physical realm, thus the need for physical armor. The Christian's battles are fought in the spiritual realm, so our armor is spiritual. Using physical armor as a metaphor, he outlined the believer's spiritual armor: truth, righteousness, peace, faith, salvation, the Word of God, and prayer (Ephesians 6:10-18). But there is one way the two types of armor—physical and spiritual—are the same: They both have to be put on.

Check your armor daily. Put on Christ by faith. Walk in truth, righteousness, peace, faith, the assurance of salvation, and prayer. Armor only defends us when it is worn—put on your armor!

I am the good shepherd. The good shepherd gives His life for the sheep.
JOHN 10:11

Matthew, Mark, and Luke wrote their accounts of Jesus chronologically. The apostle John took a different approach. While generally chronological, John focused on the themes by which Jesus could be recognized as Israel's Messiah. Jesus referred to Himself with "I am" phrases that Jews would recognize from the Old Testament, and John captured them all: I am the bread of life; the light of the world; the door of the sheep; the good shepherd; the resurrection and the life; the way, the truth, and the life; and the true vine.

These familiar images would call to the mind of observant Jews the ways in which God wanted to meet the needs of every Israelite. The bread and the vine meant daily provision; the light of the world meant guidance and revelation; the Good Shepherd meant care; the door of the sheep meant protection; the resurrection and the life meant salvation; the way, the truth, and the life meant reconciliation with God. Jesus was everything the Jews—and then the Gentiles—needed to be reconciled with God and live a life blessed by Him. All they needed to do was believe.

Ask yourself whether those images are finding fulfillment in your own spiritual experience. Jesus said, "I am" so that we could picture all He is and all He wants to be in our life.

Troubles and Trust

Let not your heart be troubled; you believe in God, believe also in Me.
JOHN 14:1

When the patriarch Job was suffering, his friend, Eliphaz, offered an observation: "Yet man is born to trouble, as the sparks fly upward" (Job 5:7). Upon reflection, Job himself agreed: "Man who is born of woman is of few days and full of trouble" (Job 14:1). All we have to do is read the morning headlines: The world is full of trouble and troubled souls. No one can escape the troubles of this life.

And that included Jesus' disciples. As He prepared His disciples for His death and return to heaven, they were troubled. He told them He had only a short time left, that where He was going they could not come (John 13:33). Seeing their discomfort, He told them not to be troubled, to trust Him just as they trusted God (John 14:1). How would trust in God be an antidote to their (and our) troubles? For the disciples, it meant God was implementing a plan they didn't understand. There would be a good outcome, but in the interim, until Jesus' Resurrection, the disciples would have to trust God's plan. The same goes for us.

We cannot be troubled and trusting at the same time. Trusting God doesn't mean our troubles disappear. It means that we focus on Him instead of what we can't solve or understand at the moment.

MAY 17
Writing for the Future

Now all these things happened to them as examples, and they were written for our admonition, upon whom the ends of the ages have come.
1 CORINTHIANS 10:11

A recent online article on a popular news website listed ten benefits of journaling—a written record of the important events, insights, and lessons learned in life. Benefits listed include self-discipline, creativity, mindfulness, and self-confidence.[9] For Christians, journaling can change self-confidence to "God-confidence." While the psalmists didn't call their writing journaling, it served a similar purpose: to record the faithfulness of God in the past to inspire faith in God in the future. For instance, David wrote in Psalm 34:4, "I sought the Lord, and He heard me, and delivered me from all my fears." Do you think that record of God's faithfulness would inspire David in the future? No doubt—and journaling will do the same for us. As Paul wrote in 1 Corinthians 10:11, the record of Israel's experience with God was "written for our admonition."

If you don't keep a journal now, consider starting. And reread it often to stay mindful of the faithfulness of God.

[9] Thai Nguyen, "10 Surprising Benefits You'll Get From Keeping a Journal," *Huffington Post*, https://www.huffingtonpost.com/thai-nguyen/benefits-of-journaling (accessed 12-12-17).

*Your ears shall hear a word behind you, saying, "This is the way, walk in it,"
whenever you turn to the right hand or whenever you turn to the left.*
ISAIAH 30:21

Documentation—it's everywhere. Your workplace may require
you to wear an I.D. tag. If you are traveling to a foreign country, you have to show a passport. If you're entering a foreign
country for an extended stay, you must produce a visa. You can't
just tell a policeman, "I'm a licensed driver"—you have to show
your license.

In other words, in much of life your word is insufficient.
And neither will it be sufficient at the gates of heaven. In a
discussion of false prophets and bad fruit, Jesus said that just
saying "Lord, Lord" will not provide access to the kingdom
of heaven. You must have documentation—evidence that you
have lived a life consistent with the will of God. That doesn't
mean a life of sinless perfection; it means a life of continuing a
path leading to Christ-likeness. It means evidence that the old,
carnal man is being replaced by the new person filled by the
Spirit.

Does your spiritual walk document your spiritual talk? Let
your life prove the power of the Gospel today.

Promises Like Precious Gems

The Lord is not slack concerning His promise.
2 PETER 3:9

During his vast citywide campaigns, evangelist Dwight L. Moody often devoted a sermon in each place to the subject of God's promises. An associate explained, "He thought that very few of us ever fully considered how much our loving Father really had promised to us. These promises, like precious gems, were to be found in every book of the Bible." Moody would sometimes ask audience members to shout out their favorite biblical promises, and the spirit of the room reverberated with one great biblical promise after another—all of which God has kept, is keeping, and will keep perfectly. He is not slack concerning His promises.

Had you been in one of Moody's meetings a hundred years ago, what promise would you have shouted? Recall it now. Then remember: We have not just one, but every one of God's unerring and infallible promises available to us.

Moody himself kept one promise close to his heart, especially when he felt overwhelmed by his work. Perhaps it's the very verse you need today: "Ah, Lord God! Behold, You have made the heavens and the earth by Your great power and outstretched arm. There is nothing too hard for You" (Jeremiah 32:17).

By Grace Alone

For by grace you have been saved through faith, and that not of yourselves; it is the gift of God, not of works, lest anyone should boast.

EPHESIANS 2:8-9

The Protestant Reformers developed five distinct sayings called the five *solae*—five *alone* sayings. The five sayings set out what the Reformers believed: Salvation is by Scripture alone, faith alone, grace alone, through Christ alone, and for the glory of God alone.

What does "grace alone" mean? The best answer is found in Paul's words. First, Paul wrote in Ephesians 2:8-9 that we are saved by grace, through faith—the gift of God—not as a result of our good works. We can't work our way to heaven. We are saved *for* good works (Ephesians 2:10) but not *by* good works. Our salvation is a grace-gift from God. A few years later, Paul wrote that "the grace of God that brings salvation has appeared to all men" (Titus 2:11)—obviously a reference to the unmerited favor that God bestowed on mankind by sending Jesus Christ into the world. Christ alone, grace alone, faith alone. What should be the effect of that grace? Godly and holy lives as we wait for the appearing of "our great God and Savior Jesus Christ" (Titus 2:12-14).

Have you received the grace of God through faith in Christ? Is that gift motivating you to live a life of gratitude manifested in godliness? It's all grace.

Moreover it is required in stewards that one be found faithful.
1 CORINTHIANS 4:2

When Joseph was sold into slavery in Egypt, he was bought by Potiphar, one of Pharaoh's top officials. Potiphar was so impressed with Joseph that he made him the manager, or steward, of his entire household. So faithful was Joseph that Potiphar "did not concern himself with anything except the food he ate" (Genesis 39:6, NIV). Potiphar turned everything over to Joseph to manage for him.

Transfer that image—a steward who is totally faithful to his master—to Paul's role as a steward of the "mysteries of God" (1 Corinthians 4:1). Was Paul thinking of Joseph when he said that faithfulness was the steward's chief requirement? Now think about Jesus as a steward of the Gospel of the kingdom of God. He said, "I do not seek My own will but the will of the Father who sent Me" (John 5:30). Joseph sought Potiphar's will; Paul sought Jesus' will; Christ sought the Father's will. In every case they exhibited the chief requirement of a steward: faithfulness to the master.

So, what is the Christian a steward of? First, we are stewards of the image of God—to live in this world in such a way that God's image is not tarnished (Genesis 1:26-27). Next, we are a steward of everything we've been given. Time, talent, and treasure are to be used to glorify God.

Furrows of Faith

Jesus, being aware of it, said to them, "Why do you reason because you have no bread? Do you not yet perceive nor understand? Is your heart still hardened?"

MARK 8:17

When Jesus spoke of "hardened" hearts in this passage, He wasn't referring to scribes, Pharisees, or Roman officials who bitterly opposed Him. Oh, their hearts were hardened too; but in Mark 8, He was speaking to His closest followers— the Twelve. Despite the miracles He performed and the instructions He gave, the truth about His power hadn't sunk into their minds. Their hearts were like fields so dry and hard that the needed rain simply ran off without soaking into the soil. They had seen Jesus feed 5,000 in Mark 6, yet they didn't know how He could feed 4,000 in Mark 8.

Healthy hearts soak up the water of the Word. They are furrowed by faith and tilled by trust. That's the kind of heart the Lord desires. Don't rebel or distrust Him. Hebrews 6:7 says, "When the ground soaks up the falling rain and bears a good crop for the farmer, it has God's blessing" (NLT).

Living Temple

You also, as living stones, are being built up [as] a spiritual
house, a holy priesthood, to offer up spiritual sacrifices
acceptable to God through Jesus Christ.
1 PETER 2:5

Temples are the dwelling places of deities; they are the place where heaven comes to earth, where heaven and earth intersect—where life is "on earth as it is in heaven" (Matthew 6:10).

There have been five temples in the Judeo-Christian tradition so far. The first "temple" was Eden, the sinless creation in which God and man had pure fellowship together (Genesis 2:8). The second was the tabernacle where God dwelt with His people in glory on their way to Canaan (Exodus 26). The third was Solomon's temple in Jerusalem (2 Chronicles 5:14), a temple God abandoned because of Israel's sin (Ezekiel 10). The fourth was the one rebuilt by the exiles who returned from Babylon (Ezra 6:13-18)—a temple to which God's glory never returned. The fifth is being built on the foundation of the prophets and apostles with Jesus as the cornerstone, followers of Jesus being the "living stones" of which it is made "into a holy temple in the Lord" (Ephesians 2:21). After centuries of the glory of God being absent, Jesus appeared and "[they] beheld His glory" (John 1:14).

As a follower of Jesus, you are part of God's spiritual temple where He dwells. In you, the world should see what it is like when heaven and earth intersect.

MAY 24
You Can't Unring the Bell

Turn my eyes away from worthless things;
preserve my life according to your word.
PSALM 119:37, NIV

In jury trials, the judge will sometimes have to admonish the jury "to disregard everything that was just said by the witness." From those courtroom settings an idiom arose: "You can't unring the bell." Once something has entered our mind through any of the five senses, it is next to impossible to erase the thought or image—to pretend it never happened.

Scripture admonishes us to be careful about what we see, listen to, and even speak—especially when there is emotion attached. The human brain has an uncanny ability to remember—a double-edged ability. For that reason, the patriarch Job said, "I have made a covenant with my eyes; why then should I look upon a young woman?" (Job 31:1) The psalmist prayed that God would "turn away [his] eyes from looking at worthless things" (Psalm 119:37). The father in Proverbs admonished his son: "Let your eyes look straight ahead, and your eyelids look right before you" (Proverbs 4:25). And it is no doubt the reason Paul listed the kinds of things we ought to think about: things that are noble, just, pure, lovely, edifying, virtuous, and praiseworthy (Philippians 4:8-9).

As much as is possible, guard the gateways to your mind. You can't unsee what you've seen or unhear what you've heard. You can't unring the bell.

But Jesus often withdrew to lonely places and prayed.
LUKE 5:16, NIV

Sometimes we withdraw *to* the lonely places, and sometimes we need to withdraw *from* them. We all need private times to detach from the turmoil and to abide in the Lord's presence. Jesus often sought lonely places to cultivate the stillness and strength He needed. But when our lonely places are too lonely for too long, our well-being is at risk. A report in *USA Today* claimed a 26 percent increased likelihood of death for those who feel lonely and 29 percent for those who have actual social isolation. According to the report, more people are living alone now than at any time in recorded human history.

Many biblical characters faced isolation and anguish in ways we cannot imagine. King David said, "I am like a pelican of the wilderness" (Psalm 102:6) and "no one cares for my soul" (Psalm 142:4). It helps to remember that even our greatest heroes in Scripture battled loneliness. It isn't a sin; it's a temporary situation and sometimes, as in Jesus' case, it is even beneficial. It provides needed time for prayer.

Whenever you're in a lonely place, remember that God is there with you, and He always cares for your soul.

The peace of God, which surpasses all understanding, will
guard your hearts and minds through Christ Jesus.
PHILIPPIANS 4:7

Almost everything Jesus did and said—teachings, parables, miracles—was illustrative of His central message: "the kingdom of God is at hand" (Mark 1:14-15). And there could have been more than one illustration given at a time.

Take the occasion of Jesus and His disciples sailing across the Sea of Galilee, trailed by other boats full of followers (Mark 4:35-41). A furious storm came up, threatening to sink all the boats. Everyone was in great fear except for Jesus who was asleep in the back of His boat. Awakened by the disciples, Jesus commanded the storm, "Peace, be still!" And the situation turned from chaotic to calm. Not only was the miracle a demonstration of Jesus' divine power, it was a picture of the kingdom of God compared to life under Roman rule: divine peace instead of pagan power. But it was also an illustration to the disciples that it was possible, through Jesus, to have the fear of death replaced by a life of peace. Being with Jesus in the midst of a storm is the safest place to be.

If you are in the midst of a storm right now, pray that the God of peace will, first, calm your heart, and second, calm the waves around you in His time.

To everything there is a season, a time for every purpose under heaven.
ECCLESIASTES 3:1

In the West, we count four seasons: winter, spring, summer, and fall. In subtropical climates, six seasons correspond to our seasonal names as spring, summer, monsoon, autumn, early winter, and prevernal or late winter. In some regions, the seasons are fixed by dates; in others, they are attuned to meteorological movements. Human experience takes us through a variety of seasons during our lifetime, and some of them are difficult for us (Ecclesiastes 3:2-8).

Solomon outlined 28 seasons—two each in 14 different categories. The seasons are contrasting: birth, death; planting, uprooting; tearing down and building; keeping and throwing away; and so on. Like most biblical lists, this list of seasons is only illustrative. Out of our own experience we could add additional sets of contrasting seasons. Solomon's point is that life is an unpredictable mix of seasons (experiences)— *unpredictable* being the key word. As he says about many things in life, trying to figure out the seasons of life is a vain pursuit. Rather than agonizing over the whens and wherefores of the seasons of life, we should remember that God "has made everything beautiful in its time" (Ecclesiastes 3:11). Our task is to search out God's eternal purposes in every season of life.

The calendar's seasons are predictable, but life's aren't. Let us discern our days so that we gain a heart of wisdom (Psalm 90:12).

MAY 28
Fan the Flame

Therefore I remind you to stir up the gift of God which
is in you through the laying on of my hands.
2 TIMOTHY 1:6

After he was released from his first Roman imprisonment, Paul appears to have made a fourth missionary journey. Toward the end of that journey he left Timothy in charge of the church at Ephesus as Paul continued through Macedonia. Not long after leaving Timothy in Ephesus, Paul wrote his young protégé the letter we call 1 Timothy.

Paul and a group of elders had laid hands on Timothy and prayed for him to receive prophetic gifts via the Spirit's anointing (1 Timothy 1:18; 2 Timothy 1:6). In his letter, Paul admonished Timothy not to neglect his gifts, to "give [himself] entirely" to using his gifts to proclaim sound doctrine (1 Timothy 4:14-16). After Paul was imprisoned in Rome, he wrote Timothy a second letter. Quickly, Paul returned to the subject of Timothy's gifts from God, admonishing him to "stir up" those gifts, to fan them into a bright flame. The image is a fire in danger of going out for lack of fuel. Don't let that happen, Paul wrote in 2 Timothy 1:6.

What gift(s) has God given you? Are you using them? If needed, return to God in prayer and ask Him for power and grace to be a good steward of His gift(s) to you. Fan the flame!

Heal the sick, cleanse the lepers, raise the dead, cast out demons.
Freely you have received, freely give.
MATTHEW 10:8

It happens at intersections—a needy person approaches your car to ask for money. Or you're walking down a street and encounter someone with a sign: "Can you help? God bless you." Or your doorbell rings and a needy-looking young person is selling some product. What do you do in those situations? What *should* you do?

The easiest thing to do is to find a reason to say "No": I don't have any money with me; I do all my giving through my church; I don't really have time right now. Legitimate questions arise: Is the money going to be used wisely? Are they telling me the truth? Am I being a good steward of God's money? The questions and reasons are never-ending. Perhaps Jesus' words to His twelve disciples when He sent them out to preach, heal the sick, raise the dead, and drive out demons, will help: "Freely you have received, [therefore] freely give." There were no instructions about motives, background checks, or worthiness. If a person had a need the disciples could meet, they were to meet that need.

Instead of reasons to say "No" (and sometimes "No" may be the right answer), look for reasons to say "Yes." God gives His grace freely to us so we can share it with others.

MAY 30
Be Prudent

A prudent person foresees danger and takes precautions. The simpleton goes blindly on and suffers the consequences.
PROVERBS 22:3, NLT

In his book *Unpacking Forgiveness*, Chris Brauns wrote, "Forgiveness does not mean the elimination of all consequences. If you believe in the Lord Jesus Christ, then you are saved (Acts 16:31). As far as east is from the west, so far does God remove the transgressions of his children from them (Psalm 103:11-12). There is *no* condemnation for those who are in Christ (Romans 8:1). Nevertheless, these truths do not teach that those forgiven by God face no consequences for sin. On the contrary! This side of heaven, we will continue to work through the consequences of our rebellion against God. One of the most famous examples of this involves the consequences that David faced for his adultery with Bathsheba."[10]

Perhaps, like David, you're grappling with painful consequences of your past. Remember, God can use those things to deter future sin; to teach you holiness and godliness; to equip you to counsel and to help others; and work all of it together for your good when you commit it all to Him. Put the sin under His blood, and put the consequences into His hands.

[10] Chris Brauns, *Unpacking Forgiveness* (Wheaton, IL: Crossway, 2008), 49.

MAY 31
No Envy

Is it not lawful for me to do what I wish with my own things? Or is your eye evil because I am good?
MATTHEW 20:15

The toxic combination of comparison, greed, and a sense of entitlement obliterates kindness and love. It is evident in families torn apart during the executing of a loved one's will.

In one parable Jesus describes a landowner who hired workers throughout the day. When it came time to pay them, each worker received the same pay, regardless of when they were hired. The workers who had been there the longest complained the loudest. Their sideways glances at what others received left them ungrateful and full of complaints.

Jesus longs to free us from the poison of comparison. He gently reminds us to look to Him for our success and blessing. If we use others as a barometer of our success, we will never be satisfied. The greatest gift He gives each of us is Himself. When we realize this, the possessions of this world stop possessing our souls. We are free to give and receive love.

JUNE

JUNE 1
The Bully Pulpit

And the Lord said to Satan, "The Lord rebuke you, Satan! The Lord who has chosen Jerusalem rebuke you! Is this not a brand plucked from the fire?"
ZECHARIAH 3:2

Bullying is an epidemic today, including cyberbullying. The goal of a bully is to make the other person feel badly about themselves, ashamed, humiliated, and alone. Bullies take their cues from Satan, the ultimate bully. In Zechariah 3, the devil ridiculed Israel's high priest, Joshua, and pointed out his filthy sins and ministerial failures. But the Lord rebuked Satan. And God removed Joshua's filthy garments and gave him rich robes and a clean turban. The Lord treated him as a brand plucked from the fire.

The Bible teaches that our great High Priest, Jesus, always lives to make intercession for us. We all go through periods of guilt, shame, and self-reproach. But the blood of Jesus Christ washes away every stain, forgives every sin, redeems every mistake, and silences the taunts of our diabolical bully.

Jesus reminds us in John 10:9-10 that "I am the door. If anyone enters by Me, he will be saved, and will go in and out and find pasture. The thief does not come except to steal, and to kill, and to destroy. I have come that they may have life, and that they may have it more abundantly." We are safe in His protective arms.

JUNE 2
Vacation With God

And when He had sent the multitudes away, He went up on the mountain by Himself to pray. Now when evening came, He was alone there.
MATTHEW 14:23

If you have a Bible concordance, you will search in vain for a number of words we take for granted today (at least in their modern sense): retirement, vacation, pension, Social Security, insurance, and more. That doesn't mean these ideas are bad or inappropriate. But it does pay for us to evaluate them in terms of biblical principles.

Take vacation, for example. What are we vacating? Typically, a vacation is a break from work; it's a chance for "R & R"—rest and relaxation. That's certainly a good thing; everyone can benefit from a refreshing break. Jesus often withdrew from His daily routine of ministering to the multitudes to pray and rest. We may be tempted to take a break from God on vacation along with a break from work. Interestingly, Jesus seems to have used His times away not to take a break from God but to draw closer to Him. David, the psalmist, found it was impossible to get away from God (Psalm 139:7-12). And God promises never to leave or forsake us (Hebrews 13:5).

When you plan a vacation, make sure to include God in your plans—time for prayer, reading, study, and fellowship with family or others. God is there, waiting to be included.

JUNE 3
The Key to Knowledge

Woe to you lawyers! For you have taken away the key of knowledge. You did not enter in yourselves, and those who were entering in you hindered.

LUKE 11:52

The word *key* appears often: book titles, product information, advice from teachers and counselors. And for good reason—all of us are looking for keys (truths) that might lead to greater success. Interestingly, the word *key* is rarely used in our English Bibles—depending upon the translation, only eight to ten times.

In Luke 11:52, Jesus accused the Pharisees of taking away "the key of knowledge" that people needed. But He didn't explain what the "key" is. It helps to note that this accusation concerning the key is one of a litany of "woes" Jesus pronounced against these religious leaders (Matthew 23:13-39; Luke 11:39-52), very similar to "woes" Isaiah pronounced upon the leaders of his day (Isaiah 5:8-25). All these "woes" have to do with arrogance, pride, and hypocrisy—a lack of obedience to the Word of God (Isaiah 5:24). Isaiah also says that "the fear of the Lord is the key to ... salvation and wisdom and knowledge" (Isaiah 33:6, NIV). Was a lack of the fear of the Lord the "key of knowledge" the Pharisees had withheld from the people?

Knowledge and wisdom begin with fearing the Lord (Proverbs 1:7; 9:10). Humility, reverence, obedience, and awe—all are keys to knowing God better.

JUNE 4
Time Is Short

But this I say, brethren, the time is short.
1 CORINTHIANS 7:29

When Moses led the Hebrew slaves out of Egypt, in short order he was overwhelmed with the task of answering questions and settling disputes. Fortunately, he took the advice of Jethro, his father-in-law, and appointed judges to help him (Exodus 18). Paul often faced similar situations with the fledgling churches. First Corinthians is an example, a letter in which he attempts to answer practical and theological questions for the church. In chapter 7, he addresses thorny questions regarding marriage, divorce, and widows—reminding them that "keeping the commandments of God is what matters" (1 Corinthians 7:19). He does his best to provide guidance regarding these issues, encouraging them to "serve the Lord without distraction" (verse 35).

Why would Paul say that? Because "the time is short"; because "the form of this world is passing away" (verses 29, 31). In other words, don't try to arrange the affairs of this world in whatever way you think will make you ultimately happy. Happiness *in* this world is not dependent on happiness *from* this world. The Lord may return at any moment; our focus is on fulfilling His command to evangelize the world. There is greater gain to be found in godly contentment than in worldly advantage (1 Timothy 6:6).

Jesus' words remain true: Seek first God's kingdom; everything else we need will be added to us (Matthew 6:33). Seek happiness, yes. But seek it first in God.

JUNE 5
Teachings on Prayer

*Now it came to pass, as [Jesus] was praying in a certain place,
when He ceased, that one of His disciples said to Him, "Lord,
teach us to pray, as John also taught his disciples."*

LUKE 11:1

In first-century Judaism, education in the Old Testament
was a matter of the teacher (rabbi, lord, master) and students
(disciples). John the Baptist had disciples (Matthew 9:14) as
did the Pharisees (Matthew 22:16). Even Moses, long dead, had
disciples (John 9:28). Saul of Tarsus was a disciple (student) of
the great rabbi Gamaliel (Acts 22:3). Disciples of any teacher
were characterized by one desire: "Teach us."

It is no surprise, then, that Jesus' disciples, seeing Him
frequently in prayer, said to Him one day, "Lord, teach us to
pray." John the Baptist had taught his disciples to pray, and
in Luke chapter 11, Jesus' disciples wanted to learn as well. So
Jesus taught them a formula (verses 2-4), a parable (verses 5-8),
a three-fold maxim (verses 9-10), and another parable in the
form of questions (verses 11-13). Two things stand out in the
maxim—the verbs imply a continual command: keep on asking,
keep on seeking, keep on knocking. That is, we are to pray
continually—illustrated by the parable in verses 5-8.

Don't give up praying. Pray the formula, meditate on
the parables, and obey the maxim. Keep on praying and your
prayers will be answered.

Therefore, since a promise remains of entering His rest, let us
fear lest any of you seem to have come short of it.

HEBREWS 4:1

In Hebrews 4:1 we are told to "fear" and in Isaiah 41:10 to "fear not." These are not contradictions, of course, but different uses of the word *fear*. For example, the fear of God is reverence and awe that leads to wisdom (Psalm 111:10). Ironically, it is such a healthy reverence for God that leads us to "fear not" (human emotional fear) in the face of life's challenges. When we rightly fear God, we will not fear anything the world sets before us.

When the writer of the Hebrews told his readers to "fear lest any of you seem to have come short of [God's eternal rest]," it is a gentle, but serious, reminder: The entirety of our life, temporal and eternal, is in the hands of God. By failing to live for Him we run the risk of not enjoying the temporal and eternal blessings He has for us. The issue is not loss of salvation, but loss of joy and eternal reward.

How focused is your fear factor? Reverence and awe of God are the beginning of wisdom and blessing.

JUNE 7
What Will You Remember?

*I will remember the works of the Lord; surely
I will remember Your wonders of old.*
PSALM 77:11

We are a forgetful people. In the heat of an argument, we forget a friend's kindness and focus on their faults. When the devastation of a financial loss occurs, we forget God's previous provision. Worry crowds out trust because they cannot co-exist. The way to shrink our worry is to meditate on God's character and truth.

What we allow our minds to ruminate on affects our thoughts, actions, and emotions. We are creatures of habit, and cycles of worry are difficult to break. One of the best antidotes to worry is a journal. Whether your journal is a list of ways God has provided for you or a rant over the concern crowding your mind, the worry antidote occurs when you read back over your journal—months or even years later. God's sustenance of you through the valleys and mountain peaks of your days will become evident. There is nothing more powerful than meditating on His Word and promises and seeing them fulfilled in our lives. Pray that He gives us the eyes to see and the mind to remember all He has done for us.

Nevertheless we, according to His promise, look for new heavens and a new earth in which righteousness dwells.

2 PETER 3:13

The caricatures of heaven in modern culture are endless. The occupants of heaven wear white robes, have angelic wings, balance hovering halos, and spend their time walking up and down streets of gold playing harps. Not surprisingly, the Bible doesn't confirm all of these images (except the main street of the New Jerusalem being gold—Revelation 21:21—and the occupants wearing white robes in Revelation 4:4; 7:9; 7:13).

If that's not an accurate description of eternity, what will eternity be like? First, the big picture. Eternity will not be lived "in heaven"; it will be lived on a "new earth" which was foreseen by the prophets (Isaiah 65:17; 66:22) and the apostles (2 Peter 3:13; Revelation 21:1). In his vision of the future, John the apostle saw "the holy city, New Jerusalem, coming down out of heaven from God" (Revelation 21:2). That vision represents the glory and righteousness that will fill the new earth. Just as God's original creation was glorious, His new creation will be also. That new earth is where we will dwell in eternal bodies, fulfilling the eternal earthly vocations for which we were created as God's image-bearers. Our eternal purpose will be to serve the purpose of God for His glory.

Prepare now to be a citizen of God's new earth, His eternal kingdom, through faith in, and faithfulness to, Jesus Christ.

Let us therefore come boldly to the throne of grace, that we may obtain mercy and find grace to help in time of need.
HEBREWS 4:16

The word *help* found in today's Scripture is also found in the story of Paul's shipwreck on Malta during his journey to Rome in Acts 27. Detailing their voyage and the challenges they encountered, Paul states the sailors "used cables to undergird the ship" (Acts 27:17). In other words, they encircled the hull with cables to keep the ship from breaking apart in the tempest.

The word *undergird* is the same Greek term as the word *help* found in Hebrews 4:16. The writer says we have a great High Priest who has passed through the heavens, the Lord Jesus, who sympathizes with our weaknesses. Let us come boldly to His throne, that we may be undergirded in the storms of life.

When we come to God in need, He undergirds us with His strong, loving arms and makes it possible for our vessel to get through the storm without sinking under the circumstances.

Because of the suffering Jesus endured, He alone can fully understand the sorrows and arrows that pierce our souls here on earth. And He alone can give us the help we need.

JUNE 10
I Offer You Work

I can do all things through Christ who strengthens me.
PHILIPPIANS 4:13

George Washington Carver rose from slavery to become a distinguished professor at Iowa State College of Agricultural and Mechanical Arts, but one day he opened a letter from Booker T. Washington of the Tuskegee Institute in Alabama, who wrote, "Our students are poor, often starving. They travel miles of torn roads across years of poverty. We teach them to read and write, but words cannot fill stomachs. They need to learn to plant and harvest crops." Washington pled with Carver to come to Tuskegee and teach, saying, "I cannot offer you money, position or fame …. I offer you in their place—work— hard, hard work."

To the shock of his colleagues, Carver accepted, saying, "I am looking forward to a very busy, pleasant and profitable time at your college and shall be glad to cooperate with you in doing all I can through Christ who strengtheneth me."[11]

God's goals for our life are far greater than our own. He opens doors and gives us inward nudges and biblical insights as to what to do. He leads us. We may not arrive at money, position, or fame; but when we work for Christ we can do all He assigns through Christ who strengthens us.

[11] William J. Federer, *George Washington Carver: His Life & Faith in His Own Words* (WJ Federer, 2002), 14-15.

JUNE 11
More Grace Than Sin

And such were some of you. But you were washed, but you were sanctified, but you were justified in the name of the Lord Jesus and by the Spirit of our God.
1 CORINTHIANS 6:11

Sometimes non-Christians are shocked when they hear the testimonies of Christians who came from rough backgrounds. Headhunters, slave traders, gangsters, addicts, thieves, and the like have all been saved. It seems unlikely that God would include people such as those in His kingdom. But Jesus said, "I did not come to call the righteous, but sinners, to repentance" (Mark 2:17).

One person who came to Christ had been "a blasphemer and a persecutor and a violent aggressor." He called himself the "foremost of all" sinners (1 Timothy 1:13, 15, NASB). Everybody who knew this man was shocked when he became a Christian. They were afraid he was a counterfeit, a spy, for those persecuting the Church. The only person more surprised than the Church at this man's conversion was the man himself—Saul of Tarsus. He would come to learn that the grace of God is greater than all sin (Romans 5:20). And the same remains true today. No one is unforgivable, beyond the reach of God's grace and mercy.

If you have ever thought that your sins were too dark for the light of God's love to reach, take the apostle's word: Jesus came into this world for sinners.

JUNE 12
Think Soberly

For I say, through the grace given to me, to everyone who is among you, not to think of himself more highly than he ought to think, but to think soberly, as God has dealt to each one a measure of faith.

ROMANS 12:3

In today's world, we have access to personality tests and IQ tests. We have competitions and awards. The media tracks highest earners, most successful entrepreneurs, and numbers of friends or followers. In other words, there are plenty of reasons for pride to make inroads.

But those are modern feedback mechanisms. Why might Christians in Rome have been tempted to think of themselves more highly than they should? First, in Romans 9–11 Paul explained God's election to salvation. Even though he emphasized that election is all a matter of mercy (Romans 11:30-32), maybe some in Rome exalted their status as God's elect. Second, maybe some had been infected by the Roman desire for power and prestige, thinking they were more important than others. Whatever their reason, Paul warns them to "think soberly" about themselves, not pridefully. Christians are saved for good works (Ephesians 2:8-10) and every person in the body of Christ is equally important—which Paul explains in Romans 12:4-8.

How do you think about yourself? Too highly ... too lowly? Think soberly, realistically—as God sees you. You are loved and gifted by God to serve Him in His Church.

JUNE 13
Jesus Paid It All

In My Father's house are many mansions; if it were not so, I would have told you. I go to prepare a place for you. And if I go and prepare a place for you, I will come again and receive you to Myself; that where I am, there you may be also.
JOHN 14:2-3

When you hear the word *heaven*, what comes to mind first? Is it the loved ones who have gone before or perhaps the absence of pain and sorrow? Although these are glorious things to look forward to, let's remember the Person who made our entrance into heaven possible. The Gospels provide glimpses into the love and welcoming nature of Christ. Each word and action of His flows from love because He is love. If you ever wondered what love sounds like—read the Gospels.

Crowds were drawn to Him. Children were invited close and He compassionately healed the sick. He saw beyond the wealth, poverty, physical appearance, and ailments of people and embraced their faith. The outcast and downtrodden were seen and included. Jesus gave generously of His time and wisdom. Even if we combined all the moments when we felt most loved, they would pale in comparison with Him. We can trust Him completely today and with our future. Let us eagerly anticipate meeting Christ face to face in heaven, the One who gave everything for us: His position, righteousness, body, and blood.

JUNE 14
Begetting Kindness

Blessed be the God and Father of our Lord Jesus Christ ... who
comforts us in all our tribulation, that we may be able to
comfort those who are in any trouble.

2 CORINTHIANS 1:3-4

Hunter Hostetler was working at a McDonald's restaurant in Scottsburg, Indiana, when an older woman came through the drive-thru and decided to pay for the customer behind her—a man with four children in the van. The woman told Hunter to tell the man and his children, "Happy Father's Day." The woman's spontaneous act of kindness caused an amazing chain reaction. The man in the van paid for two cars behind him; and they did the same for those who followed them. One customer after another passed along the blessings. By the end of the day, 167 drivers had paid for the orders of the vehicle behind them.

Kindness begets kindness, comfort begets comfort, and no one knows how far the ripples will travel. When we take time to comfort, encourage, help, evangelize, or lift up another person, we never know when, or if, the chain reaction will end. That's why we shouldn't grow weary in doing good, "for in due season we shall reap if we do not lose heart. Therefore, as we have opportunity, let us do good to all, especially to those who are of the household of faith" (Galatians 6:9-10).

Make a conscious effort to pass along kindness to someone today.

Before I formed you in the womb I knew you; before you were born I sanctified you; I ordained you a prophet to the nations.
JEREMIAH 1:5

David was forgotten. Instead of being summoned to join his father and brothers when they met with Samuel, he was left in the field tending sheep. David was only sent for after God had confirmed, one by one, that none of his brothers would be the next king. Gideon was hiding from the enemy when God called him to be a mighty warrior. God knew Gideon, his strengths and weaknesses, and what he was capable of with God's strength.

Regardless of your current situation, God sees you. Whether you are tending sheep or serving in the king's court, you are not overlooked. God has not forgotten you and knows your purpose. If you are feeling stuck or unsure, look to God. He has made each of us with unique strengths and weaknesses, even if we cannot see or articulate them.

Depend on Him for meaning, purpose, and insight into your strengths and weaknesses. You exist because He thought of you, formed you, and gave you life. Our best course of action is to trust in our loving Creator.

If any of you lacks wisdom, let him ask of God, who gives to all liberally and without reproach, and it will be given to him.
JAMES 1:5

In the last week or so you have probably made some kind of plan regarding your future. It might be short-term, like a Saturday outing, or it could be a long-range plan like a job change, a marriage, or a major financial purchase. Making decisions about the future can be challenging—especially if we try to make them without good counsel.

God makes plans, too. And because He is God, His plans take precedence over ours. After making our plans, it can be a rude awakening if they aren't fulfilled. The apostle James told a parable to illustrate how we should integrate our plans with God's (James 4:13-17): Some businessmen made plans to move to another city for a year, create a business, and make money. James reminded his readers of the vanity of such a self-centered plan—a plan that excludes God. Instead, they should say, "If the Lord wills, we shall live and do this or that" (verse 15). The best way to ensure our plans are successful is to have submitted those plans to God at the start (Proverbs 16:9).

What are you planning? Before going any further, stop and pray: "Lord, I need your direction, give me wisdom to make the right decision. Guide me in Your path and direct my steps. Amen."

*For I know the thoughts that I think toward you, says the Lord, thoughts of
peace and not of evil, to give you a future and a hope.*
JEREMIAH 29:11

Due to their sin, the ten northern tribes of Israel were exiled
to Assyria and the two southern tribes were exiled to Babylon.
Their slavery in Egypt was not due to sin, but their exile to
foreign lands was. What were they to make of God's actions?

Through Jeremiah God said His thoughts of them were
"of peace and not of evil"; His plan was to give them "a future
and a hope." In spite of their sins, this is how God thought of
His chosen people. God *thought* that way because God *is* that
way. Can we apply that verse to ourselves even though it was a
promise made to Israel? Yes, because it reflects the character of
God—a God of mercy and grace. The apostle Paul writes that
God has a hopeful future for all who are in Christ. And that
plan is to be conformed to the image of His Son (Romans 8:29)
in spite of anything that has happened en route to that goal
(Romans 8:28).

God is a God of peace for you; He is a God of a hopeful
future. Don't let anything in your past stand in the way of your
embracing His love for you.

Yet indeed I also count all things loss for the excellence of the knowledge
of Christ Jesus my Lord, for whom I have suffered the loss of all things,
and count them as rubbish, that I may gain Christ.

PHILIPPIANS 3:8

A popular British TV game show called "What Would Your Kid Do?" features small children answering questions while their parents watch off stage. In one episode, kids choose between a nice toy or a luxury family vacation. In almost every case, the kids chose the giant stuffed toy, the miniature electric car, or the bed shaped like a race car. It would be difficult to find a better example to illustrate the difference in values between a child and an adult than the choice these children made.

Scripture is clear about the difference in values. For instance, Proverbs 4:7 says, "Wisdom is the principal thing; therefore get wisdom. And in all your getting, get understanding." Jesus told a parable about a man who discovered a treasure in a field and then sold everything he owned so he could purchase the field containing the treasure (Matthew 13:44). The treasure is the kingdom of God, worth everything we have. And Paul did the same: He gave up all his position, prestige, and power in order to follow Jesus of Nazareth (Philippians 3:7-11).

The Christian life is a process of letting go of what has no eternal value and embracing what does—the wisdom of God to pursue Christ and His kingdom.

Patience, Please

Now may the Lord direct your hearts into ... the patience of Christ.
2 THESSALONIANS 3:5

In her book *Peaceful Parent, Happy Kids*, Laura Markham wrote, "Your child is fairly certain to act like a child, which means someone who is still learning, has different priorities than you do, and can't always manage her feelings or actions. Her childish behavior is guaranteed, at times, to push your buttons. The problem is when we begin acting like a child, too."

As parents, we don't need to simply act like adults; we need to act like Jesus. A Christ-like parent has patience far beyond their own resources. They know when to say, "Lord, Your patience please," when tense moments come. The patient parent knows when to redirect their frazzled emotions on God's unconditional love and the never-ending patience of Christ.

Patience is easier for some of us than others, but wise moms and dads consider it one of the most effective tools on the pegboard of parenting. It's so important, that we need the very patience of Christ circulating through our bloodstream. Today make this your prayer: "Lord, direct my heart into Your love and into the patience of Christ Himself."

JUNE 20
Lest We Forget

*This will be written for the generation to come, that a
people yet to be created may praise the Lord.*
PSALM 102:18

Have you tried journaling? Yes, you say, and it went well for
a while, then you got too busy and didn't have time to write.
Well, the great thing about journaling is you can do it your
way according to your own schedule and personality. The latest
craze is bullet journaling, in which items are jotted down in
bullet points, utilizing lists and homemade graphs and charts.

Some people use a wide-margin Bible to journal their
thoughts while reading through the Bible. Others use
journaling features on their phones. Still, it's hard to beat
the old-fashioned way of using a notebook to record a few
thoughts each morning or evening about your day and the
lessons God gives you in His Word.

When we journal our walk with God, it helps us remember
His faithfulness to us. Our lives go by in a blur, and our
memories fade with time. What a treasure to record answers to
prayer, special promises God gives, and thoughts during life's
crucial moments. Writing helps us clarify our thoughts, and it
leaves a testimony to others.

Give journaling another try—it helps document your walk
with God.

Presence of Peace

"And lo, I am with you always, even to the end of the age." Amen.
MATTHEW 28:20

A child is frightened by a crashing thunderstorm in the middle of the night. With a parent's presence and assurance, soon the child will be asleep again. Did the storm stop because the parent entered the child's room? No. Assurance was gained not by what was taken away—the storm—but by what was added—the parent's presence. Safety is not the absence of trouble; safety is the presence of Jesus.

During the year-and-a-half Paul spent in Corinth on his second missionary journey, he encountered stiff opposition from the Jews when he spoke in the synagogue. This was not unusual for Paul, but he decided he needed to move on to evangelize Gentiles (Acts 18:6). But Jesus appeared to Paul in a dream and said, "Do not be afraid, but speak, and do not keep silent; for I am with you" (verses 9-10). Jesus didn't remove the opposition; He reminded Paul that He was with him in Corinth.

Are you facing trouble, storms, opposition, discouragement? Instead of praying for God to remove them, first pray for a deeper awareness of the peace that comes from His presence. He is with you!

How to Pray

In this manner, therefore, pray.
MATTHEW 6:9

One of the best ways to describe Christianity has always been to say it is not a *religion* but a *relationship*. And nowhere is that more evident than in the way Jesus taught His disciples to pray.

The Lord's Prayer in Matthew 6:9-13 needs to be read in its context to understand what Jesus was saying to His disciples (then and now). In the Sermon on the Mount, Jesus draws attention to the formal religion of the Jews which had ceased to be a close and personal relationship with God. He pointed out many ways in which religious rituals had taken the place of intimacy with God—for example, prayer. Just before teaching His disciples how to pray, Jesus called religious leaders hypocrites for praying lengthy prayers in public to impress others. By contrast, Jesus told the disciples to pray to their Father in private using the words of the Lord's Prayer: "Our Father in heaven"—a prayer that offers the simple language of intimacy and relationship.

What was good for disciples then is good for disciples now. You can pray in the words of the Lord's Prayer or simply follow its clear and simple themes. Jesus' model prayer is a way to keep your relationship with God on a Father-to-child basis.

JUNE 23
Joy in Giving

*In the midst of a very severe trial, their overflowing joy
and their extreme poverty welled up in rich generosity.*
2 CORINTHIANS 8:2, NIV

Fundraising is big business. Generally, people hate to ask for money and people hate to be asked. When we answer a telemarketer's phone call, or open a piece of direct mail, we rarely do so with a sense of joy. And yet *joy* is the dominant theme associated with giving in the Bible.

What did it cost to raise the money to build the first temple in Jerusalem? King David asked once—and the leaders of Israel gave *hundreds of tons* of precious metals and jewels (1 Chronicles 29:6-9). Afterwards, "the people rejoiced, for they had offered willingly ... and King David also rejoiced greatly" (verse 9). Those people obviously had a lot to give. But what happens when poor people are asked to give? The same thing: joy. When the apostle Paul asked poverty-stricken Christians in Macedonia to give to the church in Jerusalem, they gave with an "abundance of their joy" that resulted in "riches of their liberality" (2 Corinthians 8:2).

When we give joyfully to the work of the Lord, we discover for ourselves what Jesus meant when He said, "It is more blessed to give than to receive" (Acts 20:35). Who wouldn't want to be blessed by God?

JUNE 24
Ought

You ought to walk and to please God.
1 THESSALONIANS 4:1

"I shall always remember [evangelist D. L.] Moody," wrote one man, "for he was the means of leading me to Christ. I was in a railway train one day when [he] came in, and sat down in the seat beside me. We were passing through a beautiful country, to which he called my attention, saying—'Did you ever think what a good Heavenly Father we have, to give us such a pleasant world to live in?' I made some indifferent answer; upon which he earnestly inquired—'Are you a Christian?' I answered, 'No.' 'Then,' said he, 'you ought to be one at once …. If you will kneel down, right here, I will pray to the Lord to make you a Christian.'"

Before the train reached the next station, this man had trusted Christ as His Savior.

We can all receive this Gospel. Jesus can set us free and wash us with His blood. If you haven't received His offer of salvation, you should. If you aren't a Christian, you ought to be!

What do you think? If a man has a hundred sheep, and one of them goes astray, does he not leave the ninety-nine and go to the mountains to seek the one that is straying?

MATTHEW 18:12

It's called "slippage" in industry: Grain falls off trucks, manufactured parts don't measure up, machines don't run at peak efficiency, oil leaks out of car engines, and so on. In other words, there are no *perfectly efficient* systems on earth. Something, somewhere, is always falling through the cracks.

But slippage never occurs in salvation. Jesus used the familiar example of a flock of one hundred sheep. When the shepherd brought his sheep into the sheepfold for protection at night, he would count them one by one. If he counted only 99, what would the shepherd do, Jesus asked. One sheep of a hundred is only a one percent loss, it could be argued. Perhaps just the cost of doing business. But not to Jesus. A good shepherd would go into the mountains and find his missing sheep and bring him safely home. Not even one sheep will ever be lost (John 10:27-29).

If you belong to Jesus Christ by faith, you are one of His sheep. You can never be lost; He will seek you and find you to bring you safely back to the fold.

For the word of God is living and powerful, and sharper than any two-edged sword, piercing even to the division of soul and spirit, and of joints and marrow, and is a discerner of the thoughts and intents of the heart.

HEBREWS 4:12

In the epic movie *The Ten Commandments*, whenever Pharaoh made a decree he sealed it: "So let it be written; so let it be done." In short, the word of Pharaoh was alive in its nation-changing power. His word was spoken, recorded, and put into action.

God's words are the same—only infinitely more so. His Word is eternal (John 1:1), made incarnate in Christ (John 1:14), and life-changing as the Holy Spirit applies it to the lives of human beings (Hebrews 4:12). God's Word is living, powerful, and sharp enough to penetrate to the deepest part of man, revealing the thoughts and intents of the human heart. The very act of reading, studying, and meditating upon the Word of God gives the Spirit opportunity to illuminate the reader's heart. The Word shows us who we are and who Christ is. Seeing the difference, the humble reader is willing to repent and be transformed into Christ's image (Romans 8:29).

Read the Word today with the expectation of being changed.

JUNE 27
Sanctified Stubbornness

Nevertheless I have a few things against you.
REVELATION 2:20

During the Reformation, Martin Luther was pressured to compromise key points involving the doctrine of justification by grace through faith. Critics said he should be more flexible with his beliefs for the sake of unity. Luther responded, "Our stubbornness on this issue is pious and holy; for by it we are striving to preserve the freedom we have in Christ Jesus and to keep the truth of the Gospel. If we lose this, we lose God, Christ, all the promises, faith, righteousness, and eternal life."

Some of the seven churches in Revelation had suffered theological erosion. The church in Thyatira, for example, had allowed "that woman ... who calls herself a prophetess, to teach and seduce" the church in heretical ways. The Lord held that against them and cautions them to "hold fast" (Revelation 2:25) till He comes.

Revelation is a solemn and sacred reminder to remain committed to the Gospel and stubborn in our beliefs. When culture tells us to compromise our core doctrine, we must say: "Our stubbornness on this issue is pious and holy; for by it we are striving to preserve the freedom we have in Christ!"

JUNE 28
Abba Father

*And because you are sons, God has sent forth the Spirit of His
Son into your hearts, crying out, "Abba, Father!"*
GALATIANS 4:6

In the West, English-speaking children refer to their male
parent with a variety of words: Dad, Daddy, Papa, Father,
Pop. In the Aramaic language that Jesus spoke, there was one
primary word for "father": *Abba*, an offshoot of Hebrew *Ab*.
Besides being a term of respect, *Abba* was also a term of warm
intimacy. Some modern English paraphrases of the Bible
translate *Abba* as "Papa," like a small child would say to a father
he loved.

Abba is only used three times in the New Testament.
Significantly, Jesus used it to address His own Father when He
was praying in the Garden of Gethsemane on the night before
His crucifixion (Mark 14:36). It was the prayer of a Son who
called out to the only Person who could sustain Him—His
own Heavenly Father. The apostle Paul suggests we do the same
in Romans 8:15 and Galatians 4:6. The Spirit in us gives us
freedom to call out to our "Papa Father" in time of need.

When you pray, picture the God who Jesus called "Papa,"
and pray the same way.

JUNE 29
Invisible Trajectory

May the God of hope fill you with all joy and peace as you trust in him, so that you may overflow with hope by the power of the Holy Spirit.
ROMANS 15:13, NIV

Traveling to another country can be exhilarating and exhausting. Seasoned travelers learn to take unexpected delays and opportunities in stride: this is part of the experience. Novice travelers often feel overwhelmed and anxious, unsure of how to proceed. Whether we are seasoned or novice travelers on our journey with Christ, we can access Him immediately through prayers for wisdom, guidance, and help.

The moment we accept Christ, our hearts are fused with His love and we are put on an invisible trajectory toward heaven. Nothing can separate us from His love. We learn to hold our positions and possessions lightly, knowing that our value and security come from Christ.

As we learn to trust Him, we are filled with hope and begin to experience the power of the Holy Spirit in our lives. He transforms us, comforts us, and gives us strength. As we walk with Christ, our eagerness for His return increases. He is our firm foundation and the home we desperately long for: the place where we are known, loved, and united with Him.

JUNE 30
Who Is My Neighbor?

And who is my neighbor?
LUKE 10:29

Jesus once advised a certain lawyer to love his neighbor as himself. The lawyer asked a burning question: "And who is my neighbor?" In response, Jesus told the story of a Jewish fellow who was waylaid by thieves on the ancient road from Jerusalem to Jericho, a trail that wound through a stark and treacherous valley. This was likely the same gorge David had in mind in Psalm 23—the Valley of the Shadow. It was a dramatic, twisting, dangerous path of several miles, riddled with thieves.

The victim was attacked, beaten, robbed, stripped, and thrown into a ditch. A priest and a Levite passed by on the other side, but it was the Samaritan who saw the wounded man, rescued him, and tended to his needs. The Samaritan knew that one's neighbor is anyone in need.

It's as simple as that. Whoever is in trouble, whoever is hurting, whoever has been abused, whoever is experiencing trials, whoever needs us—that is the neighbor we're to love as ourselves.

We're to go and do likewise.

JULY

JULY 1
The One and Only

No one has ever seen God, but the one and only Son, who is himself God and
is in closest relationship with the Father, has made him known.
JOHN 1:18, NIV

Such words were never written about Zarathustra, who
founded a religious system in Mesopotamia during the days of
David. They were never written about Confucius, the Chinese
philosopher in Asia during the days of the prophet Daniel.
Nothing like this was said of the Buddha, who is thought
to have lived in India during the biblical days of Ezra and
Nehemiah. Muhammad, the prophet of Islam who lived more
than 600 years after Jesus, never made such claims. You've
never heard words like this about Joseph Smith, Jr., or Mary
Baker Eddy or the Dalai Lama from Tibet.

Jesus of Nazareth is in a class all by Himself. He is in a field
of one. The Bible calls Him the "one and only." He is unique.
Part of our defense for the truthfulness of Christianity resides
with the uniqueness of Christ.

Of the 107 billion people who have come and gone through
the corridors of time and through the vortex of history, and
among the 7.6 billion people alive on earth today, Jesus Christ
is solitary, singular, alone, unique, and incomparable. He is
Lord. As both God and human, He can save to the uttermost
those who come to Him.

JULY 2
Rules of Contentment

So when Moses heard that, he was content.
LEVITICUS 10:20

Too many of us are contentious instead of content, but the Bible says, "be content" (1 Timothy 6:8). How can we cultivate a contented mind?

Nearly two hundred years ago an English clergyman suggested five rules, which are slightly updated here: (1) Allow yourself to complain of nothing, not even of the weather. (2) Do not imagine yourself to be somewhere other than where you are. (3) Do not compare your situation with that of anyone else. (4) Never allow yourself to dwell on wishing this or that had happened. Remember, God Almighty loves you better and more wisely than you love yourself. (5) Never dwell on tomorrow. Remind yourself that tomorrow is in God's hands, not yours. The heaviest part of sorrow is often looking forward to it with dread. Remember, the Lord will provide.[12]

The apostle Paul said, "I have learned in whatever state I am, to be content" (Philippians 4:11). We have to work to cultivate a contented heart. Perhaps it would help you to copy these five rules and post them on your mirror as a reminder of the importance of pursuing and practicing contentment.

---

[12] Updated from E. B. Pusey in *Daily Strength for Daily Needs* (Boston: Roberts Brothers, 1892), 144.

Yea, though I walk through the valley of the shadow of death,
I will fear no evil; for You are with me.
PSALM 23:4

For David, youngest of Jesse's eight sons, the life of a shepherd could be lonely. When Samuel the prophet went to Jesse's house in Bethlehem to anoint one of his sons as successor to King Saul, Samuel rejected the seven older sons. Jesse mentioned that there was one more, the youngest, who was "keeping the sheep" (1 Samuel 16:11). The implication was that David was away, in the hills with the sheep, tending the flock alone as he had to be sent for.

There are many references to David's solitary life as a shepherd, during which he had time to contemplate God, creation, and his place in it (Psalm 8). Psalm 23 is the ultimate example—David puts God in the role of shepherd, *his* shepherd (Psalm 23:1). Though often alone, and sometimes in dangerous situations (1 Samuel 17:34-36), David fell back on one truth: "You are with me"—even in the "valley of the shadow of death."

You may not be facing death today (all will one day), but wherever you are, whatever your circumstances, you are not alone. God is with you.

JULY 4
Once Enemies, Now Friends

But I say to you, love your enemies, bless those who curse you, do good to those who hate you.

MATTHEW 5:44

On April 25, 1866, a group of Confederate widows in Columbus, Mississippi, traveled to the Odd Fellows Cemetery where many of their husbands were buried. The Civil War was over, but nerves were raw. These women bore flowers for the graves of their dead. But as they decorated the Confederate graves, they were struck by the barrenness of those of Union soldiers who had perished in nearby battles and been buried there, far from home. The women spontaneously adorned those graves too. A reporter said, "No distinction was made between our own Confederate dead and the Federal soldiers who slept their last sleep by them ... Confederate and Federals, once enemies, now friends receiving their tribute of respect."

Many people hail that moment as the beginning of national healing; inspired by the story, Francis Finch later wrote "The Blue and the Gray," which was recited at civic observances for years.[13]

Nothing is gained by holding a grudge. Jesus told us to love our enemies. When wronged, we should not seek retribution, but reconciliation. Is there someone you can forgive today?

[13] Marlo Carter Kirkpatrick, *It Happened in Mississippi* (Morris Book Publishing, 2013), 30.

JULY 5
Are We Accidents?

Has not one God created us?
MALACHI 2:10

Visitors to museums of natural history typically see thousands of well-preserved samples of birds, bugs, reptiles, fish, and animals from around the world, including amazing collections of dinosaur bones. Captions on the displays often credit atheistic evolution. Somehow, say the experts, this great kaleidoscope of diversity of life arose from lifeless, thoughtless, naturalistic forces.

To hold that hypothesis, evolutionists have to believe there was a great cosmological accident resulting in the existence of the known universe. After this cosmological accident, they have to believe there was a biological accident that resulted in the existence of life. Then they have to believe that in the midst of the cosmological and biological accidents there were remarkable series of structural accidents that created such complexity and diversity that not even the greatest museums can showcase it.

There is better evidence for the reality of the creation of the world by an intelligent God who formed and fashioned us in His image. According to Psalm 139:14, we are "fearfully and wonderfully made." As such, we have purpose, meaning, and joy—all found in Him of whom it is said, "All things were made through Him" (John 1:3).

JULY 6
Peace, Be Still!

Then [Jesus] arose and rebuked the wind, and said to the sea, "Peace, be still!" And the wind ceased and there was a great calm.

MARK 4:39

In ancient literature, water often represents chaos. In Genesis 1:1-2, water covered the formless, empty, dark earth. God used a flood of waters to judge the earth in Noah's day. In Exodus, the Red Sea threatened to destroy the escaping Hebrew slaves. And during the ministry of Jesus, storms on the Sea of Galilee threatened the well-being of His disciples. In each case, God brought order out of chaos; God was bigger and more powerful than the disorder.

There is a lesson there: Whenever chaos or danger appears imminent, our concern is not how big the problem seems but whether God is with us or not. The disciples learned this lesson when a storm threatened to take their lives on the Sea of Galilee. Jesus commanded the storm (the chaos) to be still and peace was restored (Mark 4:35-41). They learned that having Jesus with them was more important than the storm that was against them.

If chaos is threatening your peace, let Jesus be your ark of safety in the storm. He can bring peace in any storm.

Abraham

*And the Scripture was fulfilled which says, "Abraham
believed God, and it was accounted to him for righteousness."
And he was called the friend of God.*
JAMES 2:23

In the early years of Facebook, the race was on to collect
"friends"—people whose posts would show up in one's news
feed. The more "friends" the better! It became a status thing,
with some users befriending tens of thousands of people,
most of whom they didn't know. So, Facebook put a cap on the
number at 5,000—still an unreasonable number if you think
about the definition of *friend*.

The Bible names only one person as being a friend of God:
Abraham (2 Chronicles 20:7; Isaiah 41:8; James 2:23). Abraham
was the person God put in place for the rescue mission for
humanity. Through Abraham the Messiah would come to
"gather together in one all things ... both which are in heaven
and which are on earth" (Ephesians 1:10). So *friend* became a
covenant term, signifying loyalty, blessing, and fruitfulness.
Jesus established that covenant relationship with His disciples
when He called them His friends (John 15:13-15).

Make a point today to thank God for the blessing of
friendship with Him.

JULY 8
Learning to Share

So let each one give as he purposes in his heart, not grudgingly
or of necessity; for God loves a cheerful giver.
2 CORINTHIANS 9:7

Parents begin early. As soon as their first child has a sibling or is around other children, the teaching begins with these words, "You need to share." The response to this counsel can be challenging at first—even to the point of experiencing temper tantrums and tears from the child.

The secret every parent knows is that when a child learns to share, they learn to value others. As parents, if we recognize that giving and sharing are vital to our child's quality of life and connection to others, it is important that we also recognize that this wisdom comes from God.

The truth is—everything comes from God—it all belongs to Him. God does not require anything from us; yet, He knows it is good for us to remember His gifts. When we give with a grateful and joyful heart, it is in response to God's goodness and love. Giving to God is also an act of faith as we trust Him not only for our daily provision but for our future as well.

The joy of giving is learned like a child who discovers how to share—it begins when we cheerfully give to God.

JULY 9
Building a Marriage Without Losing Your Mind

Therefore, putting away lying, "Let each one of you speak truth with his neighbor," for we are members of one another.

EPHESIANS 4:25

Being truthful with your neighbor is vital, but when your neighbor is your husband or wife, it's of utmost importance. A good marriage is never helped by a lie. That's why marital partners don't hide things from each other. For a marriage to work, the partners must trust one another, which means we must avoid behavior about which we will be tempted to lie.

We can paraphrase Ephesians 4:25 like this: "If you're going to build a marriage without losing your mind, both of you must put off falsehood and speak truthfully to your spouse, for you are both members of one marriage."

Avoid activities you want to hide from your spouse, including pornography, platonic friendships, undisclosed purchases, online activities, or whatever it is. Whatever you're hiding from your husband or wife will eventually damage your marriage, and it will damage you.

The one who conceals sin will not prosper (Proverbs 28:13). There is great safety in being honest and open. If you're hiding something from your spouse, confess it, get some counseling if needed, work through it, and start operating on a basis of transparency and honesty.

You can't build trust in a marriage any other way.

JULY 10
Faster or Better?

So He commanded the multitude to sit down on the ground. And He took the seven loaves and gave thanks, broke them and gave them to His disciples to set before them; and they set them before the multitude.

MARK 8:6

It's faster for a parent to pick up a toddler's toys than to watch and encourage the child to do it. But which is more educational, edifying, bonding, and discipline-promoting for the child? Obviously, to have the child (or help the child) pick up the toys. There is more to a task than the task itself.

Which raises the question: Why doesn't God just blanket the world with the Gospel message all at once? Why has He chosen to use fallible, fickle, often-faithless humans to "help" Him in this eternally significant task? Why did Jesus use the disciples to help Him feed the multitudes? For the same reason parents work with their children instead of doing things more quickly themselves. In our case, God's goal is to conform us to the image of Jesus Christ (Romans 8:29). Just as the Father worked with the Son, so the Son works with us (John 20:21).

Enjoy the blessing of doing kingdom work *with* Jesus. By the power of the Spirit, He uses us to be His hands and heart in the world.

JULY 11
Beyond Reproach

My prayer is not that you take them out of the world but that you protect them from the evil one. They are not of the world, even as I am not of it.
JOHN 17:15-16, NIV

According to a recent Gallup poll, Americans disagree about almost every issue of morality except one—infidelity. Only nine percent say adultery is morally acceptable. But on almost every other issue the moral view is softening—divorce, sex between unmarried adults, doctor-assisted suicide, pornography, and polygamy. More people are condoning behavior that, from a biblical perspective, is ungodly.[14]

The truth is—it doesn't matter what society thinks. The Word of God reflects the character of God and sets the standards of morality for humanity. At heart, Christians are counter-culturalists. We're distinct from the world. We don't adopt the convictions, standards, ways, or patterns of our society. We are determined to live above reproach, even when others are offended by our biblical lifestyle. While we don't want to needlessly offend anyone, let's never lower the standards of our godliness.

Christ calls us to live for Him—beyond reproach.

[14] www1.cbn.com/cbnnews/us/2017/may/americans-going-soft-on-moral-issues-except-one.

JULY 12
Treasured Words

And treasure my commands within you ....
Write them on the tablet of your heart.
PROVERBS 7:1, 3

Memorizing Bible verses isn't hard; it's a matter of learning one word at a time until a particular verse is installed in your mind. Nothing is more powerful, practical, and personality-changing. Nor is there a better weapon in spiritual warfare than the sword of the Spirit.

When Satan tempts you to worry, quote Philippians 4:6: "Be anxious for nothing." When tempted to speak rashly, remember James 1:19: "Be swift to hear, slow to speak, slow to wrath." When you awaken in the night with problems nagging at your mind, begin reciting Psalm 46:1: "God is our refuge and strength, a very present help in trouble."

One way of keeping track of your Bible memory verses is to write them on cards or in a small notebook. As you learn new verses and review older ones, your cards or note pages will become as valuable as a stack of hundred-dollar bills—more so—for "more to be desired are they than gold" (Psalm 19:10). As my friend Robert Morgan recalls, "The internalized truths of God's Word keep us mentally healthy. It's the greatest secret I know to personal resiliency."[15]

[15] Robert J. Morgan, *100 Bible Verses Everyone Should Know by Heart*, (Nashville: BH Publishing Group, 2010).

To the angel of the church of Ephesus .... Smyrna .... Pergamos ....
Thyatira .... Sardis .... Philadelphia ... the Laodiceans write.
REVELATION 2:1, 8, 12, 18; 3:1, 7, 14

One estimate puts the number of closed-circuit television (CCTV) cameras worldwide at 350 million as of 2016. Long used in companies and homes for security, they are now used to blanket metropolitan streets with a visual record of everything that happens. Besides CCTV, there are drones and satellites that provide a 24/7 eye-in-the-sky record.

Depending on who is watching, surveillance can seem threatening and invasive. But such "all-seeingness" is not new. God has been all-seeing, all-knowing, and all-hearing from the beginning (Genesis 16:13; Psalm 139:1-12; Matthew 12:36). How else would Jesus Christ have been able to send specific messages to the seven churches in Asia Minor about their practices and character (Revelation 2–3)? Those letters were very specific. Such letters can be a warning to us if our behavior parallels theirs, or a comfort in terms of Christ being aware of the price we may pay for serving Him. In either case, we should never doubt God's awareness of the details of our lives.

Live today as an open book before the Lord—a life you are happy for Him to see and bless.

JULY 14
A Helper for Every Need

And I will pray the Father, and He will give you another
Helper, that He may abide with you forever.
JOHN 14:16

Translation is not an exact science, especially from an ancient language to a modern one. Bible translation is a good example. Take the Greek word *parakletos*. Modern English Bibles use the following words to translate *parakletos*: helper, counselor, advocate, intercessor, supporter, friend, strengthener, and comforter. Because *parakletos* means "one called alongside," it's easy to see how any of these English words could be a viable translation.

And that's good for us, because *parakletos* is the word Jesus used to describe the Holy Spirit who would come to aid His followers after He returned to heaven. The early disciples, and we, have been given a Helper, Counselor, Advocate ... and all the rest—all in the third person of the Trinity! Jesus told the disciples to wait in Jerusalem until the Spirit was given to them which happened fifty days after His crucifixion (Acts 1:4-5; 2:1-4). The Spirit of God manifested the indwelling life of Christ in the Church (Galatians 2:20), allowing them to turn the world upside down (Acts 17:6).

Review that list of words above. Do you see one that seems fitting for a need you are facing? Live your life filled with the Spirit who has been given to strengthen you in all things (Ephesians 5:18).

Defining Moments

He will again have compassion on us, and will subdue our iniquities.
You will cast all our sins into the depths of the sea.
MICAH 7:19

If you were asked to share your life story, which events and moments would you include? The experiences we remember with the greatest clarity are those with the strongest emotions attached to them: the overcoming of obstacles, the losses that left us bereft, and the moments we felt most alive or at peace. Although the choice is often unconscious, we decide the weight and significance of our experiences.

King David chose to hide his sin with Bathsheba until the prophet Nathan told him a story about a beloved sheep stolen by a greedy man. God's truth revealed the true weight of David's sin. Although there were consequences, David's cries and brokenness drew him back to God.

When we fail, there is a temptation to allow our failures to define us and our shame to cripple us. The promise we find in David's life is that God longs to forgive and restore when we come to Him. Let's invite God's light into our lives and trust Him to take away our shame and to forgive us wholly and completely.

JULY 16
God's Timing

*And some of them said, "Could not this Man, who opened the
eyes of the blind, also have kept [Lazarus] from dying?"*
JOHN 11:37

A young man visited the father of his girlfriend to ask the
father's permission to marry his daughter. To his surprise, the
father said "No." The young man thought it was a formality; the
father took it much more seriously. The father explained to the
young man that there were character and behavioral issues in
the young man's life that concerned him. If he would agree to
work on those issues, they could talk again about marriage.

Timing in life is often a puzzle to us. We ask God for
something and we wonder why He doesn't immediately say
"Yes." Even more puzzling, God is aware of our needs even
before we ask (Matthew 6:8), so why doesn't He just provide
what we need without our having to ask? Jesus once initially
told a woman whose daughter had an unclean spirit to "let the
children be filled first" (Mark 7:27); He only healed one person
out of all the sick at the Pool of Bethesda (John 5:1-15); and He
waited four days before raising Lazarus from the dead (John
11:1-44).

Delays are only from our perspective. God's timing and
reasons are always perfect (Romans 8:28-29).

JULY 17
Like a Mighty Army

You therefore must endure hardship as a good soldier of Jesus Christ.
2 TIMOTHY 2:3

Field Marshal Bernard Montgomery, known as Monty, wrote in his memoirs, "I have always held the view that an army is not merely a collection of individuals, with so many tanks, guns, machine-guns, etc. The real strength of an army is, and must be, far greater than the sum total of its parts; that extra strength is provided by morale, fighting spirit, mutual confidence between the leaders and the led ... and many other intangible spiritual qualities."[16]

In many ways, that describes a church. In our narcissistic world, we have to remember church is not about us—our tastes, preferences, desires, comforts, and conveniences. We're in a spiritual battle, and our churches need members who do not seek their own way. We must keep Christ as our Commander and we must honor one another in gentleness and kindness. Disgruntled church members can damage a congregation's ministry. Rather than being harsh or opinionated, try being humble, gentle, and encouraging.

The Church of God is a mighty army with one Commander, marching to the rhythm of His grace.

[16] Jonathan Fennell, *Combat and Morale in the North African Campaign* (New York: Cambridge University Press, 2011), 87.

JULY 18
Panting for Glory

Now, brethren, concerning the coming of our Lord
Jesus Christ and our gathering together to Him.
2 THESSALONIANS 2:1

William Hepburn Hewitson (1812-1850) was sent by the Free Church of Scotland to the island of Madeira, off the coast of North Africa. His missionary memoir is a testimony to his brief but powerful life. On January 18, 1843, Hewitson told a friend he'd been deeply impressed while studying 2 Thessalonians 2:1-8. The personal and dramatic nature of Christ's return became exceedingly real to him.

His biographer wrote, "He not only believed in the speedy 'appearing'—he loved it, waited for it, watched for it, saying, 'Faith looks back to the cross and is at peace; it looks forward to the crown, and pants for glory.'" Then his biographer added this comment: "He used to speak of it ever afterwards as bringing with it a kind of second conversion. It is interwoven with the texture of his whole future life."[17]

It's possible for us to go through the entire day without thinking about Christ's return, but even now He is preparing to come again for us. Oh, that our hearts will be gripped with the reality of it today, that we may look forward to the crown and pant for glory.

[17] John Baillie, *Memoir of the Rev. W. H. Hewitson* (New York: Robert Carter & Brothers, 1851), 89-90.

JULY 19
Our Great High Priest

There were many priests, because they were prevented by death from continuing. But He, because He continues forever, has an unchangeable priesthood.

HEBREWS 7:23-24

Imagine buying a premium ticket to a Broadway play. Getting there early, you watch stagehands getting everything ready for the show. They move everything in place, test the lights and microphones, and double-check the props. But no actor ever arrives. No action ever takes place. The play never starts, and you spend the night watching stagehands moving the props around. You'd want your money back.

That's the theme of the book of Hebrews. The writer was saying in effect, "You know those priests and sacrifices and rituals in the Old Testament? They were simply arranging things. They were preparing for the arrival of Christ. It's the Lord Jesus who stepped onto the stage of history when everything was ready and gave meaning to what they were doing. He is the true and eternal great High Priest."

Keep your eyes on Him, press ahead, and discover the power of His priestly ministry to your soul. Our Heavenly High Priest identifies with our needs and strengthens us in time of need.

JULY 20
Shall I Go?

For You are my rock and my fortress; therefore,
for Your name's sake, lead me and guide me.
PSALM 31:3

Think of all the places you have to go on an average day—
literally. You arise in the morning and go to the shower, then
to the kitchen, then to the closet to get dressed, then to work,
then lunch, then to errands, then home … and those are only
after you decided where to get married, where to go to school,
where to live, where to work, and where to go to church.

Now—think about how many of those "where's" you
consulted God about before setting out. Where is the line in
your spiritual life between those things that you don't inquire
of the Lord about and those you do? Somewhere between what
to eat for breakfast and who to marry, you cross that line—and
it's probably different for every person. Think of it a different
way: Is anything too trivial to ask the Lord about? Perhaps the
key lies in developing what Paul called "the mind of Christ"
(1 Corinthians 2:16)—a combination of asking God about some
things and developing wisdom from Him about most other
things, knowing how God would answer before we ask.

Do you live in an ongoing conversation with God about
your next steps? Talk to God this week as if He is right beside
you (He is) and cares about every decision you need to make
(He does).

What Photos Can't Show

But the Lord said to Samuel, "Do not look at his appearance or at his physical stature, because I have refused him. For the Lord does not see as man sees; for man looks at the outward appearance, but the Lord looks at the heart."

1 SAMUEL 16:7

One of the first photographs ever taken (1839) was of an American photographer taking a picture of himself—perhaps history's first "selfie." Fast forward to today—there are tens of millions of selfies posted on social media sites around the world every year. Many of the pictures record events and relationships. But far too many are of individuals taking images of themselves alone—the "Look at me!" variety of selfie.

The problem with any picture, selfie or otherwise, is that it only records what is on the outside. The camera has yet to be invented (and never will be) that can photograph the spiritual status of the heart, soul, or mind. And that is the part of us God is most concerned about. When Samuel was sent to anoint Israel's new king, God told him not to anoint a man who looked like a king. Instead, he was to anoint a man who had the heart of a king, a heart after God's own heart (1 Samuel 13:14; Acts 13:22).

Those viewing your photos can't see your heart, but God can. Make sure He finds in you a heart that is pursuing Him.

You shall remember the Lord your God, for it is
He who gives you power to get wealth.
DEUTERONOMY 8:18

Herbert Taylor, an unassuming businessman in Chicago, was behind many of the great student ministry movements in the twentieth century. Having made a fortune as a manufacturer, Taylor shared his talents and treasures to further the Lord's work. He helped establish scores of evangelistic organizations. And he was behind the purchase of the Cedar Campus for InterVarsity on Lake Huron.

In building the Cedar Lodge in 1954, everything came down to a final payment of $10,000. About that time, Taylor was elected president of Rotary International, and the organization offered him the standard honorarium they gave to each of their presidents—$10,000. Taylor asked them to make the check out to the special nonprofit corporation set up to provide money for the conference project, and the lodge was finished.

If money comes into your hands, remember Who provides it. God allows us to have this world's goods that we might help the world have the Good News of eternal life.

This is a faithful saying and worthy of all acceptance, that Christ Jesus came into the world to save sinners, of whom I am chief.
1 TIMOTHY 1:15

Mirrors help us see ourselves as we are on the outside, but not who we are on the inside, nor the person we might become. Average athletes think they are good until they play against someone who is great—same for musicians, artists, teachers, or any other role in life. To know who we really are we must see ourselves in light of a higher standard.

That happened to the apostle Paul. Before he met Jesus Christ, he had one of the most impressive résumés in Israel. As a young man, he was brilliant, a Pharisee, a law-keeper, a defender of the faith, and destined for greatness (Philippians 3:4-6). But after meeting Christ everything changed. He had one phrase to describe himself: the chief of sinners. He was still profoundly qualified and capable, just in a different way. He suddenly realized that without the grace of God, he was nothing (Philippians 3:7-11).

The more we get to know Christ—"the image of the invisible God" (Colossians 1:15)—the more accurate picture we have of ourselves. He is our true mirror.

JULY 24
Milk or Meat?

But solid food belongs to those who are of full age, that is, those who by reason of use have their senses exercised to discern both good and evil.

HEBREWS 5:14

There is a natural progression to the foods a human being eats. First, liquids, then soft purees, then soft pieces of fruits or vegetables, then whole fruits and vegetables. Finally, when teeth are available for chewing, harder foods—solid food—can be eaten. Some variation of that progression is an indication of good nutrition and healthy development.

That's the analogy the New Testament uses for spiritual growth as well, organized in two categories: milk and solid food (1 Corinthians 3:2; Hebrews 5:12). Milk represents the "first principles of the oracles of God" (Hebrews 5:12)—teachings about repentance, faith, baptism, spiritual gifts, the Resurrection, and eternal judgment (Hebrews 6:1-2). The writer to the Hebrews suggested to his readers that they should have mastered, and moved beyond, these elementary teachings given their tenure as Christians. But they were still living like babes in Christ, capable of only milk instead of solid food. They were old in years but babes in maturity.

What is your spiritual diet? Are you nourishing yourself on the solid food of God's Word daily? Your spiritual growth depends on it.

That if you confess with your mouth the Lord Jesus and believe in your heart that God has raised Him from the dead, you will be saved.
ROMANS 10:9

Occam's razor is a principle formulated by a fourteenth-century English friar named William of Ockham: All things being equal, the answer to a problem is the one making the fewest assumptions—that is, the simplest solution. Moses hadn't heard of Occam's razor, but he expressed a form of it to the Israelites who were about to enter the Promised Land.

In Deuteronomy 28, Moses outlined the blessings (for obeying) and curses (for disobeying) God's covenant. In chapter 29, the Israelites renewed their commitment to obey. And in chapter 30 Moses reminded them that obeying God is not complicated. You don't have to travel to heaven (30:11-12) or cross the sea (30:13) to find God's Word. You have verbally confessed to believing it and it is in your heart, ready to be obeyed (30:14). So, Moses gave the Israelites a choice: believe (life) or disbelieve (death) (30:15). A complicated covenant was reduced to a simple choice. It was the same choice Paul told the Roman Christians they could make: Believe in your heart and confess with your mouth and you will be saved (Romans 10:9).

There is often a temptation to make things too complicated. Believe in the death, burial, and Resurrection of Jesus and you will be saved (1 Corinthians 15:1-4).

JULY 26
Fly on the Wall

For I delivered to you first of all that which I also received:
that Christ died for our sins according to the Scriptures.
1 CORINTHIANS 15:3

Sometimes we would like to be the proverbial fly on the wall, listening in on a momentous meeting of minds. Perhaps a history-making political or military decision is made. or an unrecorded conversation between great figures of history takes place. Unfortunately, unless somehow recorded, such moments are lost to history.

Such a conversation took place between Jesus and two men which theologians wish they could have heard. First, some background: The apostle Paul wrote to the church in Corinth that "Christ died for our sins according to the Scriptures." Paul obviously meant the Old Testament Scriptures, but which ones? And what did they say about why Christ died? Now to the conversation where Jesus likely answered those questions. After His Resurrection He walked, unrecognized, on the road to Emmaus with two men who were downcast and confused about the crucifixion. So, "beginning at Moses and all the Prophets, [Jesus] expounded to them in all the [Old Testament] Scriptures the things concerning Himself" (Luke 24:27). Oh, to have heard that conversation!

Is the Old Testament a part of your regular Bible reading? In it lies the background and foundation for the New Testament. Make it a goal to give the Old Testament its due as you seek to know Christ better.

JULY 27
Training for a Long Life

For [our fathers] indeed for a few days chastened us as seemed best to them,
but He for our profit, that we may be partakers of His holiness.
HEBREWS 12:10

When an athlete suffers a painful injury on the playing field, she is not thinking about the long-term effects of the accident. No, pain focuses our attention on the immediate task of making the pain go away. That's natural; nobody likes to be in pain—but pain keeps us from injuring ourselves even more seriously—there is purpose for pain.

The Bible points this out lest we not believe it's true. In Hebrews 11, we are told about numerous named and unnamed Old Testament characters who proved themselves faithful in the midst of suffering. Then Hebrews 12:1 says, "Therefore." That means there is a lesson for us to learn from the lives of the suffering saints in Hebrews 11. And the central part of that lesson is that God allows us to experience discomfort in this life in order to train us toward godliness in the future. Just as parents discipline (train) their children for their future benefit—including training that is sometimes uncomfortable—so God trains us as His children "that we may be partakers of His holiness."

Perhaps you are in training at this moment. (If not, you will be.) Count yourself as the blessed of God: a child in whom the Father delights (Proverbs 3:12).

JULY 28
Wait Patiently

You also be patient. Establish your hearts,
for the coming of the Lord is at hand.
JAMES 5:8

What were you doing eight weeks ago? Eight weeks seems like an eternity. But consider this: That's how long the average journey from Europe to America took, by sailing ship, in the eighteenth century. *Eight weeks*. And it could have been even longer depending on wind and weather. You send a letter to a relative in America telling them you're coming—that letter takes eight weeks. Their reply takes another eight weeks. Then, not knowing your departure date, they would begin the wait. They knew you were coming; they just had no idea when. They wouldn't even know when you arrived until you knocked on their door.

Patience was the watchword. Today, instant communications have made us impatient people. We can tell others exactly where we are at any moment of the day. Our phone's GPS will tell us exactly when we will arrive. But there is one case where patience is still needed: waiting on the Second Coming of Jesus Christ. We know He's coming, we just don't know when. What to do while we wait? "Establish your heart." That is, be resolute, unmoved, and stand firm in the expectation that *Christ will arrive*.

Are you "looking for the blessed hope and glorious appearing of our great God and Savior Jesus Christ" (Titus 2:13). Wait patiently—but be established in hope.

JULY 29
Times and Seasons

To everything there is a season, a time for every purpose under heaven.
ECCLESIASTES 3:1

Solomon's well-known passage in Ecclesiastes 3:1-8 about the times and seasons in our lives is recognized by both believers and nonbelievers in Christ. Songs have been written about its theme. The plaintive poetic verse reminds us that life has its ups and downs, laughter and pain, gains and losses, as well as joys and sorrow.

Solomon's plea encapsulates a message we all need to learn—everything has its time—there is a season for everything in God's plan and purpose. The point is not to understand the timing of every season and circumstance in life, but to trust God when they arrive: "Fear God and keep His commandments, for this is man's all" (Ecclesiastes 12:13). Remember, as the apostle Paul instructed the Thessalonians: "But concerning the times and the seasons, brethren, you have no need that I should write to you. For you yourselves know perfectly that the day of the Lord so comes as a thief in the night" (1 Thessalonians 5:1-2). Trust God with today and your tomorrow—for one day He will come and we will be caught up with Him—that is a time and season to be ready for!

JULY 30
Talk, Don't Argue

But indeed, O man, who are you to reply against God? Will the thing formed say to him who formed it, "Why have you made me like this?"
ROMANS 9:20

All parents have experienced being argued with by a toddler. Less an argument than a very small child's attempt to explain their point of view, most parents listen patiently before announcing how things are going to be. When toddlers argue with parents, things never go the toddlers' way. It's an exercise in futility.

Solomon says something similar when it comes to arguing with God. He says we "cannot contend with Him who is mightier than [we] .... How [are we] the better" for doing so? (Ecclesiastes 6:10-11) The apostle Paul asked a hypothetical debater who might challenge God's sovereign choices: "Who are you to reply against God?" Yes, Jesus entertained, and answered, questions from people, even detractors. And God even invited Israel, through Isaiah, to "come now, and let us reason together" (Isaiah 1:18). *Talking* with God? Yes. *Arguing* with God? Not a fruitful idea. Far better to cultivate trust in His ways, words, and actions.

Pour out your thoughts and concerns to God. But do so ready to trust in His will (Philippians 4:6-7; Hebrews 4:16).

Do you see a man who excels in his work? He will stand before kings.
PROVERBS 22:29

Since we live in a world of diversions, entertainment, and recreational opportunities, it's good to remind ourselves that hard work is necessary for success. King Solomon, the writer of Proverbs, extolled the need for diligence and industriousness. Proverbs 18:9 warns, "He who is slothful in his work is a brother to him who is a great destroyer." The godly woman in Proverbs 31, "Seeks wool and flax, and willingly works with her hands …. She also rises while it is yet night, and provides food for her household" (verses 13, 15).

Poet Henry Wadsworth Longfellow wrote a little verse about the power of a biblical work ethic, saying:

> The heights by great men reached and kept
> Were not attained by sudden flight,
> But they, while their companions slept,
> Were toiling upward in the night.

We all need rest; every hardworking man or woman needs time to recharge their batteries and enjoy life. But beware the spirit of this age of entertainment. God didn't place us on earth to be amused by the world, but to be employed in the work He assigns.

AUGUST

AUGUST 1
Hungry for God

Blessed are those who hunger and thirst for
righteousness, for they shall be filled.
MATTHEW 5:6

It is said that a human can live three minutes without oxygen, three days without water, and three weeks without food. Omitted from this formula is spiritual deprivation: How long can a human survive spiritually and emotionally without spiritual nourishment based on divine truth?

The point is that there is such a thing as spiritual hunger. For instance, a Pharisee named Nicodemus was hungry to know the spiritual meaning of Jesus' teachings. So he risked his position and reputation by visiting Jesus under the cloak of darkness lest his hunger be discovered by the self-satisfied around him. He was hungry for truth. On another occasion, Jesus suggested that a willingness to seek the truth was the key to finding it (John 7:17)—and not all are that hungry. He taught in parables to separate the hungry from the satisfied (Matthew 13:10-11). And Hebrews 11:6 (along with Matthew 5:6) promises that the spiritually hungry will be filled.

Don't go through life spiritually hungry. Seek God and His nourishment through prayer, worship, and His Word. And you will be filled.

AUGUST 2
In Heavenly Love Abiding

And we have known and believed the love that God has for us. God is love,
and he who abides in love abides in God, and God in him.

1 JOHN 4:16

Sometimes when we feel overwhelmed, nothing helps us like one of the great hymns of the faith. Anna Laetitia Waring is one of our greatest nearly-forgotten hymnists, but her songs have a way of finding us just where we are. She was a Welsh Quaker who became an Anglican. Her passion for Bible study was so great she studied Hebrew to better understand the Old Testament. In addition to writing, she was active in prison ministry and working with discharged prisoners. Among her hymns is this one, well worth tracking down and learning if you don't know it. It can comfort us through many pressures in life:

In heavenly love abiding,
no change my heart shall fear;
And safe is such confiding,
for nothing changes here.
The storm may roar without me,
my heart may low be laid;
But God is round about me,
And can I be dismayed?

Abide in Christ today, and let His Word abide in you.

AUGUST 3
Put Off the Old

But now you yourselves are to put off all these: anger, wrath,
malice, blasphemy, filthy language out of your mouth. ...
Put off the old man with his deeds.
COLOSSIANS 3:8-9

When people hold garage sales to declutter, three things can happen to their stuff: It gets sold or given away to yard-sale shoppers; it gets taken to charity recyclers like Goodwill®; or it goes in the trash. Unless something is really valuable or meaningful, the inviolable rule of decluttering stands: Nothing, once removed, goes back in the house!

Lots of people hold yard sales as they prepare for an in-depth cleaning of their closets or garage. Some people claim this challenging rule: If it hasn't been worn or used in a year—it needs to go. We need to be just as ruthless, on a daily basis rather than a seasonal basis, about decluttering our spiritual life. Have we gotten careless or lazy about our speech, our thoughts, our behaviors, our choices, our relationships, or how we spend our free time? Instead of putting them *out* (in the yard), the Bible says to put them *off*.

Look at your life in Christ. Is there anything you can't justify keeping? Purpose to put it off and put on the new—the new life in Christ Jesus.

Favor and Power

God anointed Jesus of Nazareth with the Holy Spirit and with
power, who went about doing good and healing all who
were oppressed by the devil, for God was with Him.

ACTS 10:38

Since 1789, presidents of the United States have been inaugurated. In monarchies like the United Kingdom, the monarch is crowned and also anointed with oil. The tradition of anointing with oil has its roots in ancient cultures, especially that of Israel.

Anointing with oil served several purposes: medicinal, cosmetic, and bestowing favor. A woman anointed Jesus' feet at a dinner as a sign of humility and respect (Luke 7:46). But when God anointed someone, through His prophets, it was a sign of divine favor and power. The prophet Samuel confirmed God's choice of David as king of Israel by anointing David with oil—"and the Spirit of the Lord came upon David" (1 Samuel 16:13). Instead of being anointed with oil at the beginning of His ministry, Jesus was anointed by the Holy Spirit Himself (Mark 1:9-13). Thus the Holy Spirit replaced oil as the sign of divine favor and power in the believer's life.

Paul commands us to "be filled with the Spirit" (Ephesians 5:18) to live out the Spirit's anointing in our lives.

AUGUST 5
Lord, You Know

Lean not on your own understanding.
PROVERBS 3:5

"There are things we know we know," Donald Rumsfeld said. "We also know there are known unknowns; that is to say, we know there are some things we do not know. But there are also unknown unknowns—the ones we don't know we don't know …. It is the latter category that tend to be the difficult ones."

When it comes to the ways of God, there is much we do not know. When God asked Ezekiel if the dry bones could live, Ezekiel simply said, "Lord God, You know" (Ezekiel 37:3). When the heavenly being asked John, "Who are these arrayed in white robes?" in Revelation 7:13, John replied, "Sir, you know."

Sometimes we need to say, "Lord, You know." The Bible tells us not to lean on our own understanding, which means we shouldn't be too confident in our ability to figure everything out. Knowing what we don't know is the beginning of humility, and humility is a precursor to wisdom.

If you're struggling to understand a particular "why" or "what if" or "if only" in your life, give it to God and trust Him with all your heart. Learn to say, "Lord, You know."

AUGUST 6
This Turn of Events

Before I was afflicted I went astray, but now I keep Your word.
PSALM 119:67

Romans 8:28 assures us that all things will work for the good of those who love the Lord, and that's a promise we greatly need. But do you realize there are a lot of Romans 8:28-like verses in the Bible? God's ability to reverse our trials is interwoven with the story of redemption. God has a way of turning things around, sooner or later.

Job said of his troubles, "Indeed, this will **turn out** for my deliverance" (Job 13:16, NIV). Nehemiah 13:2 speaks of how God **turns** curses into blessings. The writer of 1 Kings 12:15 said about an incident, "for the **turn** of events was from the Lord, that He might fulfill His word." Paul told the Philippians the things that had happened to him had **turned out** for the furtherance of the Gospel (Philippians 1:19).

"Things have a way of turning out," we sometimes say when facing difficulty. Yes, they always do for God's children, but only because of His redemptive power and grace. In His providence, trials become disguised blessings that draw us closer to God as we learn from Him and lean on Him.

So when he heard that Lazarus was sick, he
stayed where He was two more days.
JOHN 11:6, NIV

Legendary basketball coach John Wooden wrote, "Beware of doing things hastily. A productive leader is busy, and sometimes you'll be so busy that you may skim through a task without appropriate focus. You get careless. The consequences can be severe. I constantly remind players, 'Be quick, but don't hurry.' Speedy execution without carelessness was the goal. Do it properly the first time."

Wooden continued, "I pinned a card to our bulletin board to remind all of an important question: 'If you do not have time to do it right, when will you have time to do it over?'"[18]

Jesus was always active, but He never seemed rushed. He knew His Father had appointed each day's work, and Jesus was content to work or to wait, depending on the situation. He never panicked, never acted with careless haste, yet He thoroughly tackled each project with diligent care.

We often take on work that should be done by others. Somehow, we get ourselves over-committed. May the Lord teach us to do the work He assigns, and only what He gives us. And may we remain busy without being hasty, and effective without being frazzled. That reflects the steady pace of Him who accomplished His entire mission in only three years.

[18] John Wooden and Steve Jamison, *The Essential Wooden* (New York: McGraw-Hill, 2007), 97.

So Jonathan said to David, "Whatever you
yourself desire, I will do it for you."
1 SAMUEL 20:4

Rare is the person who, like David, has a faithful friend like Jonathan. We often say to others, "If you need anything, let me know. Whatever you need." We're sincere, of course—we do want to be helpful to our friends. But words like *anything* and *whatever* are all inclusive. They may represent a level of commitment we aren't ready to make.

But Jonathan and David made that kind of commitment because they made a covenant—the most binding form of contract in the ancient world. They exchanged promises, possessions, and protection—meaning "all of mine is yours, and all of yours is mine" (see 1 Samuel 18:1-4). Jonathan told David as much: "Whatever you yourself desire, I will do it for you." And he kept that promise, protecting David from Saul's murderous attempts to kill him. Sometime later, when David was king, he gave a shout-out in memory of his friend, Jonathan. He located Jonathan's exiled son, Mephibosheth, and brought him to the royal court. An act of love for, or in memory of, a faithful friend is the ultimate shout-out.

If you have a friend who has demonstrated love and loyalty, give that person a shout-out often—in word and deed.

> *Recognize those who labor among you, and are over you in the Lord and admonish you, and ... esteem them very highly in love for their work's sake.*
> 1 THESSALONIANS 5:12-13

In a recent article, Thom Rainer wrote about the epidemic of depression among pastors, and he identified five precipitating factors: (1) Spiritual warfare; the devil aims his ammunition against the leaders of God's flocks. (2) The surprising reality of pastoral leadership. Pastors don't just preach on Sunday; they deal with vexing issues of congregational life every day. (3) A sense of inadequacy, especially when the church doesn't grow or membership declines. (4) Critics and bullies. (5) Loneliness. One pastor said, "It's really hard to find a true friend when you are a pastor."[19]

Each of us should encourage our pastor and pastoral staff. Pray for your pastor regularly. Don't needlessly bother your church staff, but call on them when you need them, always expressing your appreciation. A note of encouragement can brighten a pastor's day, or a kind comment on social media can spread positive cheer. When your pastor makes a mistake (none of us are perfect), be gracious rather than critical. Remember to "recognize those who labor among you" and "esteem them very highly in love for their work's sake."

Your pastor needs your loving support today.

[19] Thom S. Rainer, "5 Main Reasons So Many Pastors Struggle With Depression," in *The Christian Post*, March 10, 2018, at https://www.christianpost.com/voice/5-main-reasons-so-many-pastors-struggle-with-depression.html

Not everyone who says to Me, "Lord, Lord," shall enter the kingdom of heaven, but he who does the will of My Father in heaven.

MATTHEW 7:21

What does it mean that Jesus is Lord? When Jerome translated the New Testament into Latin, the word *Lord* was *Dominus*, from which comes several English words, including dominate—and dominoes.

Dominoes? According to tradition, a group of monks loved playing this game, and they often played it during periods of silence when they could only speak the words, "Benedicamus Domino," which means, "Let us bless the Lord." Unable to say anything else, they shouted out this phrase when they won the game.

The Lordship of Christ is not a game, of course. It isn't an optional doctrine or something to be trifled with. The nature of Lordship is a dominate matter, and Christ wants to dominate our lives, to dominate our thinking, to dominate our affections, to dominate our schedules, to dominate our attitudes. Not in aggressive hostility, but in loving wisdom.

Is Christ everything to you? Does anything come before the surpassing greatness of knowing Christ Jesus as your Lord? Is a boyfriend or girlfriend more important to you than Christ? Is a goal or an ambition? Not everyone who says, "Lord, Lord," will enter the kingdom of heaven, but only those who do the will of the Heavenly Father.

Let Him be the dominant force in your life today.

That I may know Him.
PHILIPPIANS 3:10

Why did Paul tell the Philippians that his purpose was to "know" Christ? Had he not met Christ on the road to Damascus long ago? Had he not served Him throughout the years? Why would a seasoned Christian apostle who had introduced multitudes to Christ say that he still needed to know Him?

The Amplified Bible, Classic Edition helps us understand Paul's meaning. It renders this verse: "[For my determined purpose is] that I may know Him [that I may progressively become more deeply and intimately acquainted with Him, perceiving and recognizing and understanding the wonders of His Person more strongly and more clearly]."

We should never get to the point of being satisfied in our relationship with the Lord, for it's a joy to continue our quest to know Him more dearly and love Him more deeply. We meet Christ at the Cross through conversion; but we meet with Him in the prayer closet through conversation, talking to Him in prayer and listening to Him in His Word. As we learn to practice His presence, we keep ourselves in His love and avoid what grieves Him.

Knowing Jesus—there is no better thing.

AUGUST 12
Janitor to President

But not so among you; on the contrary, he who is greatest among you, let him be as the younger, and he who governs as he who serves.

LUKE 22:26

James A. Garfield has a remarkable history. He grew up in an Ohio log cabin—poor and fatherless—a youngster who worked in the fields to help feed his family. Wanting to improve himself, he read and attended school whenever possible. He enrolled in the Western Reserve Eclectic Institute in Hiram, Ohio, where he also worked as a janitor. The once student/janitor ultimately became the school's leading professor, and in 1857, its president. A quarter-century later, he became the twentieth President of the United States. In his teens he gave his heart and life to Jesus Christ—adding teacher and preacher to his resume.

The progress of his life—from poverty to humble service to knowledge to leadership—is a lesson for us. Everyone wants to be a leader in some form or fashion, but serving comes first. Serving others, in fact, is the very essence of leadership. Just as Garfield's leadership was enriched by his years as a farm boy and janitor, so our leadership is strengthened in the humble acts of kindness and care we perform daily.

If you have the opportunity of either serving or leading, and you can only do one—serve!

AUGUST 13
Tending to Our Future

In the day of prosperity be joyful, but in the day of adversity consider:
Surely God has appointed the one as well as the other, so that
man can find out nothing that will come after him.

ECCLESIASTES 7:14

In 1636, a devout Baptist Christian named Roger Williams was exiled from the Massachusetts Bay Colony in New England for views differing with the Puritans. He founded the Colony of Rhode Island and Providence Plantations, so-named by Williams because of what he saw as "God's merciful providence," which he believed guided him there. Providence became the capital of Rhode Island.

Providence is not only a biblical word, it also reflects biblical ideas. The word comes from the Latin word for "foresee or attend to," an appropriate way to think of God's knowledge of the future as He attends to the needs of His people. In the midst of a difficult situation, Williams credited God's providence with leading him to a new location for pursuing Christian religious freedom. It suggests to us the same: Regardless of today's trials, God knows the future and is watching over us, tending to our future, and meeting our needs.

Whatever your need today, trust in the providence of a good and gracious God.

AUGUST 14
Serve With Gladness

Wisdom is with aged men, and with length of days, understanding.
JOB 12:12

When Charles McCoy retired at age 71, he didn't know what to do with the rest of his life. A friend invited him to preach in India, and McCoy accepted against the advice of friends. It led to the most fruitful period of his life. He preached around the world, and his influence penetrated the highest levels of academia and government.

On one occasion, McCoy arrived by ship in Yokohama to find a telegram informing him of his own death! A mistaken report announced he had died and been buried at sea, and the news had been reported in papers and pulpits across New York. Looking out the window of his hotel, McCoy saw crowds of soldiers and army trucks. He saw streets of asphalt. He noticed an ambulance with its siren shrieking. He knew he wasn't in heaven yet, for in heaven there will be no soldiers or ambulances, and the streets will be gold. So Dr. McCoy resumed his schedule, went on traveling and teaching, and kept serving the Lord until age 88, when he finally made it safely to his heavenly home.

Does age bring wisdom? Not necessarily. But it should. As long as we remain on earth, we should be faithful at whatever the Lord gives us to do, serving with humility and gladness.

AUGUST 15
The God Who Speaks

Blessed is the one ... whose delight is in the law of the Lord.
PSALM 1:1-2, NIV

Allan Rex Sandage, noted observational cosmologist, said, "It is my science that drove me to the conclusion that the world is much more complicated than can be explained by science."[20]

As Mark Clark suggests in *The Problem of God*, an honest look at the evidence—the necessity of a first cause, the explanation for marvels such as the human eye, the gaps in the fossil record, the fine-tuning of the universe, and the undeniable moral code permeating the cosmos—would lead an objective thinker to the assumption there is a Creator-God. It rationally follows He would be able to communicate, that He would want to do so, and that He would do so truthfully. The nature of Scripture, then, is that it is breathed out by God and inspired by the Holy Spirit. It deserves to be read, demands to be obeyed, and delights those who seek out its truths.

According to Psalm 1, as we read God's Word and meditate on it day and night, we are as blessed as trees by the river bearing our fruit in season, and whatever we do will prosper. Don't let a day go by in your life without delighting in the Word of God.

[20] Quoted by Mark Clark, *The Problem of God* (Zondervan, 2017), 38.

*And in Your book they all were written, the days fashioned
for me, when as yet there were none of them.*
PSALM 139:16

In 1726, the author of a volume titled *The Primitive Liturgy*
dedicated his book, in part, "to all honest admirers of the Good
Old Days, of their Best and Wisest Forefathers." "The good old
days" is a nostalgic longing for the past. The assumption is that
the future, about which we know nothing, surely will not be as
good as the past, about which we know everything.

Deficient as that reasoning might be, it's hard to talk people
out of their longing for the comfort of the past. But wait—
what if we could have confidence that the future, regardless
of what it holds, could be trusted in every way? That is surely
true for those who look to God. The psalmist tells us that all the
days of our life—past, present, and future—were written in
God's "book" before any of them came to pass. That means we
can trust God with our past, present, and future days. None are
better than others because they are all in the hands of God.

We may not know what the future holds, but we know
Who holds the future.

AUGUST 17
Plateaued or Climbing?

As newborn babes, desire the pure milk of
the word, that you may grow thereby.
1 PETER 2:2

In Central Asia, a warlike tribe employs a certain curse against their enemies. They don't call down fire from heaven or hurl insults or threaten violence. They simply say, "May you stay in one place forever." What a denunciation! Yet if we don't keep growing, that's what happens to us. We reach a certain point in our spiritual life and we just stop thriving. We plateau when we should keep climbing.

The Lord wants us to grow in grace, in knowledge, in love, and in effectiveness. Psalm 92:12 tells us to "grow like a cedar in Lebanon." Paul described the true Church as one building, which, he said, "being fitted together, grows into a holy temple in the Lord" (Ephesians 2:21). Peter commands us to "grow in the grace and knowledge of our Lord and Savior Jesus Christ" (2 Peter 3:18).

Each day we're either growing closer to the Lord or inching further from Him. We are becoming loving or more hardened, more joyful or more depressed, more biblical or more compromised, more patient or more irritable. Which way are you moving?

Don't get stuck in your spiritual life. Desire the pure milk of the Word of God, commit yourself to the study, memorization, and meditation of Scripture—and grow thereby.

AUGUST 18
Gone Upstairs

Having a desire to depart and be with Christ, which is far better.
PHILIPPIANS 1:23

In 1901, Rev. Handley Moule became Bishop of Durham and moved to Auckland Castle, where he and his wife, Harriot, entertained people from all stations of life. One day their daughter, Tesie, passed away. Shortly afterward, Harriot died too. The castle suddenly became a lonely place, but Moule penned a letter to a friend and spoke of the divine comfort "dropt like an anodyne (pain-killer) from the hand of the Physician into my great wound .... I bless Him who is more near and dear to me than ever, in His mercy. My beloved one is not far from me. And I bless the Lord for calling her to go upstairs, and meet Him there, and our Tesie with Him, and for trusting me to meet the solitude here, and to find Him very near in it."[21]

Moule didn't think of his wife and daughter as dead, for they were Christ-followers. In his mind, they had simply gone upstairs to be with Christ and with each other as they waited for him to join them.

The Lord understands our grief, but He doesn't want us to live in chronic loneliness and sorrow. When those we love in Christ are taken home, they aren't far away. They have simply gone upstairs to wait for us. That's a wonderful picture to keep in mind if you're heavy-hearted today.

[21] Quoted by Amy Carmichael in *Gold by Moonlight* (Fort Washington, PA: Christian Literature Crusade, u.d.), 34.

AUGUST 19
A Joyful Life

Without him, who can eat or find enjoyment?
ECCLESIASTES 2:25, NIV

In an episode of the popular animated television program *The Simpsons*, Homer Simpson had the opportunity of asking God—or a god-like figure who represents God—an important question: What is the meaning of life? But just as God opened his mouth to answer, the show's credits began to roll and the viewers never learned the answer.

That seems emblematic of the whole world. So many people are asking the right questions, but somehow the answers keep getting interrupted by the closing credits—things like death. Solomon felt that way in the book of Ecclesiastes, but he kept coming back to one basic truth. Everything in life is meaningless without a personal relationship with God, for only God can impart lasting joy to our hearts.

When we learn to enjoy God, we can learn to enjoy life. As Solomon put it, "So I decided there is nothing better than to enjoy food and drink and to find satisfaction in work. Then I realized that these pleasures are from the hand of God. For who can eat or enjoy anything apart from him?" (Ecclesiastes 2:24-25, NLT) That's the answer we need.

AUGUST 20
Nobody's Perfect

*If we confess our sins, He is faithful and just to forgive us
our sins and to cleanse us from all unrighteousness.*
1 JOHN 1:9

Christian perfection refers to living without sin in this life. Only a very small number of Christians have ever taught this doctrine. There is no biblical support for it and no practical evidence that it is achievable. When one preacher suggested that he had attained Christian perfection, a woman in the congregation turned to her friend and whispered, "I'd like to ask his wife to verify that!"

The apostle John would have agreed with that lady: "If we say that we have no sin, we deceive ourselves, and the truth is not in us" (1 John 1:8). In other words, professing to be sinless is a lie, and lying itself is a sin. And toleration of sin in our life is what provides Satan with a foothold (Ephesians 4:26-27). The apostle John would have had no reason to pen the words of 1 John 1:9 if there was the possibility of us not ever needing to confess our sin. Instead, the testimony of Scripture is that by confession and repentance we can be forgiven and restored to fellowship.

Instead of boasting of perfection, let's boast in the grace of God that leads to forgiveness when we sin.

AUGUST 21
The Wise Doctor

The fear of the Lord is the beginning of wisdom.
PROVERBS 9:10

Alexander Grigolia emigrated to America from Soviet Georgia, earned three doctorates, and started teaching at the University of Pennsylvania. Despite his achievements, he was unfulfilled. One day while getting a shoeshine, he noticed the worker went about his task with joy, and Grigolia asked, "Why are you always so happy?" The bootblack replied, "Jesus. He loves me. He died so God could forgive my badness. He makes me happy." Those words brought Grigolia to the Savior. He later became one of Billy Graham's professors at Wheaton College.[22]

According to the Bible, wisdom transcends intellect and education; it's a mindset that adopts God's view of the meaning and morality of life. It's the skill of living. Without God's wisdom, we're without purpose or direction.

To make the best decisions, speak the best words, and understand situations from the best perspective—ask God for daily wisdom and seek out His Word for His will. The fear of the Lord is the beginning of wisdom, and Jesus alone can make us happy.

[22] Ruth Bell Graham, *Legacy of a Pack Rat* (Nashville: Thomas Nelson Publishers, 1989), 187.

AUGUST 22
Plane Words

Do not fear, for I am with you; do not be afraid, for I am your God. I will strengthen you; I will help you; I will hold on to you with my righteous right hand.
ISAIAH 41:10, CSB

One day when Jim Harvey was traveling by plane to Sacramento, a family of Russian immigrants sat across the aisle. Jim's heart went out to them; they looked anxious. During the flight, Jim stood up in the aisle and extracted his brown leather Bible from the overhead bin. Seeing him, the Russian man did the same. Both men lowered their tray tables and opened their books, and Jim could tell by the way the pages were laid out that the man had a Russian Bible.

Motioning with his hand, Jim took the man's Bible and located Isaiah 41:10. Though he didn't speak Russian, he could find the arrangement of the books and the numbers were the same. The stranger read the words, the anxiety fading from his face, and smiled. It was the promise he needed.[23]

Perhaps it's the verse you need too.

Notice the two "I am" statements and the three "I will" statements. You don't need to be afraid today. The Lord is with you. He will hold on to you with His righteous right hand.

[23] Jim and Val Harvey, *What a Difference a Name Makes* (Bloomington, IN: CrossBooks, 2011), 95-97.

Job

*So it was, when the days of feasting had run their course, that
Job would send and sanctify [his children], and he would rise early
in the morning and offer burnt offerings according to the number
of them all. For Job said, "It may be that my sons have sinned
and cursed God in their hearts." Thus Job did regularly.*

JOB 1:5

There is no end of worrying by parents on behalf of their
children—especially after they have left home and are living
their own adult lives. Parenting never ends. In spite of the
many ways to communicate electronically, parents no longer see
their children daily. Parents want to know how their children
are doing, especially how they are doing spiritually.

The best way for parents to safeguard their children's lives
no matter where they are is by intercessory prayer. The father
and patriarch, Job, maintained a steady practice of intercession
on behalf of his seven sons and three daughters. He offered
sacrifices and prayers for them in case they had stumbled and
sinned against God (Job 1:1-5). Just as Jesus Christ intercedes
for us (Romans 8:34; Hebrews 7:25), fathers and mothers can
intercede for their children.

If you have children and grandchildren, let intercessory
prayer be your lifeline to heaven on their behalf.

AUGUST 24
Spirit-Filled

*It is the Spirit who gives life; the flesh profits nothing. The words
that I speak to you are spirit, and they are life.*

JOHN 6:63

We are being pulled in opposite directions. Our flesh is magnetized to sin. It pulls, draws, and entices us. The Holy Spirit
dwelling inside Christians is magnetized to holiness. While
the war within may leave us exhausted and overwhelmed, this
simple truth can transform our perspective on the tension we
feel: The Holy Spirit has come to set us free.

Sin, although still as enticing as the forbidden fruit Eve ate,
ensnares and enslaves us. A seemingly small sin leaves our souls
constricted and heavy. When we choose sin, we are building a
prison for ourselves.

When we follow the gentle prodding of the Holy Spirit, we
are set free from our prison and sin begins to lose its hold on us.
Only the power of the Holy Spirit can equip us to withstand sin
and can transform us. As we learn to depend on and accept the
Holy Spirit's guidance, we experience the joy of living a Spirit-
filled life.

AUGUST 25
Another Day to Serve Jesus

Light is sweet; how pleasant to see a new day dawning.
ECCLESIASTES 11:7, NLT

Put a finger to your pulse. Are you alive? Then be thankful! God has given you another new day on this earth. You can see the clouds floating in the sky, feel the soft breeze on your face, hear the birds in the trees, smell the roses, and tell someone you love them. Enjoy those blessings, but remember we have things to do! While we are here on earth, we have a mission and a purpose to fulfill for Jesus.

We don't know if we'll be able to do those things tomorrow, for we don't know what tomorrow holds—we might be in heaven. Yes, in many ways, that would be better; but it would mean ceasing our earthly life and service for the Lord. Paul told the Philippians that while he preferred to go on to heaven, he also desired to stay awhile longer on earth to serve them (Philippians 1:23-24).

So we have this day. Don't waste it in sin, depression, self-pity, or laziness. Live it to the fullest "that our God would count you worthy of this calling, and fulfill all the good pleasure of His goodness and the work of faith with power, that the name of our Lord Jesus Christ may be glorified in you, and you in Him, according to the grace of our God and the Lord Jesus Christ" (2 Thessalonians 1:11-12).

AUGUST 26
God Is Bigger

Listen to Me, O house of Jacob, and all the remnant of the house of Israel,
who have been upheld by Me from birth, who have been carried from the
womb: even to your old age, I am He, and even to gray hairs I will carry
you! I have made, and I will bear; even I will carry, and will deliver you.
ISAIAH 46:3-4

One of the most important verses in the Bible for linking the Old and New Testaments is 1 Corinthians 10:11: "Now all these things happened to [Israel] as examples, and they were written for our admonition." The way God cared for Israel tells us He will care for us.

God birthed the nation of Israel and has carried and cared for her and will deliver her at the end of the age. Nothing Israel has experienced will be more than she is able to bear for those who trust in the Lord. Likewise, God elected believers in Christ and called us to Himself. Nothing can separate us from His love and His divine purpose to conform us to the image of His Son (Romans 8:28-29, 35-39). When we face difficulties in life, we can rest assured they will not be stronger than God's power to deliver and save us.

If you are experiencing tests or trials, remember that God is bigger than them all. Nothing will derail His plans for your eternal destiny.

AUGUST 27
The Importance of Walls

Whoever has no rule over his own spirit is
like a city broken down, without walls.
PROVERBS 25:28

Nehemiah rebuilt the walls of Jerusalem that lay in ruins during Israel's Babylonian captivity. When he heard a report that the gates and walls were in ruins, he wept and called out to God for help (Nehemiah 1:5-11). King Artaxerxes granted permission for Nehemiah to return and rebuild the walls around Jerusalem.

The importance of city walls in the ancient world cannot be overstated. A wall in disrepair could be easily breached; a broken-down wall allowed enemies ready access to a city and its population. King Solomon used walls as a metaphor for a certain part of human behavior. He didn't compare walls to love, joy, peace, or other godly traits. Instead, he said walls around cities are the equivalent of self-control in a person's life. As walls protect a city from harm, so self-control protects people.

Think of all the harm that could have come to an ancient city whose walls were broken down. Now consider the same dangers on a personal level. Self-control, enabled by the Spirit, is part of your spiritual and moral protection (Galatians 5:22-23).

AUGUST 28
Do Miracles Occur?

Immediately the girl arose and walked, for she was twelve years of age. And they were overcome with great amazement.

MARK 5:42

Throughout Scripture we encounter times when God performed supernatural wonders. During His earthly ministry Jesus went about doing miracles, and in Mark 5, He raised a little girl from death to life. Those who disparage the Bible often reject it because of its miracles, whether it's plagues of Exodus, the miracles of Elijah and Elisha, the story of Jonah, or the wonders performed by Christ.

But the rationality of miracles depends on presuppositions. An atheist, by definition, must reject any and every miracle; there can be none, ever. But to those who accept the first four words of the Bible—"In the beginning God"—the miracles of the Bible are intellectually reasonable and philosophically legitimate. If there is a God, by the definition of who He is, there is the potential for the miraculous.

That's a good thing, because unless Christ can raise the dead and give us eternal life, we're in deep trouble. The God of miracles can keep our hearts strong, and the Christ of wonders can keep our eyes looking upward. When we see the power and blessings flowing from supernatural grace, we're like the people in Mark 5; we are overcome with great amazement.

As an old hymn says, we're "filled with His goodness, lost in His love."

Lord, Have Mercy

Blessed are the merciful, for they shall obtain mercy.
MATTHEW 5:7

American Southerners have grown up hearing the phrase, "Lord, have mercy!" It's an expression of amazement or bewilderment in a perilous circumstance. "Lord, we need your help here. Lord, have mercy!" It is not surprising that the expression was common in the Bible Belt as it occurs often in the four Gospels. Two blind men call out to Jesus for mercy in Matthew 20:30-31; a Canaanite woman cries out for mercy in Matthew 15:22; blind Bartimaeus begs for mercy in Mark 10:46-47. The phrase is also the core of one of the most famous liturgical prayers in both the Western and Eastern Church, the *Kyrie eleison*: "Lord, have mercy; Christ, have mercy."

What is mercy? It is compassion and help directed toward the helpless or toward one who is otherwise not deserving of help, but rather of judgment. God has obviously had mercy on undeserving sinners by sending His Son to save us from our sins. But Jesus says something unique about mercy related to people: Those who extend mercy will receive mercy. It's another application of Galatians 6:7: We reap what we sow in life.

Don't fail to extend mercy today wherever you can. Mercy is God-work. It reveals the kindness of God to a needy world.

Be Faithful

Let your light so shine before men, that they may see
your good works and glorify your Father in heaven.
MATTHEW 5:16

The Old Testament story of Joseph is filled with lessons for the child of God, not least of which is the importance of integrity (faithfulness). While a captive in Egypt, Joseph was made the chief steward of Potiphar, an official of the Pharaoh. Potiphar trusted Joseph implicitly: "So [Potiphar] left everything he owned in Joseph's charge; and with [Joseph] there he did not concern himself with anything except the food which he ate" (Genesis 39:6, NASB).

Joseph was the same when Potiphar was absent as when he was present. Potiphar worried about nothing in his household because Joseph was honest and loyal. That is the heart of integrity and faithfulness. Joseph reflected the unchanging nature of God: always the same, always faithful, always loyal to His children (2 Timothy 2:13). As God conforms us to the image of Christ, we should be the same. Jesus said that our character—our works and words—is one way our lives can reveal the person of God to a world not used to such integrity.

Think about your life today. How faithful will you be? How trustworthy and loyal? Let integrity and faithfulness set you apart from this world.

And [Ananias] kept back part of the proceeds, his wife also being aware of it, and brought a certain part and laid it at the apostles' feet.

ACTS 5:2

There are huge canals like the Panama Canal and the Suez Canal. And there are channels that help fuel commerce and trade on a smaller scale: the Erie Canal in New York, the Royal Canal in Ireland, and the Alter Strom in Germany. A canal is a channel that allows movement between two points.

As God's stewards, we are channels of His blessings. Part of God's reason for blessing us is so we might channel His blessings to others. In the early days of the Church in Jerusalem, believers sold their possessions and gave the funds to the apostles to give to the needy. One couple, Ananias and Sapphira, lied about the amount they donated; they held back part of God's blessing out of greed. And their decision cost them their lives. When we fail to channel God's blessings to others, we must examine our motives.

Giving becomes a joy when we realize that what we are giving is not ours but God's. When we open our hands to others, God can fill our hands again.

SEPTEMBER

SEPTEMBER 1
Guard Your Heart

Let the word of Christ dwell in you richly in all wisdom.
COLOSSIANS 3:16

The Wall Street Journal ran an article entitled "One Habit to Make You Happier Today." The writer said, "Repeating a positive phrase, or mantra, to yourself creates new pathways between neurons in your brain, conditioning you to feel calmer and healthier. ... Research shows that thinking of a word or phrase that affirms our values—and repeating it over and over—produces powerful physiological changes .... Mantras can create and strengthen new neural pathways that are positive and not toxic. And that can make our brain much calmer and happier."

For some odd reason, the writer neglected to mention the power of quoting the Bible to oneself. It isn't a mantra we need but manna from heaven. It's not a positive sentence but a promise from God. We don't need clichés; we need Scripture. Colossians 3:16 says, "Let the word of Christ dwell in you richly."

Self-control is a battle that begins in our minds. Our minds as well as our hearts need to be focused on God and His Word. Daily Bible reading and meditation really is the one habit that will make you happier—and holier—every day.

Now the man Moses was very humble, more than
all men who were on the face of the earth.
NUMBERS 12:3

Somewhere along the way, meekness was made a synonym of weakness. Granted, there is a fine line between the words in the semantic range of *meek*: "gentle, soft, submissive, humble, compliant." They sound more weak than strong. Modern Bible versions have taken steps to correct the problem. In the King James Version, "meek" occurs fifteen times; in the New King James Version, it only occurs once in the New Testament. "Humble" is now used in many verses instead of "meek." And humility, biblically speaking, should never be confused with weakness.

For instance, in Numbers 12:3, Moses is described as "very meek" in the King James Version, but in the New King James Version he is "very humble." Would anyone say Moses was weak or compliant? No, but he could easily be seen as humble before God (in spite of occasional outbursts). Indeed, it takes strength to be humble, strength demonstrated by Jesus when He humbled Himself, and "became obedient to the point of death, even the death of the cross" (Philippians 2:8). Paul says we should also be humble (verse 3, NIV).

Arrogance and pride are not strengths but weaknesses. Conversely, humility is a Christ-like strength that should characterize all who follow Him.

SEPTEMBER 3
Our Birth Certificate

And this is the testimony: that God has given us eternal life, and this life is in His Son.
1 JOHN 5:11

For nearly a century, Martha Mossberg celebrated her birthday on August 11. Then she needed her birth certificate for a cruise, and imagine her surprise when she saw the real date of her birth—August 4, 1917. She was a week older than she thought. When she turned 100 in 2017, she celebrated on the right day. Her birth certificate left no doubt.

As Christians, we have a birth certificate. The moment we trust Christ as Savior, our names are recorded in the Lamb's Book of Life, and the whole Word of God becomes a personal birth certificate—our document assuring us of salvation.

The Lord doesn't want His children worrying about whether they are truly His children—whether they have really been born again. When we believe on the Lord Jesus, we are saved. The Lord Jesus rose again so we needn't toss and turn at night worried about our eternal destination. If you have doubts about your salvation, don't depend on your own understanding. Open your birth certificate and read: "This is the testimony: that God has given us eternal life, and this life is in His Son."

SEPTEMBER 4
The Spin of Grace

Nevertheless the Lord your God would not listen to Balaam, but the Lord your God turned the curse into a blessing for you, because the Lord your God loves you.
DEUTERONOMY 23:5

God turns curses into blessings. In His great redeeming purposes for us, He works every situation for the good of those who love Him. This is the spin of grace. God's ways, though mysterious, are marvelous.

In the book of Numbers, the king of Moab hired a pagan soothsayer named Balaam to curse the Israelites. But whenever Balaam tried to utter his curses, only blessing came from his mouth. Centuries later, Nehemiah reminded the exiles who were repopulating Jerusalem of this story, saying, "Our God turned the curse into a blessing" (Nehemiah 13:2).

We need to develop the confidence that while God's plans may be mysterious, they are ultimately for our good. A host of enemies seek to unravel our lives, and the devil finds every opportunity to curse us with problems. Sometimes the circumstances of life seem against us. But through the power of Christ, God moves to redeem all our problems, sooner or later, both in time and eternity. He does it because He loves us.

As Psalm 109:28 says, "Let them curse, but You bless."

Treasure From Heaven

The law of Your mouth is better to me than
thousands of coins of gold and silver.
PSALM 119:72

Not long ago, a Russian cargo plane malfunctioned in mid-air when one of its doors mysteriously opened. The aircraft was carrying more than $370 million worth of platinum, gold, and diamonds, which fell to earth like sparkling raindrops. Russian authorities managed to recover most of the 170 gold bars, but the precious cargo was scattered over a fifteen-mile stretch, so somewhere along the route some fortunate people discovered treasure from heaven.

That's the way we should feel whenever we open our Bibles. Proverbs 3 says, "Happy is the man who finds wisdom, and the man who gains understanding; for her proceeds are better than the profits of silver, and her gain than fine gold. She is more precious than rubies" (verses 13-15).

Just as a woman sorts through her jewelry each morning to decide what to wear—a bracelet, a broach, a necklace, a ring, a watch, a set of earrings—so we should sit down with our Bibles each morning and select a verse to take into the day with us. We might write it on the calendar or on an index card as our "verse for the day." Meditate on that verse all day long, and God's Word "will be a graceful ornament on your head, and chains about your neck" (Proverbs 1:9).

SEPTEMBER 6
The Burden Bearer

Your will be done on earth as it is in heaven.
MATTHEW 6:10

In her memoirs, *Remembering*, Bula Dell Blanchard describes her anguish when her young daughter Darlene battled a serious illness in India. Bula prayed and wept but had no inner peace, only relentless anxiety. One day little Darlene looked up and said, "Must I always be sick?" That sent Darlene into a determined time of prayer. The Lord seemed to ask, "Will you accept My will?" "Yes, Lord," Bula prayed, "Your will be done. Do what you will. Take Darlene or let us keep her."

"What relief!" Bula later wrote. "What release! What a good feeling! The burden was now on the Great Burden Bearer. All on Him. I could smile again. I could talk about our little daughter to callers at the mission bungalow and not cry …. What peace!"

Over time, and with the help of the Christian Medical Center at Vellore, Darlene recovered.

Our burdens are sometimes too heavy to bear, but the Great Burden Bearer says, "Cast your burden on the Lord, and He shall sustain you" (Psalm 55:22). When you can't understand your circumstances, you can still pray, "Yes, Lord. Your will be done."

Who is like the Lord our God, the One who sits enthroned on high, who stoops down to look on the heavens and the earth?
PSALM 113:5-6, NIV

The Bible describes God's throne as shimmering in majesty, established on a foundation of crystal, radiating blinding light, surrounded by rainbows, encircled by angelic worshipers, and humming with omnipotent power.

Yet according to Psalm 113, the King who is eternally established on this glorious throne, stoops over and peers down at His heavens and earth. His eye misses nothing. He knows the flight and fall of the smallest sparrow. He counts your heartbeats, knows when you are sighing or singing, and He knows every anxious thought.

He stoops over to help us, reaching an invisible finger into the very situations that most distress us. He stoops over to heal us, giving us comfort in conflict and strength in weakness. He stoops over to protect us, keeping us safe from the evil one. He bends over to forgive us, for He knows our frame and remembers that we are but dust.

If He were a Comforter but not a King, His presence would be appreciated but powerless. If He were a King but not a Comforter, He would be a fearsome authority that would leave us terrified and without hope.

But your King sits enthroned on high, yet He stoops down to look at you and to share your concerns. Hallelujah!

Broken-Down Altars

He repaired the altar of the Lord that was broken down.
1 KINGS 18:30

In the story of Elijah on Mount Carmel in 1 Kings 18, it seems someone had once built an altar to God on Mount Carmel, but it had crumbled with time. Elijah repaired it, prayed earnestly, and God answered with fire.

Has an altar in your life crumbled? You once knew the Lord. You once walked with Him. You once lived for Him. You once loved Him. But your spiritual life has deteriorated. In our Western world, there was once a greater fear of God than now. We once walked with Him, but the spiritual vitality of our culture has crumbled, and the altars have broken down. We need to repair the broken-down altars. First Kings 18:31-32 says: "Elijah took twelve stones, one for each of the tribes descended from Jacob .... With the stones he built an altar in the name of the Lord" (NIV).

We can do that too, through confession and commitment. We can say, "Lord, this area of my life has broken down. But I confess it to You and I rededicate myself to live for You with all my heart. I am coming back to You full force."

To alter things, let's repair the altars; that the fire of God will fall fresh upon us.

SEPTEMBER 9
The Most Important Thing

Keeping the commandments of God is what matters.
1 CORINTHIANS 7:19

The Early Church was birthed in a Gentile, pagan world. Many new Christians suddenly found themselves in unique situations: slaves and slaveholders became Christians; new Christians found themselves married to a non-Christian spouse. Besides those personal situations, the culture itself was stressful, dominated by the heavy hand of Rome. Finally, the Church lived with the expectation of Christ's Second Coming. What were new Christians to do?

Paul said, "Nothing—stay where you are." There is no command in Scripture to be married or single, to be a slave or to be free. So remaining single, as Paul himself was (1 Corinthians 7:7), was completely acceptable. In light of a troubled world (1 Corinthians 7:26) and the hope of the returning Christ (1 Corinthians 7:29), Paul gave no new commands except this: Keep the commandments of God; live a holy and righteous life; be content in the place to which God has called you.

Whether you are single or married as you serve Christ in anticipation of His return is not as important as serving Him faithfully—being a witness to Him in this world.

How to Learn Obedience

Though He was a Son, yet He learned obedience
by the things which He suffered.
HEBREWS 5:8

A child learns nothing of obedience when his parent instructs him, "Take the cookies and eat them." But when the parent says, "Do not eat the cookies before supper"—oh, the suffering begins! Obedience is only learned through the things we suffer. What suffering? The suffering of resisting temptation; the suffering of not gratifying our desires; the suffering of doing another's will instead of our own.

One of the most amazing descriptions of the humanity of Jesus Christ as Son of Man regards how He learned obedience: "by the things which He suffered." As a human man, Jesus was tempted the same way we are, though He never yielded to those temptations (Hebrews 2:18; 4:15). His ultimate suffering came as He fulfilled the Father's will for His life by dying for the sins of the world. He lived His entire life in service to God's will (John 4:34; 5:19, 30; 6:38; 7:28-29). Like Jesus, our love and loyalty to God is proved when our obedience is tested.

The next time you suffer, look first to see if your obedience is being tested. Then, like Jesus, submit your will to God's.

For if these things are yours and abound,
you will be neither barren nor unfruitful.
2 PETER 1:8

Aldous Huxley, the twentieth-century British author, said, "There is only one corner of the universe you can be certain of improving, and that's your own self."

What area of your life do you want to improve? Just take a moment and think about that. In what area would you most like to grow? With God's help, you can improve your one corner of the universe. What it really takes is the power of God in our lives, and there is a passage of Scripture on this very subject.

The apostle Peter wrote, "His divine power has given us everything we need for a godly life through our knowledge of him who called us by his own glory and goodness …. For this very reason, make every effort to add to your faith goodness … knowledge … self-control … perseverance … godliness … mutual affection … love. For if you possess these qualities in increasing measure, they will keep you from being ineffective and unproductive" (2 Peter 1:3-8, NIV).

God will do His part ("His divine power has given us"), but we must also do our part and "make every effort." Find an area of your life to improve, and start right now.

SEPTEMBER 12
The Midnight Ride

I would rather be a doorkeeper in the house of my
God than dwell in the tents of wickedness.
PSALM 84:10

On April 26, 1777, Sybil Ludington, 16, learned the British were about to attack Danbury. Her father, Colonel Henry Ludington, had a militia of 400 men, but they were on furlough and needed to be alerted. Sybil jumped on her horse, tore out through the pouring rain, and raced from village to village assembling the soldiers. At one point, she fought off a bandit. She rode all night, covering forty miles—twice the distance of the ride by Paul Revere. Yet few of us have heard of Sybil Ludington because Henry Wadsworth Longfellow wrote: "Listen, my children, and you shall hear of the midnight ride of Paul Revere."

We owe a lot to all the Revolutionary midnight riders—there were several—but they also show us the uncertainty of fame. Real heroes are often neglected and few are remembered for long. But we have a God who sees every sacrifice, knows every effort, rewards every kindness, and carries every burden. He never forgets the smallest task we do for Him.

Fame isn't all it's cracked up to be, but the steadfast love of the Lord never ceases.

SEPTEMBER 13
What Doest Thou Here?

What are you doing here, Elijah?
1 KINGS 19:13

When Julie Wayner was twelve, her parents came to her and her siblings, explaining they needed to move to Philadelphia for employment reasons. "We would really like you children to pray about this too," they said. In her room, Julia prayed, "Lord Jesus, I know that whatever You show Mom and Dad about Philadelphia will be Your will for me because I'm still young. But I would really like You to show me too." Each morning Julie read the Bible and prayed, and one morning while reading 1 Kings 19 (KJV), she saw verse 13: "And, behold, there came a voice unto him, and said, What doest thou here Elijah?"

Instantly Julie felt God was speaking to her through that verse, telling her He didn't want her to stay where she was. He had plans for her in Philadelphia. "Deep within my heart," she recalls, "God had spoken His will to me and peaceful assurance flooded me throughout. I learned at that moment the assurance of God speaking through the Scriptures and of hearing His voice. From that time on, no important decision was ever made without following this pattern: Circumstances leading, God's Word confirming, and God's peace following."[24]

We can learn a lot from a child like Julie.

---

[24] Julie Wayner, *Love's Gentle Voice* (Marion, IN: The Wesley Press, 1986), 17-18.

SEPTEMBER 14
Use Hite's Pain Cure

Prepare to meet your God.
AMOS 4:12

Robert Sheffey was an American frontier original, a nineteenth-century, circuit-riding Methodist preacher known for being eccentric. He was also far-famed for the power of his prayers and the passion of his soul-winning efforts. It's both amusing and convicting to read stories about his life. On one occasion, for example, his brother said, "Bob, I want you to stop being so peculiar."

"I won't do it, for the Bible says God's people are a peculiar people."

"Yes," said his brother, "but there is no use in being childish!"

"Oh yes, there is, for the Bible says, 'that except ye be converted and become as little children, ye shall not enter the kingdom of God.'"

One day Sheffey saw a wide rock alongside the road, and he wrote the words: "What must I do to be saved?" Later, he passed the place again and noticed a medicine salesman had written beneath his words: "Use Hite's Pain Cure." Dismounting his horse, Sheffey added in even larger letters: "AND PREPARE TO MEET THY GOD!"

In this day and age, it's not a good idea to deface the landscape, but shouldn't we share the childlike, peculiar enthusiasm of the old-time evangelists? They transformed the frontier by compelling people to prepare to meet God. That's a message the world needs now more than ever.

SEPTEMBER 15
Freely Given, Freely Give

Heal the sick, cleanse the lepers, raise the dead, cast out demons. Freely you
have received, freely give.
MATTHEW 10:8

A well-known quip says that you never see a hearse pulling a trailer. That is a modern paraphrase of Paul's words to Timothy in 1 Timothy 6:7: "For we brought nothing into this world, and it is certain we can carry nothing out." That truth is the basis for the Bible's principle of generosity: Everything we have, we have been given. Therefore, we should be a channel, a conduit, of God's grace and gifts to others.

That's what Jesus told His disciples when He sent them out to minister in His Name. Everything they were taking with them—the power to "heal the sick, cleanse the lepers, raise the dead, cast out demons"—had been given to them to give to others—"Freely you have received, [therefore] freely give." That lies at the heart of goodness and generosity in a godly life. Even King David recognized that God was the source of his wealth: "For all things come from You" (1 Chronicles 29:14). Therefore, he gave generously for the building of a temple for God in Jerusalem.

Look for opportunities today to be good, to be generous, to others. Whatever God has done for you, do for others in His Name.

What Is That in Your Hand?

So the Lord said to him, "What is that in your hand?"
EXODUS 4:2

Moses didn't have much—a handful of sheep on the slopes of a blistered mountain. He also had eighty years of memories, some of them sad and regretful. He had some clothes, a family, a wise father-in-law, and a tent in the desert. That's about it. Oh yes, he had a staff.

He'd probably found a broken branch from some sturdy tree, maybe six or seven feet long and reasonably straight. He'd seasoned and smoothed it to become his walking cane; plus it was useful in herding sheep and warding off predators. But it was quite ordinary—just a rod.

On rugged Mount Horeb that day, as Moses argued with the Lord about his inadequacies for the mission being assigned him, God asked a simple question: "What is that in your hand?" It was a broken branch, a piece of dead wood, a rod. But the Lord wanted it, and the Lord touched it, and the Lord used it to baffle the magicians of Egypt, to turn the Nile to blood, to part the waters of the Red Sea, create streams in the desert, and to deliver His people again and again.

What's that in your hand?

Do not avenge yourselves, but rather give place to wrath; for it is written,
"Vengeance is Mine, I will repay," says the Lord.
ROMANS 12:19

Suppose a hit-and-run driver smashes your car, causing thousands of dollars of damage. If it happens too fast to get a license number, you're left with repair costs and the knowledge you could have been killed. What if there's no way to hold the perpetrator accountable? You can stew about it, or you can turn the case over to the Lord.

Romans 12:19 in the NIV, says, "Do not take revenge, my dear friends, but leave room for God's wrath, for it is written: 'It is mine to avenge; I will repay,' says the Lord."

Faulty thinking leads us to feel that injustice on earth is final. But God will ultimately right the wrongs, settle the scores, and square the accounts. Though we can't always claim our legal rights, we can turn the hard cases over to the Lord and leave room for His justice. The Bible tells us our Defender is strong (Proverbs 23:11, NIV) and we have a powerful Advocate (1 John 2:1).

Trust Him with wrongs you cannot right.

SEPTEMBER 18
Sequoia-Sized Grace

The grace of our Lord Jesus Christ be with your spirit. Amen.
PHILEMON 1:25

Grace is just about the biggest word in the Bible, so big it's impossible to get your arms around it. It's like the Giant Sequoia trees in California. Without seeing them with your own eyes, you can't imagine how massive they are. No one has arms that are long enough to encircle them. With some of the trees, fifty people side-by-side could barely get their arms around the gigantic trunks of those colossal trees. Grace, as we see it in the Bible, is an endless forest of Sequoia trees. It's a word with an infinite circumference that includes every blessing, every benefit, and all the bounty that flows from God's hand. From the fullness of His grace He gives us one blessing after another (see John 1:16). We can define grace as:

- God's
- Riches
- Available to
- Christ-Followers
- Every day

Why don't you take some time soon to go hiking in the endless forest of God's Sequoia-sized grace? Open your Bibles and spot His blessings. May the grace of our Lord Jesus Christ be with your spirit today!

He has made everything beautiful in its time. Also He has put eternity in their hearts, except that no one can find out the work that God does from beginning to end.
ECCLESIASTES 3:11

One's vocation often takes the most time and energy—it's how we earn a living, and it hopefully provides satisfaction. But there is another way of looking at vocation: the "covenant of vocation," a phrase popularized by British theologian N. T. Wright. The covenant of vocation is the "task" given to every human being: Reflect the glory of God into the world and the praises of creation back to Him.

The primary difference between the two types of vocation is that one is temporal and the other is eternal. While our earthly vocation can be part of our covenant of vocation—as we work "heartily, as to the Lord and not to men" (Colossians 3:23)—it will inevitably come to a close. But our vocation as image-bearers for God (Genesis 1:26-27) is an eternal one. As we transition to a new heaven and a new earth (Revelation 21:1), we will continue our eternal vocation of glorifying God.

God put eternity in your heart for a reason—to remind you of your eternal purpose of honoring Him.

Those who are wise shall shine like the brightness of the firmament.
DANIEL 12:3

Many city dwellers who visit the countryside comment on how bright the stars are compared to where they live. In reality though, the stars have not gotten brighter. Rather, the darkness surrounding them has gotten darker, making them stand out.

Being a Christian in the world today can be discouraging at times when we look at how dark our surroundings are becoming. But just as stars shine brightest when enveloped by a pitch-black night sky, the light of Christ should be most radiant in our lives when we are surrounded by the darkness of this day and age.

Jesus said, "Let your light so shine before men, that they may see your good works and glorify your Father in heaven" (Matthew 5:16). Christian, do not be disheartened by the increase of evil in the world; it is simply our cue to take center stage and shine with all our might for the glory of our Savior.

The unfolding of your words gives light.
PSALM 119:130, NIV

Okay, you want to begin studying God's Word, but you don't know how to begin. Try the *read* and *mark* method. Find a newer version of the Bible and a pencil. Open to a manageable book, like Matthew, Philippians, or Proverbs. Ask the Lord to speak to you, then read the first paragraph. Look for something to underline, circle, or highlight. Read the next paragraph and do the same. Is there a truth to learn? A promise to claim? A prayer to echo? A command to obey?

If a verse confuses you, put a question mark by it. If it thrills you, use an exclamation mark. If you find a verse to memorize, circle it and spend time working on it, word by word. When you finish a book, go to another.

If you have a study Bible, the notes will help you understand the text. Don't grow discouraged. The more you study, the more you learn; the more you learn, the more you'll want to read—and mark.

SEPTEMBER 22
Thy Father Calleth Thee

For God so loved the world, that he gave his only begotten Son, that whosoever believeth in him should not perish, but have everlasting life.
JOHN 3:16, KJV

The story is told of an aged Quaker named Hartman who had a son in the Army during the 1700s. When he received news that a dreadful battle had taken place, the concerned father went to the scene of the conflict to find his son. The officer in charge said they believed the boy was dead because he had not answered to his name. This did not satisfy the father, and so he set out across the battlefield calling for his beloved son who was dearer to him than life. Night set in and Hartman continued searching by lantern until a gust of wind extinguished the light. In desperation, he began shouting, "John Hartman, thy father calleth thee." Finally, in the dark distance, Hartman heard his boy's voice crying, "Here, father." He then took him in his arms, carried him to headquarters, and nursed him back to health.

God loves us more than life itself; as His beloved Son hung on the cross and died for our sins, He shouted to us in a dark world, "(*your name here*), thy Father calleth thee." Have you cried, "Here, Father"?

The World Is Your Neighborhood

For all the law is fulfilled in one word, even this:
"You shall love your neighbor as yourself."
GALATIANS 5:14

If our English word *neighbor* had stuck to its etymological roots, determining who our neighbor is might have been a bit easier. *Neighbor* is derived from a German word that was a compound made up of words meaning "near" and "dweller, especially a farmer." In other words, in centuries-ago Germany, a *nahgabur* was someone, likely another farmer, whom you knew because he lived near you.

But when Jesus told the story of the Good Samaritan, He established a definition even older than Europe's Middle Ages. Your neighbor is not someone who necessarily lives near you, nor does it have to be someone with whom you are acquainted. According to Jesus in Luke 10:25-37, my neighbor is any person who has a need that I am able to meet. Jesus made the point in His parable that the man the Good Samaritan helped was a stranger—not a near-dweller. Yet the Samaritan assumed the responsibility for doing everything he could to help.

Today we think of neighbors as those who live on our street or in our neighborhood. Yet, using Jesus' definition, we have many more neighbors than those. We need to broaden the boundaries of our neighborhood to include the whole world.

SEPTEMBER 24
Thought Therapy

Be anxious for nothing, but in everything by prayer and supplication,
with thanksgiving, let your requests be made known to God; and
the peace of God, which surpasses all understanding, will
guard your hearts and minds through Christ Jesus.

PHILIPPIANS 4:6-7

It begins with a thought. Peter thought he would drown and looked away from Jesus. Moses thought he was inadequate and looked away from God's calling. The disciples thought the soldiers were more powerful than Jesus and fled into the night. Every one of our actions flows from a thought: conscious or subconscious. Often our thoughts are automatic and reactionary.

It takes effort to examine the thoughts running on repeat in our minds. A thought repeated becomes a belief.

This explains why God's first words to His people time and time again are, "Do not be afraid." He knows our fears and anxious thoughts. He only asks that we bring them to Him and replace them with the truth of His power, love, and wisdom. Although each of us will face challenges and deep loss, God invites us to trust Him. As we do, our anxious thoughts are replaced with His peace. He is with us. He loves us. He is working on our behalf.

The Cost of Compassion

But when he was still a great way off, his father saw him and had
compassion, and ran and fell on his neck and kissed him.
LUKE 15:20

The word *sacrifice* is the costliest word in the biblical lexicon, especially when it comes to the price God paid—allowing His Son to be sacrificed for our sins. Sacrifice means to offer up something of one's own—to relinquish ownership, to give it up for a higher purpose or calling. But there is another word that has a high price attached to it, one that gets less attention than sacrifice.

The cost of compassion, while perhaps not as high as sacrifice, is nonetheless high—as all compassionate people can attest. Take the father of the prodigal son in Jesus' parable, for instance (Luke 15:11-32). When the rebellious son returned home after a period of profligate living, the father welcomed him home with compassion. What price did he pay for his compassion? How about the sleepless nights that he agonized over the fate of his son? Or the forgiveness he extended? Or the large sum of money that the son wasted in riotous living?

Compassion's price is the loss of whatever we could be doing for ourselves instead of spending ourselves on another. Keep your compassion account balanced, ready to spend when needed.

First Line of Defense

[The Bereans] received the word with all readiness, and searched the
Scriptures daily to find out whether these things were so.
ACTS 17:11

For years, Bible teachers and preachers have used the following illustration: The U.S. Treasury uses only one method when training new agents to detect counterfeit currency: Trainees study the appearance of actual currency so long that they can immediately detect a counterfeit when they see it.

Though the illustration makes for good preaching, it is not actually true. But consider the premise generally: The more intimately we know the details of the truth, the more readily we can detect error. Such preparation would apply to theological truth as well. When false doctrines are presented to us, how will we know they are false unless we know what is true? If someone says he knows the date of Christ's Second Coming, we might believe him if we don't know what Jesus said in Mark 13:32. We should be like the Jews in Berea when they heard Paul preach—they studied the Old Testament daily to verify what Paul was preaching about the Messiah.

Make sure your first line of defense against theological error is a thorough knowledge of the truth.

SEPTEMBER 27
Down the Drain

Honor the Lord with your possessions, and
with the firstfruits of all your increase.
PROVERBS 3:9

In 2017, a strange story showed up in European newspapers. Swiss authorities in Geneva launched an investigation about tens of thousands of paper currency—Euros—that had been shredded and flushed down the toilets of several restaurants in Geneva, clogging the pipes. No one knows how or why this occurred, but the police believe someone was trying to depose of large amounts of cash for unknown but illicit reasons. The mystery has yet to be solved.

We can't imagine flushing our money down the toilet, but have you ever heard expressions like, "That's money down the drain" or "It's like throwing good money after bad"?

Many of our purchases and expenditures, if not prayerfully and wisely made, represent money down the drain. But whenever we invest our funds faithfully in our local churches and in the worldwide cause of the Gospel, we are honoring God and He will honor us with blessings untold.

"Honor the Lord with your wealth and with the best part of everything you produce. Then he will fill your barns with grain, and your vats will overflow with good wine" (Proverbs 3:9-10, NLT).

Ambassadors, Not Citizens

For our citizenship is in heaven, from which we also
eagerly wait for the Savior, the Lord Jesus Christ.
PHILIPPIANS 3:20

Diplomats are protected from prosecution and harm while representing their country in another nation. Even a nation's embassy is considered the sovereign territory of the visiting nation. In other words, diplomats are subject to the laws of their own nation, not the laws of the nation to which they have been appointed.

Likewise, Christians should think of themselves as diplomats, or "ambassadors for Christ" (2 Corinthians 5:20) during their stay in this world. While we are subject to the civil laws of the governments under which we live (Romans 13:1-7), we operate under the spiritual laws of our home nation: the kingdom of heaven. We live under Christ's law of love (John 13:34) and the "law of the Spirit of life in Christ Jesus" (Romans 8:2). The "fruit of the Spirit" marks our behavior and "against such there is no law" (Galatians 5:22-23). If you feel constrained to obey the laws of this world, you need to be set free from "the law of sin and death" (Romans 8:2).

We are ambassadors to, not citizens of, this world—and should live accordingly.

Then Nathan said to David, "You are the man!"
2 SAMUEL 12:7

The great theologian and preacher of the Great Awakening in New England, Jonathan Edwards, described what happened in his work, *A Faithful Narrative of the Surprising Work of God in the Conversion of Many Hundred Souls in Northampton* (1736): "Many that came to Town, on one occasion or other, had their Consciences smitten, and awakened, and went home with wounded Hearts."

A guilty conscience in the presence of the holiness of God is not a happy situation for the guilty one. Just the very presence of purity, joy, honesty, and love is enough to cause conviction to arise. Part of the ministry of the Holy Spirit is to convict the world of sin, righteousness, and judgment (John 16:8). It can happen without a word being spoken, or it can happen when God uses a righteous person to confront the sinner—as Nathan the prophet did with King David after he concealed his sin for almost a year. Either way, nothing makes a guilty sinner more miserable than the presence of the righteousness of God.

If you are harboring sin in your heart, you no doubt feel guilty whether you are a Christian or not. The only solution to such misery is to confess that sin to God and receive His forgiveness.

SEPTEMBER 30
Once and for All

And for this reason He is the Mediator of the new covenant, by means of death, for the redemption of the transgressions under the first covenant, that those who are called may receive the promise of the eternal inheritance.

HEBREWS 9:15

Very few things in life are one and done, never needing to be repeated. That has given rise to the complaint people have about life in general: "Life is so *daily*!" Most of what we do today has to be repeated tomorrow and the day after.

And that is true of most spiritual practices as well—except for one. The death of Christ put an end to the offering of sacrifices for sin. That is the main reason the Bible refers to the death and Resurrection of Christ as the institution of a "new covenant," a "better covenant": "He is also Mediator of a better covenant, which was established on better promises" (Hebrews 8:6). What is better about the new covenant? It never has to be repeated. Jesus is "the Lamb of God who takes away the sin of the world" (John 1:29). No sacrifice under the Mosaic Covenant could do that.

Be glad today that your sins are forgiven once and for all through Christ. Nothing can separate you from His love.

OCTOBER

OCTOBER 1
Tell the Truth

Therefore, putting away lying, "Let each of you speak truth with his neighbor," for we are members of one another.
EPHESIANS 4:25

What many Americans remember most about the Rio Olympics in 2016 is the scandal created by swimmer Ryan Lochte and his friends when they lied about getting robbed. That one falsehood cost Lochte his major sponsors, his prime endorsements, millions of dollars of income, and his good name. But Lochte isn't the first to swim in a pool of lies. Because of our sinful nature, lying comes to us as naturally as talking. When faced with damaging or embarrassing situations, we somehow try to invent lies on the spot; then we fabricate more lies to sustain the original ones. Before long, we're in the deep end of the pool of deception.

The best way to prevent lies is to live above reproach and avoid doing anything which we'll be tempted to lie about. If we don't misbehave in the first place, we have less reason to want to lie. But even if we do find ourselves in a situation tempting us to lie, we must not do it. The Bible commands us to speak truthfully to our neighbors—which includes our husband or wife—and to live by a simple maxim: Jesus-followers are truth-tellers.

OCTOBER 2
The Cover Up

Above all, keep loving one another earnestly,
since love covers a multitude of sins.
1 PETER 4:8, ESV

When Peter said "love covers over a multitude of sins," he was quoting Proverbs 10:12 and was using a powerful verb—*to cover*. If you buy a piece of furniture from a junk shop, it might be scratched and unattractive. But put on a fresh coat of paint, and it can look like new. Think of a pasture full of mud holes and weeds. But let a heavy snowfall come, and the whole scene is so bright and beautiful you'll want to take a picture of it. Think of the apostle Paul when they strung him up to flog him. His whole body was a mass of scars and wounds. But give him back his robe so he can cover his body, and all you will notice is the glow of his face.

When you love someone it's as if you see them through a thick pane of frosted glass. You look at them without emphasizing or clearly recognizing their faults and flaws. Love covers a multitude of faults and sins. That doesn't mean we excuse bad behavior or allow others to abuse us. It simply means we lean into forgiveness easily. We tend to be people of grace because we are people whose sins have been covered by the blood of Christ.

Do you need to show grace toward someone today?

*Whatever you do, do it enthusiastically, as something
done for the Lord and not for men.*
COLOSSIANS 3:23, HCSB

Meng Fei was a lowly gym cleaner in China who spent a lot of
time on his knees. During timeouts, he would pounce onto the
basketball court like a cat, sprint to wherever there was sweat
or spit, furiously attack it with rags in both hands, and race
back to his spot like an Olympic runner. His blinding speed
and intense focus took crowds by storm, and some fans enjoyed
watching him more than the game itself. Meng's video clips
went viral, and several NBA teams in America tried to hire
Meng for their games before he found a new vocation working
in a tech company.

Meng Fei is a good example for us all. Whatever we do, we
should do it enthusiastically, with all our hearts. But notice the
last part of the verse: "as something done for the Lord and not
for men." It isn't enough to perform our work with faithfulness
and enthusiasm if we're doing the wrong work, or if we're
doing it for the wrong reason. We will find fulfillment only
when our work is done enthusiastically—and rendered for His
glory.

OCTOBER 4
How Much Is Enough?

He who loves silver will not be satisfied with silver; nor he who loves abundance, with increase. This also is vanity.
ECCLESIASTES 5:10

John D. Rockefeller was America's first billionaire, a goal he attained in the early 1900s. At the peak of his wealth, at age 74, he was worth more than $400 billion in current dollar values. (Today's richest persons have wealth approaching $100 billion.) On one occasion a reporter asked Mr. Rockefeller, "How much money is enough?" He is said to have replied, "Just a little bit more."

King Solomon's wealth made Rockefeller's look small by comparison. Although it's impossible to say exactly, estimates put Solomon's wealth at more than $2 *trillion*. Yes, this is the same man who wrote that money can never satisfy. The love of gold and silver as a source of satisfaction is "vanity," the famous king wrote in Ecclesiastes. That means it is a fruitless pursuit, one that can never bring temporal or eternal contentment or peace. Jesus said that the best treasures are those laid up in heaven rather than on earth—treasures that will last forever (Matthew 6:19-21).

Only heavenly treasures can bring the peace and contentment which we seek.

OCTOBER 5
Befuddled

Righteousness will go before Him, and shall make His footsteps our pathway.
PSALM 85:13

Firefighter Constantinos Filippidis disappeared while skiing on Whiteface Mountain in New York State. When his friends couldn't find him, search crews arrived and combed the Adirondacks. At one point, a helicopter and 140 workers were trying to find him. Six days later Filippidis ended up in California, 2,500 miles away, confused and unable to give answers. He had no idea how he had gotten there, but he said he thought he had suffered a head injury, ridden in a "big rig-style truck," and slept "a lot." He's now reunited with his family and trying to piece together the missing six days of his life.[25]

We hope the best for firefighter Filippidis, but his story reminds us that many people in the world are wandering through life in a daze, befuddled about where they have been and where they are going. They are lost. They are morally confused and in a spiritual stupor.

According to Psalm 85:13, the Lord walks ahead of His people, creating footprints so we can follow in His steps. Putting Jesus Christ first in our lives, living righteously, praying daily, studying His Word, and doing whatever we do for His glory—that's the clear pathway to joy on earth and life in heaven. Because of Christ, we're not befuddled; we're blessed!

[25] Finance.yahoo.com/news/skier-lost-york-no-idea-012303495.html.

The Unlovable Guard

If we love one another, God abides in us, and
His love has been perfected in us.
1 JOHN 4:12

In the mid-1930s, a German Protestant pastor was abducted from his church. Suspected of aiding and abetting Jews, he was thrown into prison without a hearing, a trial, or even a phone call to his family. The prison guard outside his cell hated everyone associated with Jews. He purposefully skipped the pastor's cell when meals were handed out, made him go weeks without a shower, and gave him the most difficult job on the labor gang. The pastor, on the other hand, prayed that he would be able to love this guard with God's love. As the months went by, the pastor smiled at the guard, thanked him for the few meals he did receive, and even got to talk about *agape* love. The guard never said anything; but he heard it all, and one night he cracked a smile. The next day the pastor received two meals and was able to shower for as long as he wanted. Finally, one afternoon the guard personally made the long-awaited call to the pastor's family, and a few months later, he was released.

It is against our human nature to love someone like that prison guard, but through His power God can give us the ability to love the unlovable.

Therefore receive one another, just as Christ also received us.

ROMANS 15:7

A frail old man went to live with his son, daughter-in-law, and grandson. Every night, the family ate dinner together; but because of the old man's shaky hands and blurred vision, he had difficulty eating. Peas would roll off of his spoon, and milk was almost always spilled on the table as he tried to take a drink. His son and daughter-in-law became very frustrated and decided to have him sit at his own table in the corner where they wouldn't have to deal with the mess. Because he had broken a dish or two, they also gave him a wooden bowl to eat out of. One night, the father noticed his son playing with some wood scraps, and he asked him what he was doing. The son answered, "I am making a wooden bowl for you and mommy to eat from when I grow up." The parents were speechless and in tears. From that moment on, the grandfather ate at the table with the rest of the family and somehow, the messes he made never bothered them again.

Impatience can occur when expectations are not met. No one is perfect, and wanting that from someone is frustrating and unproductive. Choose to love people for who they are, as they are. That's how God loves us, and He asks us to do the same for others.

In Him we live and move and have our being.

ACTS 17:28

Eric Metaxas told of Sarah Irving-Stonebraker, who was one of the brightest academics in the atheist community. One day Sarah attended lectures by Peter Singer, an atheist who believes some forms of animal life have more worth than humans. He sees no basis for any intrinsic human dignity. Singer asserted that nature provides no grounds for believing a human being is any more valuable than a snake or snail. Sarah said: "I remember leaving Singer's lectures with a strange intellectual vertigo. I began to realize that the implications of my atheism were incompatible with almost every value I held dear."

Months later, someone challenged Sarah to consider the possibility of the existence of God. Sarah realized if human value and ethics mattered, the question of God's existence was viable. She began reading *Mere Christianity* by C. S. Lewis, and one night, she said, "I knelt in my closet in my apartment and asked Jesus to save me, and to become the Lord of my life."[26]

Imagine! An atheist led to Christ by listening to a fellow atheist and by questioning the implications of her own hollow philosophy. Our faith in God is reasonable, sound, and based on solid logic. It's God who bestows our dignity, for we are made in His image. In Him, we live and move and have our being.

[26] www.christianpost.com/news/saved-by-an-atheist-do-humans-matter-or-not-187709/

When anyone hears the word of the kingdom, and does not understand it,
then the wicked one comes and snatches away what was sown in
his heart. This is he who received seed by the wayside.
MATTHEW 13:19

Humanly speaking, the hope of the human race is stored on the Norwegian island of Spitsbergen about 800 miles from the North Pole. It is the Svalbard Global Seed Vault, an underground storage facility for billions of seeds from millions of crop species from around the world. It is designed to be a source for replanting food crops in the aftermath of a global catastrophe.

Seeds represent the essence of life. Physical life depends on seeds as does the spiritual life. Spiritually, the seed that leads to new birth is the Word of God. This is such an important concept that Jesus' longest parable is spent on the necessity of good soil (hearts) to receive the Word (Matthew 13:1-23). In fact, He suggested this parable was a critical one among all His parables (Mark 4:13).

The Word of God is the source of spiritual life and reproduction. We should preserve and protect it and let it bear fruit in us.

OCTOBER 10
Staying Focused

Do not turn from [the law] to the right hand or to the
left, that you may prosper wherever you go.
JOSHUA 1:7

In the early centuries of the Christian Church, a movement of ascetics developed. These individuals became hermits, living in caves and other isolated places as a way to remove themselves from the impurities of the world and enhance their own holiness. One of the most famous was Symeon the Stylite, who lived atop a stone pillar for 37 years, dying in A.D. 459.

It would be spiritually safe, though thoroughly impractical, for us to retreat to a cave or climb atop a pillar to live. There is much in life to distract us as we journey through this world, but no physical protection can guard the thoughts and intents of the heart. We need a way to keep our priorities, values, and decisions focused only on the will of God for our life. The Bible refers to such choices as obedience—the outworking of the believer's committed faith. When Joshua was heading into the spiritually dangerous pagan land of Canaan, God cautioned him to obey *all* the Word of God, staying focused—turning neither to the right nor to the left.

A daily prayer for obedience is how we keep our eyes focused on Christ. But it's up to us to pray the prayer.

OCTOBER 11
Life Lesson

God resists the proud, but gives grace to the humble.
JAMES 4:6

Few people would dare write a book on the subject of humility—we feel innately disqualified. But one man did write a wonderful book on this subject—the South African pastor Andrew Murray. In all, Murray wrote 240 books and tracts, many of them about holiness. In his mid-fifties, he contracted a strange throat ailment that took him from the pulpit for two years. Many years later, recalling the life lessons of that period, he preached twelve sermons on the topic of humility; they were published when he was nearly eighty.

"There is nothing so divine and heavenly," wrote Murray, "as being the servant and helper of all. The faithful servant, who recognizes his position, finds a real pleasure in supplying the wants of the master or his guests. When we see that humility is something infinitely deeper than contrition, and accept it as our participation in the life of Jesus, we shall begin to learn that it is our true nobility .... When I look back upon my own religious experience, or round upon the Church of Christ in the world, I stand amazed at the thought of how little humility is sought after as the distinguishing feature of the discipleship of Jesus."

It is a reminder to "Do nothing out of selfish ambition or vain conceit. Rather, in humility value others above yourselves" (Philippians 2:3, NIV).

OCTOBER 12
Peculiar

Go your way; behold, I send you out as lambs among wolves.
LUKE 10:3

The history of Christianity is dotted with the unusual. For example, Robert Sheffey (1820-1902) was known as the "Peculiar Preacher." One day he was called to a cabin in the mountains. He had previously tried to win this family to Christ, but without success. As he rode up this time, things were different. One of the family members had been bitten by a rattlesnake, and the family was sobered and fearful. Entering the house, Sheffey sank to his knees and prayed, "O Lord, we do thank thee for rattlesnakes. If it had not been for a rattlesnake they would not have called upon You. Send a rattlesnake to bite Bill, and one to bite John, and send a great big one to bite the old man!"

Before we recoil in horror, we should remember that Sheffey's unorthodox prayers and sermons ushered multitudes of mountaineers into the kingdom of God and earned him the title of the "Peculiar Preacher."

God has given different gifts and personalities to all His children, and it's important that we faithfully use those gifts to serve Him. Wherever He sends us, He goes as well.

We do not look at the things which are seen,
but at the things which are not seen.
2 CORINTHIANS 4:18

Jesus' followers live by invisible realities and are guided by an unseen hand. The rest of the world operates on the basis of physical materials. But Paul said he did not lose heart because his eyes were focused on things unseen. He wrote in 2 Corinthians 4:18, "The things which are seen are temporary, but the things which are not seen are eternal." He said in Colossians 3:2, "Set your mind on things above, not on things on the earth." The writer of Hebrews 11:1 added: "Now faith is the substance of things hoped for, the evidence of things not seen."

In other words, faith is living by unseen realities.

What, then, are these unseen things? God the Father is invisible. God the Son is currently outside our range of vision. God the Holy Spirit lives unseen within us. Heaven is unseen. The angels hovering around us are invisible to our normal vision. The unfolding promises of God regarding the future are fulfillments not yet seen. Yet these unseen realities are more important than all that is visible around us, for what is unseen is eternal.

If you're troubled by the problems you see around you, turn your eyes upon Jesus. Trust His presence and His promises; and begin living by the invisible realities of God.

OCTOBER 14
The Battle Within

*For the flesh lusts against the Spirit, and the Spirit against
the flesh; and these are contrary to one another, so
that you do not do the things that you wish.*
GALATIANS 5:17

A Native American elder told his grandson about two wolves
who live in every heart. One is evil—anger, jealousy, pride—
and the other is good—joy, love, peace, humility. The grandson
asked his grandfather, "Which wolf wins?" The elder replied,
"The one you feed."

While not exactly a biblical illustration, it makes an
important point: There is a battle raging in the heart of the
Christian. As the apostle Paul put it, the flesh wars against the
Spirit and the Spirit against the flesh. Becoming a Christian
does not mean the flesh—our sinful human nature—is
eradicated. Instead, we have been given power by the Spirit to
overcome the flesh and conquer it. But the battle will not cease
until we have been glorified in the presence of Christ in our
new, resurrection body. The more we feed the Spirit by faith in
Christ—by obedience, prayer, Bible study, worship, and holy
living—the weaker the flesh becomes.

Don't be discouraged if you cannot escape the struggle
within. Instead, feed the Spirit! Give the Spirit complete access
and lordship over your life.

OCTOBER 15
All at Once

Behold what manner of love the Father has bestowed on us,
that we should be called children of God!
1 JOHN 3:1

Isaac Newton worked on it in the seventeenth century, then Albert Einstein wrote about it in the early twentieth century: time. Generally, time has three dimensions: past, present, and future. Right now you are in the present. But a few seconds from now, this moment will be in the past. There is a seamless transition at work in our lives as the present retreats to the past and gives way to the future. God exists outside of time; past, present, and future are one to Him. God sees our redemption (past), sanctification (present), and glorification (future) at the same "time."

The Bible speaks of both God's and man's perspective on time. God is both eternal (Deuteronomy 33:27) and infinite (Psalm 147:5). And the apostle John speaks of our past, present, and future with God in 1 John 3:1-2. God has bestowed His love on us (past; verse 1), resulting in our being children of God (present; verse 2). And the future is ahead of us when "we shall be like Him, for we shall see Him as He is" (verse 2).

Praise Him today that His love is all-encompassing. Our past, present, and future are in His hands.

OCTOBER 16
Stirring and Being Stirred

And let us consider one another in order to stir up love and
good works, not forsaking the assembling of ourselves together,
as is the manner of some, but exhorting one another, and
so much the more as you see the Day approaching.
HEBREWS 10:24-25

There are more Americans who claim to be Christians than
those who attend church. The difference represents an obstacle
to the spiritual maturity of the Body of Christ. The writer of
Hebrews draws a distinct connection between the "assembling
of ourselves together" and the love, good works, and encouragement of Christians.

The writer names something we are to do and something
we are not to do. We are to consider how to contribute to one
another's spiritual growth and we are *not* to exempt ourselves
from meeting with the Body of Christ. The connection is
apparent: It is in meeting together for fellowship, instruction,
worship, and service that we "stir up love and good works" and
encourage (exhort) one another. As the end of the age looms,
and the return of Christ draws near, we need all the stirring up
and encouragement we can get.

Are you intimately involved in your church—stirring and
being stirred by fellow believers? If not, prayerfully consider
getting more involved, for it's God's plan for your spiritual
growth.

Patriarchs

Then Joseph sent and called his father Jacob and all his relatives to him, seventy-five people. So Jacob went down to Egypt.

ACTS 7:14-15

We don't often use the word *patriarch* in modern conversation, and it may be to our detriment because of its rich meaning. *Patriarch* is a biblical term, occurring four times in the New Testament. The Greek word behind *patriarch* is made of two words: *patria* ("lineage" or "family") and *archon* ("ruler" or "leader"). Put them together and *patriarch* refers to the head of an extended family—like the patriarchs Abraham, Isaac, and Jacob.

Unlike modern families, ancient families in the biblical era often lived intergenerationally—there might be three or four generations of the extended family living in close proximity. And the patriarch had oversight over them all. When Jacob and his descendants left Canaan to go to Egypt in search of food, there were around seventy-plus people in all (Acts 7:14; see also Genesis 46:27). Regardless of the exact number, it was a large family. Today, whether living in proximity or not, grandfathers can exercise the role of patriarch over their extended family by offering love, encouragement, example, counsel, and provision to all their descendants.

The role of patriarch (and by extension, matriarch) was an honored role in Scripture—and should be today as well.

OCTOBER 18
Invisible Wisdom

The fear of the Lord is the beginning of wisdom, and
the knowledge of the Holy One is understanding.
PROVERBS 9:10

Waking up each morning, we use our eyes to gauge our surroundings. Is it morning? What time is it? Throughout the day, we rely on our sight. When Balaam traveled to the princes of Moab, he was most likely lost in thought or focused on his physical surroundings. He knew God had given him permission to go, but he did not realize the importance of relying on God for the words to speak. The moment God opened Balaam's eyes to see the Angel of the Lord, he realized that God's wisdom was the difference between life and death.

Foolishness starts small. We rely on our own understanding based on what our eyes can see and our past experiences. God is untainted by the past or bias of people. He is omnipresent. When we draw close to God, we draw close to wisdom. This is good news. We can rely on Him and rest in quiet trust, even if we are unsure of what to say or how a situation will unfold.

The Fool's Tongue

The words of a wise man's mouth are gracious,
but the lips of a fool shall swallow him up.
ECCLESIASTES 10:12

Medieval royal courts employed a jester, or fool, to entertain the monarch and courtiers with tricks, jokes, and songs or recitations making fun of those in high position. Because no one took the fool seriously, his words and actions were allowed to slip past the court censors.

In the book of Proverbs, the fool had a moral, not a comic, dimension. The fool is used some 39 times in Proverbs as the opposite of the wise man or woman. Whereas the wise man feared God, the fool did not. Indeed, the fool was the epitome of a person who was "right in his own eyes" (Proverbs 12:15); he was a person who failed to learn from experience. Take speech, for example: Eventually, most people learn that barbs, sarcasm, arguments, put-downs, and distasteful humor are not acceptable. They get the message and change their speech. But a fool does not. The fool continues sowing seeds of speech that produce a harvest of destruction: "the lips of a fool shall swallow him up."

Be wise and gracious in your speech. Don't be consumed by the errors of a foolish tongue.

He who believes in Me, as the Scripture has said,
out of his heart will flow rivers of living water.
JOHN 7:38

God delighted in running His finger across the planet and creating rivers. Four of them watered the Garden of Eden. The Promised Land was watered by the River Jordan, and other rivers provided picturesque settings for many Bible stories, such as the call of Ezekiel by the River Chebar and the founding of the church in Philippi by the riverside in Acts 16:13. This summer, many of us will enjoy the great outdoors alongside a scenic river.

Jesus used the metaphor of rivers to describe how spiritual ministry should flow from our lives. We quench our spiritual thirst by taking a drink of Him (John 7:37), and believing in Him for eternal life (verse 38). That "drink" soon becomes a "river" flowing from our inmost being into a parched world.

This is an image we can visualize. As you move through your day, meeting people and tackling jobs, see the people around you as thirsty ground, and imagine a river of refreshment flowing from you to them. Be a refreshing person today. Let the river of God's Spirit stream through you.

OCTOBER 21
Relentless Pursuit

Be sober, be vigilant; because your adversary the devil walks
about like a roaring lion, seeking whom he may devour.
1 PETER 5:8

In the 1969 comedic Western film, *Butch Cassidy and the Sundance Kid*, the two main characters have committed a robbery and are being pursued by a posse of lawmen. Every time the main characters look over their shoulder, the posse is still there. The robbers repeatedly ask, "Who *are* those guys?"

Relentless pursuit is part of the Christian life. That is, we are constantly being stalked by "[our] adversary the devil." It was the same with David in the Old Testament; he was pursued by King Saul who sought to put David to death. Unlike the film characters, we are not being pursued for a specific sin or action. In fact, it is the opposite: We are on God's side and are relentlessly pursued and attacked by our spiritual enemy, Satan. For that reason, we must "be sober, be vigilant"—we must never let our guard down. We must clothe ourselves daily in the believer's spiritual armor, our only defense against the "fiery darts of the wicked one" (Ephesians 6:10-18).

Be vigilant, but not fearful. In Christ, we have all the defense we need against our spiritual enemy. We are victorious in Christ.

The Blame Game

Let no one say when he is tempted, "I am tempted by God"; for God cannot be tempted by evil, nor does He Himself tempt anyone.
JAMES 1:13

It's a terrible argument: "If God didn't want me to leave my wife and fall in love with (name) and marry her, why did He bring her into my life?" Given the number of complex situations we encounter in life, blaming God for all of them would become a full-time job.

The Bible is clear that God doesn't tempt anyone to sin. If we respond sinfully to any temptation it is our problem, not God's (James 1:13-15). God is a giver of good gifts, not tempting or evil gifts (James 1:16-17). In fact, Solomon warns us that we should be careful about being "rash" with our mouth; about uttering "anything hastily before God" (Ecclesiastes 5:2)—such as, "God, why did You ...?" "Therefore," Solomon writes, "let your words be few" (verse 2). Words of accusation or blame, that is. If you have a question for God about your circumstances, ask Him. Then let His peace guard your heart and mind in Christ (Philippians 4:6-7).

There is no peace in playing the blame game with God.

Life With Purpose

"But let him who glories glory in this, that he understands and knows Me, that I am the Lord, exercising lovingkindness, judgment, and righteousness in the earth. For in these I delight," says the Lord.
JEREMIAH 9:24

When you buy an expensive item that comes with a warranty, the warranty often requires that any service on the item be performed exclusively by an authorized repair center. Why the *authorized* requirement? Because the manufacturer's technicians know the workings of your item better than anyone else.

Just as an inventor knows the best practices to follow to maintain the value and use of the product he or she created, the same is true for us and our Creator. For prolonging our life and living it with the utmost purpose and fulfillment, nothing is more important than being guided and known by our Creator. The world boasts of finding purpose in strength, riches, status, or power (Jeremiah 9:23), but we must agree with the apostle Paul who wrote: "But of Him you are in Christ Jesus, who became for us wisdom from God—and righteousness and sanctification and redemption—that, as it is written, 'He who glories, let him glory in the Lord'" (1 Corinthians 1:30-31; 2 Corinthians 10:17).

Life is lived against the backdrop of eternity, and eternal life is knowing God and Jesus Christ whom He has sent (John 17:3).

Great Is Thy Faithfulness

He who calls you is faithful, who also will do it.
1 THESSALONIANS 5:24

In his book about preaching, Pastor Charles Bugg recalls a day when he didn't feel like giving the sermon. His son had been diagnosed with a critical illness and had suffered radiation treatments and surgeries. Pastor Charles, overcome with fear and fatigue, wasn't sure how he could stand in the pulpit. "I have no energy to preach," he told himself as the congregation opened the service by singing, "Great is Thy Faithfulness, O God our Father. There is no shadow of turning with Thee ...."

"That wasn't a new song," recalls Charles. "That Sunday, however, those familiar words became manna from heaven. I was tired; I was anxious; my faith in God was brittle. If preaching that day depended on my feelings, I could have the benediction and go home. Singing that song, though, was a searing reminder .... I was singing about a God whose faithfulness changes not."[27]

The constancy of God in every situation allays our fears. He who calls us is faithful. He gives us "strength for today and bright hope for tomorrow."

---

[27] Charles B. Bugg, *Preaching and Intimacy* (Macon, GA: Smyth & Helwys, 1999), 26.

*I will lift up my eyes to the hills—from whence comes my help? My help
comes from the Lord, who made heaven and earth.*

PSALM 121:1-2

A vacation in the mountains provides majestic vistas, hiking
trails, high altitudes, and cooler temperatures. The hills also
provide an opportunity of reminding us of Him from whom
comes our help.

To the writers of the Psalms, the mountains were
testimonies of God's durable strength. If you see mountains
outside your window this summer, consider these verses from
Psalms: *Your righteousness is like the great mountains. Before the
mountains were brought forth, or ever You had formed the earth and
the world, even from everlasting to everlasting, You are God. As the
mountains surround Jerusalem, so the Lord surrounds His people
from this time forth and forever. [He] established the mountains by
His strength, being clothed with power. Mountains and all hills, let
them praise the name of the Lord* (Psalm 36:6; 90:2; 125:2; 65:6;
148:9, 13).

Whenever you're outdoors, take time to reflect on the
artistry of God. His handiwork is visible in every pine cone,
lofty crag, winding trail, and wildflower. Lift up your eyes,
notice His workmanship, and sing His praises.

Hard to Imagine

But as it is written: "Eye has not seen, nor ear heard, nor have entered into the heart of man the things which God has prepared for those who love Him."

1 CORINTHIANS 2:9

Moving to a new town or state, going to new schools, working at new jobs—what will it be like? Most of the time, things work out. Once we settle in, our worries subside and we get in the flow.

If moving to a new city is a big transition, what about moving from our earth to a new earth? And what about finding yourself in very difficult circumstances, wondering if things will ever change? That was Israel's experience—under God's judgment. Isaiah the prophet wrote first about judgment (Isaiah 1–39) and second about restoration (Isaiah 40–66). In the second, God promised new heavens and a new earth (65:17; 66:22), telling the Jews it would be hard to even imagine what God has prepared for them (64:4-5). As that theme of blessing unfolded through Jesus the Messiah, the apostle Paul quoted Isaiah's words in 1 Corinthians 2:9—we can't imagine what God has prepared for us.

Living in a new earth will be quite a transition, but it's one with which we can trust God.

Whose Plan?

Instead you ought to say, "If the Lord wills, we shall live and do this or that."
JAMES 4:15

Everybody plans; everybody dreams. Surely that is part of the image of God we bear. After all, the animal kingdom does not plan for, dream about, or consider the future. Only we humans do—a gift of God to use in carrying out our mandate as stewards of His kingdom-creation.

But planning has one caveat in Scripture: Who is the beneficiary of those plans? Proverbs 16:1-9 provides several guidelines for planning. Summed up, they say this: God's plans take precedence over man's. When we plan, we should leave room for God's plans to change ours. James even provided an example to illustrate this principle (James 4:13-17)—businessmen made plans for the future but failed to remember God and are chided for their failure. We ought always to say, "If the Lord wills, we shall live and do this or that." When we plan and dream with God in mind, we will always be content with His changes.

We are not on earth to pursue our own glory or satisfaction, but God's. Pursuing God's best is what turns out best for us.

The Coming One-World Government

All inhabitants of the earth will worship the beast—all
whose names have not been written in the Lamb's book of life,
the Lamb who was slain from the creation of the world.
REVELATION 13:8, NIV

Just before his death, the brilliant physicist, Stephen Hawking, told an interviewer that the technological revolution threatens the well-being of the entire world and demands a global, one-world government. Since civilization began, he claimed, there is a certain aggression hard-wired into our genes, which has enabled humans to survive. But now technology has advanced to such a place that this aggression may destroy us all unless we develop, as he put it, "some form of world government" to keep humanity from annihilating itself.[28]

According to biblical prophecy, the entire world will one day come under the domination of a demonic dictator, called the Beast and the Antichrist. Foreshadowing of that time is seen today. The technological revolution is setting the stage for the fulfillment of all that the Bible predicts.

Followers of Christ have front-row seats to the unfolding history of the world as we await the return of Jesus Christ. As we observe the signs of the times, let's keep our eyes on the Lamb of God. The future belongs to Him, and so do we!

[28] "Left's No. 1 Physicist: 'World Government' Only Way to Save Humankind" in *The Washington Times*, March 9, 2017.

But, beloved, do not forget this one thing, that with the Lord one day is as a thousand years, and a thousand years as one day.

Time management could be an oxymoron—two words that are contradictory. We know what management means: adjusting resources to accomplish a goal. And we know what time is: the progress the earth makes in circling the sun. But let's face it; nobody manages time. We can manage our activities, but we do not manage time—speed it up, slow it down, put it on hold, go back in time, go forward in time.

But God? God doesn't manage time either because time doesn't apply to Him. He is aware of the marking of time on earth, but God Himself is *timeless*. God is eternal: "Even from everlasting to everlasting, You are God" (Psalm 90:2). God is "the Alpha and the Omega, the Beginning and the End, the First and the Last" (Revelation 22:13). So, what does that mean for us? Unlike us, God is never surprised—by anything.

The next time you are surprised by an unforeseen event, remember: God saw it before it happened. He knows what you will need. You can trust Him.

OCTOBER 30
The Trinity

He who promised is faithful.
HEBREWS 10:23

The nineteenth-century Irish clergyman, Robert Traill, once pondered the "He" in Hebrews 10:23. Who did the writer have in mind? God the Father, the Son, or the Holy Spirit?

"It is no great matter," Traill said. "We find that the promises that are the ground of the Christian's faith are the promises of God the Father as the author (Titus 1:2); but we find promises ascribed unto Jesus Christ, and He is the promiser. When He left His people and went out of this world, He left them with an abundance of promises (John 14:3). The promises are also given by the Holy Ghost; He is called the Spirit of promise (Ephesians 1:13)."

All Three Persons of the Godhead work in concerted effort to make and keep every promise in the Bible. God the Father ordains them. Christ purchased them for us with His blood. The Holy Spirit brings them to fruition in our daily experiences.

Broken promises are the source of pain here on earth, but God is changeless. His promises are as sure as His immutable nature; they are tripled in power for they come from Him who is One yet Three.

Finally, all of you be of one mind, having compassion for one another;
love as brothers, be tenderhearted, be courteous.
1 PETER 3:8

Sometimes the origins of words help us understand their meaning. For instance, the Greek word for *compassion* refers to the inward parts of the body (heart, liver, lungs, and so on). A slightly modified version of that word came to be used for the feelings associated with the inward parts. When we have *passion*, it comes from deep within. And when we have *compassion* (in English, *com* + *passion*), it means we "feel with or for" another person.

For instance, when Jesus traveled through the region of Galilee preaching and healing, He saw the condition of the people and "was moved with compassion for them, because they were weary and scattered, like sheep having no shepherd" (Matthew 9:36). Like the high priests before Him, Jesus is able to "have compassion on those who are ignorant and going astray" because of His humanity (Hebrews 5:2). Jesus knew, and knows, what it is like to endure suffering and pain. Compassion is a godly trait—first in Jesus Christ and then in those who follow Him.

Let Christ in you stir your heart to feel passionately and to care for those around you today.

NOVEMBER

NOVEMBER 1
Advice About Advice

For by wise counsel you will wage your own war,
and in a multitude of counselors there is safety.
PROVERBS 24:6

Don't believe everything you read, because many people with
strong opinions are simply wrong. Take John B. Watson, for
example. He was an American psychologist who established the
psychological school of behaviorism. Watson wrote extensively
about child rearing, and his advice was widely practiced in
the 1920s. But today, with the passing of time, his approach
is considered patently wrong. He said: "Never hug and kiss
[children], never let them sit in your lap. If you must, kiss them
once on the forehead when they say good night. Shake hands
with them in the morning." Our Lord's approach was so much
better as He took the little children in His arms, "laid His
hands on them, and blessed them" (Mark 10:16).

The Bible's words are infallible, and Scripture gives us
unfailing advice. As a result, those who love and ponder the
Bible are more apt to give seasoned and sound advice. But no
human being is infallible. So if you need counsel or advice
concerning an issue in your life, ask your friends for counsel—
then measure their words by the Bible itself. As you do so, the
Lord will provide the wisdom you need.

Jehoiachin was eight years old when he became king, and
he reigned in Jerusalem three months and ten days.
2 CHRONICLES 36:9

James A. Baker's influence in Washington was legendary. He could walk in and out of the Oval Office at will. One day while serving as Presidential Chief of Staff, Baker was traveling home in his limousine. He noticed a man walking alone. No reporters were around him. No security. Just a man on an empty street. Baker recognized him as the Chief of Staff of a prior administration.

"There he was alone," Baker said. "No reporters, no security, no adoring public, no trappings of power—just one solitary man alone with his thoughts." That image became a constant reminder to Baker of the fleeting nature of power. "That man had it all," Baker said, "but only for a time."[29]

History is littered with the names of people who rose and fell, who lived and died. But we serve a God whose power will never diminish and whose rule and reign will never end. Our God doesn't rule for three months and ten days. His kingdom is forever.

[29] From James Baker's Address at the 1990 National Prayer Breakfast

NOVEMBER 3
Pants on Fire!

Can a man scoop fire into his lap without his clothes being burned?
PROVERBS 6:27, NIV

Miami lawyer Stephen Gutierrez was defending a client accused of arson. As he made his closing arguments, he made a quick exit as his pants caught fire. The culprit was an e-cigarette battery, which ignited at the worst possible moment. Gutierrez was unharmed, but his client was convicted.

Allowing a bad habit to reside in the pockets of your mind or heart is dangerous, for you never know when it will ignite in shame, harmful consequences, or judgment. The apostle James warns about this twice. James 3:6 says, "The tongue is a fire." When we allow the wrong words to slip into our conversations, it can burn up our testimonies. James later also warns against the selfish accumulation of wealth, saying, "Your gold and silver are corroded, and their corrosion will ... eat your flesh like fire" (James 5:3).

Likewise, Proverbs 6:27 describes sexual immorality as taking fire into our laps, hoping not to be burned. Wrong words, covetousness, and sexual sin—these and other hidden sins—will come back to burn us. If you're tolerating anything in your life that could flare up into sin, confess it to God. Don't let Satan fan temptation into a flame.

Be imitators of God as dear children. And walk in love.
EPHESIANS 5:1-2

Walking is the world's favorite exercise. A global study found that seventy percent of people say walking is their primary form of exercise, followed by running and bicycle riding. Many experts claim that a brisk walk is better than running, but that's a matter of debate.

There's no debate, however, on the exercises Paul recommended for believers in the book of Ephesians. Though we once walked according to the course of the world (Ephesians 2:2), now we are to walk in the good works God has prepared for us (2:10). We must walk worthy of the calling we have received (4:1); no longer walk as the Gentiles (4:17), but walk in love (5:2); walk as children of light (5:8); and "walk circumspectly, not as fools but as wise, redeeming the time, because the days are evil" (5:15-16).

The word *walk* implies a steady forward pace, and the emphasis is on our daily behavior. If two people are walking side-by-side down the street—a Christ-follower and a non-believer—there should be a radical difference in the way they treat others, the values they hold, the goals they pursue, and the way they use their time and resources.

Walking in the Spirit is the Christian's most enjoyable exercise. When you walk out the door today, make sure you are walking in newness of life.

I will open rivers in desolate heights, and
fountains in the midst of the valleys.
ISAIAH 41:18

"The marvelous richness of human experience would lose something of rewarding joy if there were no limitations to overcome," said Helen Keller. "The hilltop hour would not be half so wonderful if there were no dark valleys to traverse."

To travelers enjoying the great outdoors, valleys are a sight to behold. Certain websites suggest the most beautiful valleys in the world. Usually, the list includes the Valley of Geysers, a remarkable three-mile basin in the Russian Far East with ninety pulsating geysers sending plumes of steam into the air like tea kettles.

All of us occasionally end up in our own Valley of Geysers. Valleys are symbols of suffering and shadows. But when we're walking with God, He creates rivers from the heights and fountains in the valleys. Isaiah 41, addressed to people in captivity, assures us that God knows how to refresh us in the valley as well as on the mountaintop. If you're in a valley today, remember, "Though I walk through the valley … I will fear no evil, for You are with me" (Psalm 23:4).

Valleys are great places to enjoy your walk with God.

Do not be conformed to this world, but be transformed
by the renewing of your mind.
ROMANS 12:2

South American newspapers were running stories of a young man in Argentina who decided to transform himself into an elf through plastic surgery. His jaw was broken and reassembled; his chin was reshaped; his ears were cut open and stretched out; his eyes were made cat-like; and he is having four ribs removed to be thinner at the waist. "I have my own beauty ideal and want to achieve it no matter what," he said.

Romans 12:1-2 has a better approach to total transformation: (1) receive the mercy of God available through Christ; (2) offer your body a living sacrifice to Him; (3) refuse to let the world push you into its mold; (4) renew your mind daily with Scripture; (5) trust God to transform you from within; (6) and commit to fulfilling His good and acceptable and perfect will day by day.

When we encounter the holiness of God, we are transformed, not by plastic surgery but by spiritual renewal. True transformation isn't from the outside in, but from the inside out.

You have a few names even in Sardis who have not defiled their garments; and they shall walk with Me in white, for they are worthy.
REVELATION 3:4

In speaking to the church in Sardis in Revelation 3, Jesus said bluntly, "You are dead." Visitors to the church noticed a lot of activity, but in terms of spiritual life and doctrinal truth the congregation was dead in God's sight. But not everyone. There were a few true Spirit-filled believers in the city of Sardis who were commended by Jesus.

It's discouraging to see churches die, church buildings abandoned, and ministries struggling to keep their doors open. It's even worse to see thriving churches that have abandoned the truth of the Gospel. Yet every generation has "a few names"—a handful of faithful servants of God who are committed to following Christ without turning back.

In 1 Kings 19, the prophet Elijah complained he was the only prophet left in Israel, "and they seek to take my life" (verse 14). But the Lord told him, "Yet I have reserved seven thousand in Israel, all whose knees have not bowed to Baal" (verse 18).

Let's be among the few who say, "Though none go with me, still I will follow."

The Lord is my shepherd; I shall not want.
PSALM 23:1

We've all been in situations, perhaps as a parent, where we say, "I don't have time to explain the details, but trust me—I've got it covered. Everything will work out." And sure enough, it does. It's nice to know the details, but even if we don't we can have faith that things will work out.

Psalm 23 is like that. It could consist of one verse if that's all David had chosen to write: "The Lord is my shepherd; I shall not want" (verse 1). That's really all we need to know about God as our divine Shepherd: We shall not want. Or, as the New Living Translation puts it, "The Lord is my shepherd; I have all that I need." Sheep are entirely dependent on their shepherd for guidance, protection, food, and rest—which happen to be the things we need as well. In the rest of Psalm 23, David enumerates how God provides for him and, by extension, for us. If we have a need, we should go to God our Shepherd who has promised to provide all that we need.

It's a challenge to separate our wants from our needs. The longer we live with God our Shepherd, the more we will understand our needs from His divine perspective. And the more we will commit our needs to Him.

The goodness of God endures continually.
PSALM 52:1

We have some examples of things happening continually in our world: the thunderous flow of water over Niagara Falls or Victoria Falls in Africa. Or consider the constant flow of energy from our solar system's Sun, or the continual pull of gravity that keeps us grounded. Some things happen so continuously that we don't think about them; we take them for granted and thus fail to appreciate them.

While the continual action of some things in nature might one day be interrupted, there is one continual reality that will never be—God's goodness: "The goodness of God endures continually." The Hebrew word translated "goodness" in Psalm 52:1 is the foundational word for God's chief attribute in the Old Testament: *hesed*. It is most often translated "lovingkindness" or "mercy," but a more illustrative way of rendering *hesed* is "loyal love." What do you think of when you think of loyalty? In a friend, loyalty means a person who is always faithful, always dependable, always there, and always good. That is a person you count on through thick and thin.

That is how the psalmist describes God when he says, "The [loyal love] of God endures continually." Waterfalls, sunlight, and gravity may end, but God's goodness will not.

NOVEMBER 10
Fear Not

There is no fear in love; but perfect love casts out fear, because fear involves torment. But he who fears has not been made perfect in love.

1 JOHN 4:18

At first, very small children are reluctant to admit to their wrongdoings. At the heart of their reluctance is fear. But in a loving environment a transformation gradually takes place. Children become willing to admit their misdeeds because their confidence in their parents' love for them is unwavering. When love is given and received—when love becomes the unconditional norm—it removes fear from the relationship.

The same is true in our relationship with God. John wrote, "There is no fear in love; but perfect love casts out fear." Fear of what? Fear of punishment, of banishment, of the end of the relationship. But such is never the case with God's unconditional love. His love for us is not based on our good deeds but on His choice. His love is the reflection of His character. Even if we sin, God "is faithful and just to forgive us our sins" (1 John 1:9). God has demonstrated His love for us in Jesus Christ (Romans 5:8). We should never fear being separated from His love by anything (Romans 8:35-39).

Are you secure in God's love? Ask Him to remove all fear from your heart and mind.

Who shall not fear You, O Lord, and glorify Your name? For You alone are holy. For all nations shall come and worship before You, for Your judgments have been manifested.

REVELATION 15:4

As much as modern cultures have tried to assimilate citizens, "identity" is still an issue: race, religion, gender, economics, personality, vocation, education. Humanity has compartmentalized itself now more than ever.

That is not true with God. From the beginning, God's plan has been clear: to bless "all the families of the earth" (Genesis 12:3) without regard to the categories we force people into today. God called Abraham, through his descendants, to be a light to the world. If we are in Christ, then we are Abraham's seed and heirs of God's promises to Abraham without distinction (Galatians 3:28-29). This is what John saw in his vision of heaven—all nations coming before God to worship Him. This had been God's plan from the beginning: to reveal His holiness to all of humanity and offer them an eternity in His presence (Psalm 86:9; Isaiah 45:22-23; Malachi 1:11; Philippians 2:9-11).

Regardless of who you are on earth, the worship of our holy God is your purpose in Christ. Your true identity is found in Him, now and forever.

NOVEMBER 12
Looking for a Friend?

A man who has friends must himself be friendly.
PROVERBS 18:24

One day the noted Bible teacher Henrietta Mears counseled a college student who was battling loneliness. The young woman was beautiful and smart, but she had few friends. Dr. Mears asked her to name the qualities she would like in a friend. The student began listing the traits she longed to find in another person—someone who would accept her, who would not misuse her, who could be counted on, and who would listen to her hopes and dreams. Dr. Mears then said an amazing thing: "Go be that kind of friend to other people, and you will find that is what they will be to you." The young woman left Dr. Mears office radiant, as though she had found the secret to making and keeping friends.[30] She had!

The best way to find a friend is to be one, and this is very old advice. The Bible said years ago, "A man who has friends must show himself friendly." Don't sink into self-pity or assume others are talking about you behind your back. Self-centeredness focuses on our own needs; when we are Christ-centered, we have a way of seeking to meet the needs of others. Try a warm smile and become the kind of friend to others that you want and need for yourself.

[30] Lloyd John Ogilvie, *The Essence of His Presence* (Eugene, OR: Harvest House, 2007), 55.

NOVEMBER 13
Leave It There

Humble yourselves ... casting all your care upon Him.
1 PETER 5:6-7

Charles Tindley lived a remarkable life. Born into slavery in 1851, he taught himself to read so he could read his Bible. He had a special heart for the Lord. After emancipation, he moved to Philadelphia and found a job as a church janitor. Eventually he became the church's pastor. One day a Christian came to him overwhelmed with worry and asking what to do. "Put all your troubles in a sack," said Tindley, "take 'em to the Lord, and leave 'em there." Later, Tindley composed a popular hymn, "Leave It There."

That requires faith, but it also takes humility. First Peter 5:5 says, "God ... gives grace to the humble." Verse 6 says, "Therefore humble yourselves under the mighty hand of God." And verse 7 says, "Casting all your care upon Him."

When we bring our burdens to the Lord and leave them there, we're acknowledging that we cannot solve every problem. We look in humble faith to Him who can do more than we can and who cares for us more than we know.

For the Scripture says, "You shall not muzzle an ox while it treads out the grain," and, "The laborer is worthy of his wages."

1 TIMOTHY 5:18

Next time you pick up your clothes from the dry cleaner, pick up food at the grocery store, or pick up your car from the mechanic, try leaving without paying the bill. You wouldn't do that, of course. But because no one gives you a bill when you attend church, it's easy to forget that those who labor in the ministry must support their families as well—not to mention pay for the expenses of maintaining a building and other ministry endeavors.

From the first century, financial support of those who minister the Gospel has been understood. Jesus told His disciples that "the laborer is worthy of his wages" (Luke 10:7). Paul told the Corinthians that he and his co-laborers had the right to claim financial support even though they gave up that right (1 Corinthians 9:7-14). And he wrote to Timothy that the church leaders in Ephesus were "worthy of [their] wages" (1 Timothy 5:17-18).

Are you a faithful and generous financial supporter of the church you attend? Remember that God's laborers are worthy of their hire.

Having a desire to depart and be with Christ, which is far better.
PHILIPPIANS 1:23

Washington, D.C.'s National Gallery of Art has four paintings by Christian artist Thomas Cole, entitled, "The Voyage of Life." Each of the four panels shows a different stage of life—childhood, youth, manhood, and old age. The last is particularly tranquil: an older person on a boat accompanied by a guardian angel under the dark skies pierced by brilliant sunbeams.

We never know if we'll make it through these stages, for life is uncertain. But Cole understood that for the believer, death wasn't something to be feared but anticipated. While we want to tarry on earth in service to God, the voyage of life inevitably takes us upward into heaven, "which is far better."

Death is certain for all. Denying it does no good; it doesn't change the reality. We must be ready at any moment. Jesus came for one great purpose: "that by his death he might break the power of him who holds the power of death—that is, the devil—and free those who all their lives were held in slavery by their fear of death" (Hebrews 2:14-15, NIV).

How important to know Him as our Savior and Lord! How wonderful to enjoy His presence throughout the voyage of life!

NOVEMBER 16
A Little Human Kindness

Pure and undefiled religion before God and the Father is this:
to visit orphans and widows in their trouble, and to keep
oneself unspotted from the world.
JAMES 1:27

A California newspaper published a picture of a note scribbled by a woman named Wanda. She slid it under the front door of her neighbor, whose name she did not even know. The note said: *Mrs.? Would you consider becoming my friend? I'm 90-years-old—I live alone and all my friends have passed away. I am so lonesome and scared. Please—I pray for someone.* Thankfully the neighbor, Marleen Brooks, found the note and went right over to Wanda's house with cupcakes, and the two formed a wonderful friendship. Furthermore, Marleen has now campaigned on social media to encourage others to be on the lookout for lonely neighbors who may live right next door.

When we express our loneliness to someone, whether written or verbalized, we feel better about our circumstances and it can lead to friendship. It doesn't do any good to internalize all our feelings when we should instead be letting others know of our needs.

On the other hand, some of us simply need to look next door, down the street, and into the nursing homes, hospitals, and retirement communities. People need people, and people who need people often need the Lord.

The Adequacy of Jesus

*Then Peter said, "Silver and gold I do not have, but what I do have I give
you: In the name of Jesus Christ of Nazareth, rise up and walk."*
ACTS 3:6

It is likely true that life presents us with more challenges for
which we feel *inadequate* than for which we feel *adequate*. We
often find ourselves wanting to be part of the solution, but
feel unequal to the task. Needs seem to be unlimited while our
resources and abilities seem limited, but that is only true when
we look at ourselves, and not what we can do with God's help.

In the early days of the Church in Jerusalem, after Christ's
ascension, Peter and John encountered a lame man—"lame
from his mother's womb"—begging outside an entrance to the
temple courts. The man sought money from the two apostles,
but they had none. What could they do? No doubt three years
of experience, watching Jesus heal the sick, flashed through
their minds. So, Peter said, "What I do have I give you: In the
name of Jesus Christ of Nazareth, rise up and walk." And the
man was healed. Even when we have nothing in ourselves to
meet a need, we have Jesus. We are never without the riches of
God's grace, mercy, and power to meet the needs of others.

When you feel weak or inadequate, remember the ade-
quacy of Jesus in all things. When we are weak, He is strong
(2 Corinthians 12:7-10).

NOVEMBER 18
Becoming What We Worship

We all, with unveiled face, beholding as in a mirror the glory
of the Lord, are being transformed into the same image from
glory to glory ... by the Spirit of the Lord.
2 CORINTHIANS 3:18

"When my daughters, Hannah and Nancy, were about two or three years old, I noticed how they reflected my wife and me," wrote Professor G. K. Beale. When they played house, they used the same activities and attitudes they saw in their parents. "God has made humans to reflect Him," wrote Beale, "but if they do not commit themselves to Him, they will not reflect Him but something else in creation .... What people revere, they resemble."[31]

Some people create a god to fit their lifestyle, but this is simply modern-day idolatry. If money is our god, we'll become materialistic. If it's pleasure, we'll become hedonistic. If it's ego, we'll be narcissistic. Psalm 135:18 says those who make idols will become like them.

But if we worship the God of the Bible, we'll imitate Him and by the power of the Spirit be transformed into His image, from one degree of glory to another.

[31] G. K. Beale, *We Become What We Worship* (Downers Grove: InterVarsity, 2008), 15-16.

With Gratitude

Stand every morning to thank and praise the Lord, and likewise at evening.
1 CHRONICLES 23:30

At fifteen, Martin Greenfield was seized by Nazi soldiers and sent to Auschwitz, where he was put to work scrubbing Nazi uniforms. When he damaged one of them, he was beaten. "A nice man pulled me aside," he said, "and taught me how to sew and [to make] a simple stitch. It was my first tailoring lesson." Martin was eventually liberated by American soldiers, though his family perished. Immigrating to the United States, Martin became a tailor. Today he's known as the best suit-maker in America, and among his customers are presidents of the United States. The primary attitude in Greenfield's life is thanksgiving. "Everything I am or will ever be I owe to God and the sailors, soldiers, airmen and Marines of the US Armed Forces who fought and died to liberate me .... I am overwhelmed with gratitude."[32]

Our Lord Jesus came to liberate us from sin, death, and hell. He equips us to serve Him and uses us to bless others. He clothes us with righteousness. Everything we are or ever will be, we owe to Him. Let's be overwhelmed with gratitude and say "Thank You" to Him every day.

[32] nypost.com/2014/11/10/thank-you-us-vets-a-survivors-story-of-gratitude/

I will bless the Lord at all times.
PSALM 34:1

We all have a lot of anxieties and aggravations in life, but "God is our refuge and strength, a very present help in trouble" (Psalm 46:1). We have endless trials and troubles, but our Savior has "overcome the world" (John 16:33). Every day brings uncertainty, but God will never leave us or forsake us (Hebrews 13:5). Tomorrow's events are unknown to us, but our eternal God knows the future as well as He knows the past (Psalm 139:1-4). For every blow, we have a fistful of promises from our Sovereign God—and not one jot or tittle of His Word will pass away (Matthew 5:18).

That's why James 1:2 tells us, "My brethren, count it all joy when you fall into various trials."

In all the moments of life, we should be quick to praise the Lord and to bless Him. When you have a good day, thank God for it. When the day turns dark and troubling, praise the Lord anyway, for His lovingkindness is fresh every morning and His faithfulness endures every night. Let's bless Him every moment today.

For all things come from You, and of Your own we have given You.
1 CHRONICLES 29:14

My is a possessive pronoun, a word we use when we want to express ownership ("that's mine") or status ("it's my turn"). It's not a bad word, but the frequency of its use suggests we use it carelessly.

The truth is, nothing is "mine." "Indeed heaven and the highest heavens belong to the Lord your God, also the earth with all that is in it" (Deuteronomy 10:14). Everything we have has come from God, given to us to use for Him. We are stewards of His creation. And one thing is required of stewards: faithfulness. What does that mean? It means that, as stewards of God, we receive from Him different degrees of provision at different times. If we receive less, it is not because God is running short of funds. It is because His plans and purposes for our work for Him have changed. In times of plenty or times of want, faithfulness is our calling (Philippians 4:10-13).

Are you content today as God's steward—content with what He has entrusted to you? He owns everything and has all you will ever need.

The Certainty of God

He who observes the wind will not sow, and he
who regards the clouds will not reap.
ECCLESIASTES 11:4

When television meteorologists miss a weather prediction, their only consequence is being ribbed by friends. But it's a different story for farmers—their very livelihood depends on being right about the weather.

The primary crop in biblical days was grain—specifically wheat and barley. Those crops were sown and harvested by hand. When it was time to sow grain seeds, a high wind could scatter the seeds before they ever hit the ground, providing patchy coverage in the field. So it was better to sow on a calm day. At harvest time, rain was the enemy. The grain would be cut by hand and lie in the field until it could be bundled and stored. Rain could ruin a harvest laying in the field. A farmer would check the wind and check the clouds and make his best guess as to the approaching weather. A farmer bound by uncertainty would never sow and never reap a harvest.

Life is filled with uncertainty. But that should never keep us from making decisions based on prayer and counsel and trusting God with the outcome. Submit all your uncertainties to the certainty of God's providence.

Martha was distracted with much serving, and she approached
Him and said, "Lord, do You not care that my sister has
left me to serve alone? Therefore tell her to help me."
LUKE 10:40

Why are family functions some of the sweetest times of our lives, but also some of our most stressful? Well, every family has problems, tensions, and dysfunctions, and those challenges don't take breaks for holidays. It requires a lot of energy to care for a crowd, no matter how much we love them. Even the godly Martha became overwrought when Jesus brought His disciples for supper.

Here are two suggestions to keep you from being swept away by the stress of family functions. First, don't be afraid to establish healthy boundaries. Sometimes we need to duck out of the room, escape the mob, let them fend for themselves, and take a nap or enjoy a hot shower. If we're the ones dropping in on others, sometimes it's best to get a hotel room rather than crash in the spare room.

Second, make sure you don't skimp on your devotional time with Christ. Martha needed to take a lesson from Mary's book and sit at Jesus' feet a while—and so do you. We love others best by loving Him more.

A Patient Father

*The Lord is not slack concerning His promise, as some count slackness,
but is longsuffering toward us, not willing that any should
perish but that all should come to repentance.*

2 PETER 3:9

A mom or dad can put a toddler's shoes and socks on, and tie them, in a fraction of the time it takes the little one to do the same things. And a neighborhood walk takes several times longer when a child is allowed to stop and explore bugs, rocks, leaves, and flowers along the way. Loving parents understand what's happening in those moments. Their little one is learning and exploring at his own speed. Patience is the speed of the parent until the learning is done. Patience is an expression of a parent's goodness and love.

That's an imperfect way to think about God's patience with us. He is a perfect Heavenly Father; we are imperfect (still learning) earthly children. God is patient with humanity, believers and unbelievers alike. He knows our weaknesses and is patient with us (Hebrews 4:15). He knows unbelievers' hearts and is longsuffering toward them, "not willing that any should perish" (2 Peter 3:9).

When you feel impatient with yourself or with others, remember God's loving patience with you.

*As you therefore have received Christ Jesus the Lord, so walk in Him,
rooted and built up in Him and established in the faith, as you
have been taught, abounding in it with thanksgiving.*

COLOSSIANS 2:6-7

When a person is "rooted and built up" in Christ, they are secure even when persecution and challenges come their way. Although the pain of hardship is felt and grieved, they see beyond their current circumstances to a God who is strong, loving, and good. Despite the rollercoaster of betrayal by his brothers, and later, by a spiteful woman, Joseph looked to God for protection. He remained rooted in his faith despite and amidst his circumstances.

As our faith roots deepen, we realize, God alone is steadfast and unchanging. The world and its people are constantly shifting, like shadows. As we practice gratitude and communion with God, our eyes are opened to His gifts and goodness. This world is temporary. As the reality of our relationship with God becomes tangible, we trust Him as our shield and fortress. Fear dissipates. God is with us. He will never forsake us. As we orient ourselves to Him, we are equipped for the challenges of today. He welcomes us and gently moves us toward His life, healing, and love.

His brother's name was Jubal. He was the father
of all those who play the harp and flute.
GENESIS 4:21

In their book on worship, Keith and Kristyn Getty suggest we are singing people because God has created us to sing. When we sing we're simply doing what the rest of creation does. Singing comes as naturally to children as breathing, and music seems written into our DNA. It's also written into the Bible. Beginning with Genesis 4:21, we meet musicians and musical instruments; from that point onward, the Bible rings with music.

"We may sound differently," wrote the Gettys, "but each of us has the same vocal apparatus (you, us, Bono, Pavarotti, Sinatra)—breath flowing up from the lungs, vibrating through the vocal cords in our throat, and pushing sound out through the articulators of our mouths, tongues, and lips."

We are not only *created* to sing, we are *commanded* to sing. "Repeatedly and throughout Scripture, we are commanded to be a singing people."[33] There's something about singing to the Lord—whether it's a great old hymn or a modern song of praise—that lifts our spirits and settles our nerves.

Let's all be children of Jubal, and "Sing praises to God, sing praises! Sing praises to our King, sing praises! For God is the King of all the earth" (Psalm 47:6-7).

[33] Keith and Kristyn Getty, *Sing!* (Nashville: B&H, 2017), 2, 14.

NOVEMBER 27
Doctrinal Drift

Therefore we must give the more earnest heed to
the things we have heard, lest we drift away.
HEBREWS 2:1

As a theory, continental drift was first suggested in 1596—the idea that today's continents were originally together, gradually drifting apart. That idea is now discussed under the theory of plate tectonics—the motion of the world's seven major (and other minor) tectonic plates. The movement of those plates is the major cause of earthquakes as we know them today.

Have you ever seen one of earth's tectonic plates move? Probably not, unless you have seen the action of a major earthquake. Plates drift imperceptibly, but the effects of such drifts are all too real. The same is true of doctrinal drift, warned about by the writer of the letter to the Hebrews. He warned his readers about drifting away from the truth by not giving "earnest heed" to doctrine. Such drifts happen slowly, but their effects are eventually seen: lukewarm affections, apathy, disinterest in worship, changes in values and priorities, and a loss of love.

How to prevent doctrinal drift? Bible study, fellowship, prayer, worship, and "earnest heed" to matters of the faith. Send the roots of your faith deeply into Christ to avoid drifting from Him.

And be thankful.

COLOSSIANS 3:15

"Some years ago I bought a house on Gratitude Street," wrote J. Ellsworth Kalas of Asbury Seminary. "I can't say when I made the purchase, because getting this house wasn't like signing a conventional contract .... But of this I am absolutely sure, that I never intend, ever again, to live anywhere else."

It's one thing to celebrate Thanksgiving Day every year. It's another to live on Gratitude Street all the time. People who intentionally count their blessings, express their thanks, and cultivate the quality of finding thanksgiving items in every circumstance—those are the people who live on Gratitude Street. They recognize there's no such thing as Black Friday. There can be no day *after* Thanksgiving because every day *is* Thanksgiving.

Today as you gather with family or friends—or if you're alone—find a few moments to start a thanksgiving list. Jot down something every day for which you're thankful. It costs nothing to improve your property, add rooms to your house, or cultivate your landscaping—when you build your life on Gratitude Street.

NOVEMBER 29
Your Tribe

And when [Barnabas] had found [Saul], he brought him to
Antioch. So it was that for a whole year they assembled
with the church and taught a great many people.

ACTS 11:26

The Internet has expanded the definition of *tribe*. Whereas *tribe* historically had geographical as well as cultural implications, today geography has been superseded by the Internet. Today one can be part of a tribe—an affinity group with cultural, social, or other ties—that is linked digitally rather than constrained geographically. Tribes provide identity, support, education, and social links not available outside the tribe.

In that sense, the Body of Christ is a giant tribe. But to gain the social and spiritual benefits, tribes need to be smaller—a church, family, or other close-knit group. The apostle Paul's tribe was the church at Antioch. They sent him out on his first missionary journey and it was to them he returned. The people in our tribe deserve a shout-out. They miss us, welcome us, encourage us, correct us, and mature us as we grow.

What is your tribe? Let them know how much you appreciate them being there for you. Give them a shout-out soon.

NOVEMBER 30
Happily Wise

Happy is the man who finds wisdom, and the man who gains understanding.
PROVERBS 3:13

In the Old Testament, what did weavers, artists, tentmakers, carpenters, and ship captains—among others—have in common? They all possessed wisdom. More accurately, they possessed *skill*. The Hebrew word for *wisdom* is the word for *skill*. So, as a craftsman built the tabernacle with skill, Proverbs teaches us to build a life with skill.

What is skill (wisdom) in living? Proverbs 9:10 says it begins with "the fear of the Lord." From there, it means living life from God's perspective. Understanding His ways, values, plans, expectations, and methods. Most people spend their life searching for true happiness; the book of Proverbs says that happiness comes from finding wisdom, and wisdom begins with the fear of the Lord. God is eternal; knowing Him means eternal happiness (Psalm 16:11). Only God, His Word, and His counsel will stand forever (Psalm 33:11; Isaiah 40:8). Like the grass and flowers, everything else will fade away.

What is your source of happiness today? Is it temporary or eternal? Find wisdom and happiness in your relationship with God.

DECEMBER

DECEMBER 1
The Measure of Love

But God, who is rich in mercy, because of His great love with which He loved us, even when we were dead in trespasses, made us alive together with Christ.

EPHESIANS 2:4-5

How long is an inch? What is the volume of a quart? America's Founding Fathers gave the responsibility to Congress to establish "standards of weights and measures throughout the United States." President George Washington ordered Thomas Jefferson to create a plan for maintaining uniform standards. And the sixth president, John Quincy Adams, wrote while serving as Secretary of State in 1821, "Weights and measures may be ranked among the necessities of life to every individual of human society." Today, the National Institute of Standards and Technology keeps track of measurements.

But there is one measurement, more important than all the rest, for which the NIST has no standard. And that is how love is measured. We are not left without a standard, though. Jesus said that love is measured by sacrifice, the greatest sacrifice being to lay down one's life for another (John 15:13). It is no surprise that the God who is love sacrificed His own Son so we might be reconciled to Him and have eternal life (1 John 4:8, 16).

Sacrifice is how we know that God loves us, and how we know we truly love others.

Completely Saved

Therefore He is also able to save to the uttermost those who come to God through Him, since He always lives to make intercession for them.
HEBREWS 7:25

Have you heard this expression: "She is *really* pregnant; she could deliver at any moment!" How about this: "After his bath, my little boy ran out the back door *completely* naked!" We know what is meant, but in each example adverbs like *really* and *completely* are unnecessary. A woman is either pregnant or not; a child is either naked or not. There is no in-between.

So then, why does Hebrews 7:25 say that Christ is able to save *completely* (or "to the uttermost") those who trust in Him? Aren't we either saved or not saved? Yes, but the author used a Greek word that is imprecise in meaning. *Completely* could mean "in every way" or "forever"—or both. And most likely, the meaning is both—similar to Paul's words in Romans 8:1: "There is therefore now no condemnation to those who are in Christ Jesus"—no condemnation of *any kind*, at *any time*. We are saved from everything, forever, in Christ.

If you ever wonder about the extent of your salvation in Christ—don't. You are saved completely, to the uttermost, forever.

He Who Understands

You know my sitting down and my rising up;
you understand my thought afar off.
PSALM 139:2

The famous prayer usually associated with Saint Francis of Assisi begins, "Lord, make me an instrument of your peace"— thus often called the Peace Prayer. It is a prayer that asks for things that are counterintuitive to natural human impulses, such as, "O Master, let me not seek as much to be consoled as to console, to be understood as to understand." Consoling and understanding (instead of being consoled and understood) are not natural to us.

Most teenagers say, "You just don't understand!" to their parents at least once. And that may be true—parents are long past their own misunderstood teenage years. Yet even as adults we wonder if anyone really understands us. Saint Francis' prayer seems to be modeled after the life of Christ, for surely He was one who came to serve rather than to be served, to console and understand rather than being consoled and understood (Mark 10:45). Indeed, the Bible tells us that Christ understands our life experiences since He endured every human emotion we do (Hebrews 4:15).

When you think no one understands, turn to Jesus in prayer (Hebrews 4:16). Not only will He hear, He will understand.

DECEMBER 4
The Gift of Music

And so it was, whenever the spirit from God was upon Saul, that David would take a harp and play it with his hand. Then Saul would become refreshed and well, and the distressing spirit would depart from him.

1 SAMUEL 16:23

It's a natural instinct—singing to calm a fussy infant. Yes, there's usually rocking and bouncing involved, so maybe it's not just the singing. But most parents don't rock or walk with a fussy infant in silence. There's just something about gentle singing that seems to help.

And not just with infants. Very few people, after a tiring and stressful day at work, come home and turn on hard rock or heavy metal music. But they will turn on something soothing, uplifting, or encouraging. Given the amount of music that apparently fills the halls of heaven (Revelation 5:9-10, 13; 14:1-3; 15:3-4), it should be no surprise that we, made in the image of God, respond so positively to edifying music. Such music certainly helped King Saul when he was distraught. David playing on the harp soothed Saul's soul when nothing else would.

We are so surrounded by music via various media that we can easily forget the power of edifying music. Remember to incorporate beautiful music into your daily routines.

And seven times shall pass over you, till you know that the Most High rules in the kingdom of men, and gives it to whomever He chooses.

DANIEL 4:25

Most leaders of nations don't have dreams of ruling the whole world—perhaps Adolf Hitler was a modern exception. But they often speak and act as if they are sovereign rulers of at least their own domains. In other words, the temptation to think of one as sovereign is always present. And not just for world leaders. We can view ourselves as sovereign over the nation of our own life if we aren't careful.

An ancient ruler, Nebuchadnezzar, king of Babylon, had designs to rule the part of the world to which he had access. It fell to Daniel the prophet to remind him this wasn't true. God sent Nebuchadnezzar a dream showing the destruction of his kingdom and seven years of insanity and exile that awaited him until he learned that God rules in the kingdom of men and assigns human rule to whomever He wants. Fortunately, Nebuchadnezzar learned his lesson and humbled himself before the sovereignty of God.

Let God be the sovereign over your life. He exalts those who allow Him to be God over all (James 4:6).

DECEMBER 6
Never Alone

To this end I also labor, striving according to
[Christ's] working which works in me mightily.
COLOSSIANS 1:29

As children, we hated having to go places alone without the
security of a parent—like walking into a new school building
alone on the first day of school. Little has changed. As adults
we still fear being alone—in times of trouble or crisis or
discouragement, when facing responsibilities and challenges
that only we can undertake. God noticed the unnatural state of
aloneness shortly after creating Adam (Genesis 2:18).

There's another way that little has changed: the presence
of Christ with those who follow and serve Him. Before His
death, Resurrection, and ascension, Christ was always with His
disciples. He taught them, modeled life for them, and trained
them. After His ascension, His *physical* presence changed but
not His *spiritual* presence. By the presence of His Spirit, He
was with them as much as He had been. Paul gave testimony to
this fact more than once (Galatians 2:20; Colossians 1:29). Jesus
promised He would be with His disciples (Matthew 28:20) and
He was (Mark 16:20).

If you are Christ's, He is with you in every situation of your
life. You never have to go anywhere or do anything alone.

DECEMBER 7
Just a Prayer Away

And there is no creature hidden from His sight, but all things are naked and open to the eyes of Him to whom we must give account.
HEBREWS 4:13

An idea that we now take for granted used to be the stuff of science fiction. Technology now allows us to track the movements of cars, phones, and people with digital devices. We can pull up maps to that effect on our computer screens. This is not actually omniscience since there are limits.

True omniscience is one of God's attributes; because He is love, His exhaustive knowledge is used for our benefit. The psalmist, David, wrote eloquently about God's all-knowing awareness of his life (Psalm 139:2-11). The phrase "misery loves company" comes to mind: When we are suffering, the knowledge that God knows about our pain is comforting. He is with us (Hebrews 13:5) and, even before we tell or ask Him, He knows what we need (Matthew 6:8). Whether in good times or bad, God is with us, never more than a prayer away.

Are you standing on troubled ground today? Be assured that you do not stand alone. God is with you 'til the end of the age (Matthew 28:20).

DECEMBER 8
Closer Than a Brother

A man who has friends must himself be friendly, but there is a friend who sticks closer than a brother.

PROVERBS 18:24

The burgeoning world of social media has redefined the notion of friend—on one platform in particular. When that platform debuted in 2004, early users raced to accumulate as many friends as possible; high numbers were a status symbol. Then people realized most of their friends weren't friends at all and they started "unfriending" (the word entered the dictionary in 2009). This process raised a good question which continues today: What is a true friend?

The Bible talks about friendship. Abraham and God were friends (Isaiah 41:8; James 2:23). Jonathan and David were friends (1 Samuel 18:1)—they were friends that were closer to one another than to their own brothers (Proverbs 18:24). These friendships imply something deeper than a blood connection—intimacy, love, and loyalty. The ultimate expression of such friendship was expressed by Jesus when He declared His disciples to be His friends for whom He was prepared to die (John 15:13-15). Jesus extends His hand (His life) of friendship to all who will accept His invitation.

Jesus has declared His friendship for us—His intimacy, love, and loyalty. It is up to us to do the same for Him. Friendship is a two-way relationship.

DECEMBER 9
Godly Mothers

*Charm is deceitful and beauty is passing, but a woman
who fears the Lord, she shall be praised.*
PROVERBS 31:30

As a teenager, Elizabeth Tilley traveled with her parents to
the New World from Plymouth, England, in September 1620,
aboard the *Mayflower*. One of her fellow passengers, John
Howland, fell overboard but was miraculously rescued. Shortly
after their arrival, the two were married. They had ten children
and 88 grandchildren, providing a rich legacy of *Mayflower*
descendants. Among the number: Franklin D. Roosevelt,
George H. W. Bush, George W. Bush, Sarah Palin, Ralph
Waldo Emerson, Henry Wadsworth Longfellow, Humphrey
Bogart, and Phillips Brooks, the author of "O Little Town of
Bethlehem."

Elizabeth outlived her husband by fourteen years, and she
was an extraordinarily active mother and grandmother, always
busy cooking, sewing, cleaning, gardening, and caring for loved
ones. If you visit her gravestone, you'll see it inscribed with
these words: "It is my will and charge to all my children that
they walk in fear of the Lord, and in love and peace towards
each other."

Mothers who do their work enthusiastically for the Lord
leave a legacy that shapes history.

DECEMBER 10
The Perfect Gift

Thanks be to God for His indescribable gift!
2 CORINTHIANS 9:15

A few people have finished their holiday shopping, but most of us are being swept away by the stress of completing our list. Christmas shopping can leave us frazzled—and for some head over heels in debt. Perhaps these four facts will help you.

(1) No one wants you to go into debt for them. Think of how terrible your loved ones would feel if they knew it took months for you to pay off your credit card after buying gifts for them.

(2) Thoughtfulness is better than expensive. A good book, a homemade treat, or a lovely photograph is more personal than the boxes of goods stacked at department stores.

(3) Wrap each gift in prayer. People need prayer more than paraphernalia. Tell them you paused while wrapping their gift to pray for them and their needs.

(4) There's only one perfect gift. The world's first Christmas gift was its best—a Baby wrapped in swaddling cloths and placed in a manger. If you could spend a million dollars on Christmas this year, you could never do better than that. So, ask God to give you shopping wisdom, and praise Him for the best gift of all.

DECEMBER 11
A Bag of Cement

Today, if you will hear His voice, do not harden your hearts.
HEBREWS 3:7-8

A certain man was driving down a bumpy country road when he spotted a bag of cement that had apparently fallen out of the back of a truck. Not wishing to see a perfectly good bag of cement go to waste, he stopped to pick it up believing he could get some use out of it. But when he reached down to pick up the bag, it was surprisingly heavier than he expected due to the fact that it had solidified into an immovable piece of cement. The bag of cement was created to be used for a specific purpose, but because it never reached its intended destination, it became a useless rock.

Just like that bag of cement, many people appear to be useable on the outside; but when God tries to draw near to them, they have hardened their hearts to His love and purpose.

Fortunately for us, it is never too late to listen to the voice of God. If you have made no room in your life for Almighty God and you wish to have a relationship with Him, pray and ask Him to soften your heart through His saving grace. You will then become a person with a purpose and a destination.

Because they do not change, therefore they do not fear God.
PSALM 55:19

We often grumble about change. We don't like the new songs at church, the new exits on the freeways, the new shows on television, or the new prices at Starbucks. President Woodrow Wilson once lamented, "If you want to make enemies, try to change something." Some changes aren't for the better, but nothing improves without some change, and being flexible is the best way to keep from being bent out of shape. That said, the hardest change is the kind we determine to make in our own lives.

Let's suppose we could look at ourselves from the outside in. Pretend you were a total stranger and you spent a day with yourself, just objectively observing you. What changes would the "objective you" suggest to the "real you"?

Every once in a while, we have to take a look at ourselves and say, "I'm not going to live like this anymore. I'm going to change."

We can be our own change agents as we find an area of life needing improvement and start on it at once.

Your Heart Is His Priority

Keep your heart with all diligence, for out of it spring the issues of life.
PROVERBS 4:23

Pulitzer Prize-winning American writer Ernest Hemingway lived an eclectic life that was reflected as a reporter in war-torn Europe and other locations around the world. During his life, depression besieged Hemingway, and that, along with heavy drinking and many near-death accidents, took a toll on him. Seeking a cure for his state of mind, he was unsuccessfully treated with electric shock therapy. In the end, Hemingway took his own life in 1961. In the foreword of his book *A Moveable Feast* that was published after he died, Hemingway stated that he was trying to write his memoir from storage places of his memory and heart, though, he said, one had been tampered with and the other no longer existed.

Life is often harder than any of us expected. It tries to beat us up and tear us down. The devil looks for places to get a foothold in our hearts—especially if we become discouraged. We must keep our hearts with all diligence, and that means putting Jesus Christ first, trusting every word He speaks, and leaning on Him with every care.

Make knowing Christ your highest priority, the object of your praise, and the pursuit of your life. He will never fail you, and His strength will bear you through the anxious moments in life. His priority is to watch over you.

DECEMBER 14
He Is God

Know that the Lord, He is God.
PSALM 100:3

Those words—*Know that the Lord, He is God*—are what separates Christian optimism from the rest of the body of literature about positive thinking. There's a wide array of material about optimism and positive thinking. Books, magazines, seminars, courses, workshops, and websites. But positive thinking is worthless unless it's grounded in God's theology. It's nothing but cotton candy and vaporous thoughts without this truth—the Lord, He is God.

On the other hand, the existence and perpetual reign of the Lord Himself as God of the universe is sufficient to fuel anyone's optimism. Those words—*the Lord, He is God*—is the answer to every problem, the solution to every heartache, and the remedy for every perplexity we ever face.

The Lord, He is God. He is on His throne. He is in control. He is our God, and nothing can withstand Him. God is the sovereign ruler of the earth to whom everyone will give an account. He wants us to make a joyful shout to Him, to serve Him with gladness, and to come before Him with singing. That's something we can be positive about.

The Lord reigns; let the earth be glad!

DECEMBER 15
Awkward Gifts

Every good gift and perfect gift is from above,
and comes down from the Father of lights.
JAMES 1:17

The Wall Street Journal once ran an article on the awkwardness of exchanging gifts in the office or among business associates. "As if it's not hard enough to buy gifts for the family," said the paper, "consider having to get a colleague something that doesn't break the bank but seems thoughtful at the same time." The newspaper described one boss who gave his secretary a beautiful set of candles he found packed away in his home closet. Unfortunately, it was the same set she had given him the Christmas before, and the hurt feelings haven't quite healed yet.

God's gifts are never awkward, inappropriate, or thoughtless. He puts infinite care into His blessings, and every gift is good and perfect. John 1:16 says that from the fullness of His grace, we have all received one blessing after another. Psalm 68:19 says, "Blessed be the Lord, who daily loads us with benefits."

God's greatest gift is Jesus Himself, and it's up to us to receive or decline this blessing. As we give and receive gifts this Christmas, the theme of our hearts should be: "Thanks be to God for His indescribable gift!" (2 Corinthians 9:15)

Then Joseph, being aroused from sleep, did as the angel of the Lord commanded him and took to him his wife [Mary].

MATTHEW 1:24

When one's spouse does something that seems wrong or out of the ordinary, it takes faith to love anyway, to love unconditionally. It takes faith to say, "I'm going to assume the best; I'm going to wait to discuss this until the right time; I'm going to give my spouse the benefit of the doubt." Loving unconditionally means seeking the best for another person even when feelings might dictate otherwise.

Think about Joseph of Nazareth and the difficult situation he found himself in when he discovered his beloved Mary was pregnant—before they were married. His first inclination was to do what was best for Mary which meant ending their relationship privately to avoid any public shame or embarrassment for Mary and her family. Then, when he discovered the reason for Mary's pregnancy, he stood by her completely during her pregnancy and after. Joseph stood by Mary in every way, even when he didn't understand completely.

Love "bears all things, believes all things, hopes all things, endures all things" (1 Corinthians 13:7).

*Behold, there was a man in Jerusalem whose name was Simeon,
and this man was just and devout, waiting for the Consolation
of Israel, and the Holy Spirit was upon him.*

LUKE 2:25

Among the wondrous lessons of the Christmas story is this
one: We don't have to be famous, great, wealthy, talented,
experienced, or an extrovert to serve the Lord. The "stars" of
the Nativity story are unknowns—a young laboring couple
from Nazareth, an unknown resident of Bethlehem who loaned
them a stable, a handful of smelly shepherds, a devout fellow
named Simeon, and an aged widow named Anna.

They were ordinary enough to be used by God.

When we see this, it helps us overcome our fears of being
unqualified to serve the Lord. It isn't highly trained specialists
the Lord needs most, but devout people who, like Simeon,
are faithful to the house of the Lord and who wait for God
to work. Remember what Paul said: Not many great people
are chosen. Not many wise or noble or famous. It's the simple,
humble, ordinary people that God most often uses so that the
glory will be His alone.

Let's all be sons of Simeon—just and devout, touched by
the Holy Spirit, and available at a moment's notice.

Now by this we know that we know Him, if we keep His commandments.
1 JOHN 2:3

A time-honored saying warns us that "a chain is only as strong as its weakest link." There were more than 600 legal links in the chain of the Old Testament law—so many that no one could keep them all. It took the death of an innocent animal to remove the guilt of those who failed to keep the law. The apostle James clarified in the New Testament what was implied in the Old: To break one of God's laws made a person guilty of breaking them all.

The yoke of the law weighed heavily on the minds of the Jews. Besides the laws given through Moses, the religious leaders added hundreds more traditions that made the yoke even heavier and harder to bear (Mark 7:1-5). But when Jesus came, He announced a different kind of yoke, one that is "easy and … light" (Matthew 11:30). It is not a yoke free from law, but a yoke that is easy to bear since we are given the Holy Spirit to help us glorify God and offered forgiveness when we don't. Christmas is a time to celebrate the fact that Christ has come to show us how to keep God's laws.

The weakest link for us is our sinful human nature. But when we accept the Christ of Christmas, we are given His nature—a nature that wants to keep God's law.

DECEMBER 19
A Shepherd's Faith

As it is written, "The just shall live by faith."
ROMANS 1:17

A man lost in the desert was near death for lack of water. Soon he came across a pump with a canteen hung on the handle along with a note. The note read: "Below you is all the fresh water you could ever need, and the canteen contains exactly enough water to prime the pump."

For a lot of us, it would be difficult to believe the note and empty the entire contents of the canteen for the promise of unlimited water. Such an act would require tremendous faith. The Bethlehem shepherds exhibited this kind of faith when they were told of the birth of Jesus. If they had not trusted God's guidance to the manger, they might have missed meeting and worshiping the Savior of the world!

Thankfully, when we are asked by God to step out in faith, we are not putting our trust in a note that may or may not be trustworthy. Instead, we are following the directives of the Lord who "is a shield to all who trust in Him" (2 Samuel 22:31).

The next time God asks you to trust Him, remember the shepherds; for theirs is an amazing example of how we should exercise our faith.

And when [the Magi] had come into the house ... they presented
gifts to Him: gold, frankincense, and myrrh.
MATTHEW 2:11

Frankincense is a clear, yellowish resin obtained from certain trees grown in northern India and the Arabian Peninsula, treasured for its aroma and healing properties (Exodus 30:34). Myrrh is a spice that was valued as a medicine and cosmetic (Mark 15:23). And gold is gold, the most valuable commodity in human history. These were the three gifts presented by the Magi to the baby Jesus in Bethlehem.

The Magi's gifts were valuable, indeed. But the impression given by Scripture is that the Magi could afford the gifts they brought. They were scholars, perhaps astronomers, likely in the upper echelons of their own society. It would be a mistake to assume that only gifts of extreme value are appropriate to give to God. To the contrary, the Bible commends those who gave out of their poverty—like the poor widow who gave two small coins, "her whole livelihood" (Mark 12:44), and the Corinthians who gave out of their "deep poverty" (2 Corinthians 8:2). It is not the size of the gift, but the size of the heart, that matters most.

The next time you give to God, look first at what's in your heart before counting what's in your hand.

And behold, an angel of the Lord stood before [the shepherds], and the glory of the Lord shone around them, and they were greatly afraid.

LUKE 2:9

A gospel group called The Williams Brothers had a hit with their song, "I'm Just a Nobody." It was about a down-and-out man who lived on the streets and spent his days telling people about Jesus. He was laughed at and harassed by passersby, but that didn't stop him. The chorus of the song was his life message: "I'm just a nobody trying to tell everybody about Somebody who can save anybody."

The shepherds in the fields outside Bethlehem might have felt the same way when the angels from heaven appeared to them: "Why did God choose us, a bunch of nobodies, to be the first to hear of the birth of the Messiah in Bethlehem?" They were just a bunch of nobodies who probably later told everybody about the Somebody in Bethlehem who could save anybody. Why did God reveal Himself to shepherds instead of to important royal officials? Perhaps to signal the kind of King who was coming into the world: gentle and humble, a Servant-Shepherd who came to tend to God's flock.

If you sometimes feel like a nobody, rejoice! God seems to gravitate to the nobodies of this world when He wants them to meet Somebody who can save everybody.

DECEMBER 22
Songs of the Season

Praise the Lord! For it is good to sing praises to our God;
for it is pleasant, and praise is beautiful.
PSALM 147:1

If anything characterizes the Christmas season, it is music—especially George Frideric Handel's *Messiah*. But in addition to formal choral presentations, there are the traditional Christmas hymns sung by choirs in churches and by carolers in neighborhoods.

How did Christmas become the season of glorious songs? Besides the fact that music is woven into the fabric of the Old Testament, beginning with the song of celebration following the exodus from Egypt (Exodus 15), the first Christmas was marked by psalm-singing and songs. Mary said what is now called the Magnificat when she visited Elizabeth (Luke 1:46-56), and Zacharias lifted his voice in praise when his son John (the Baptist) was born (Luke 1:67-79). And when Jesus' parents presented Him in the temple, Simeon spoke a song of praise (Luke 2:29-32). All of these songs are crowned by the glorious words the angels declared to the shepherds (Luke 2:13-14).

This Christmas season, don't fail to lift your voice in song as you praise God for the indescribable gift of His Son, Jesus Christ.

Before the mountains were brought forth, or ever You had formed the earth and the world, even from everlasting to everlasting, You are God.

PSALM 90:2

If you stretched a 2,700-mile-long piece of string from the East Coast to the West Coast, that would represent eternity. Then if you went to Kansas and put a pencil dot on the mid-point of the string, that would represent time as we know it on earth. Then if you went up to the Space Station and looked down on the string with the little dot in the middle, you'd see time relative to eternity—the way God sees everything at once.

Our little pencil dot is small compared to the "everlasting to everlasting" that God sees, yet it's still significant to Him. But because He sees our dot all at once, He sees past, present, and future at the same time. So when God moved the prophets in the Old Testament to tell of the coming Messiah to be born in Bethlehem, the prophets had to wait for it to happen. But God saw the prophecy and its fulfillment all at once. Prophecy is important because it represents a completed event in God's sight. Jesus was born in time, but God saw it in eternity.

Don't ever doubt God's promises and prophecies. Once spoken, they're as good as done.

God With Us

Behold, the virgin shall conceive and bear a Son,
and shall call His name Immanuel.
ISAIAH 7:14

Immanuel consists of two Hebrew words: *im* (the preposition "with" coupled with the plural "us" yielding *immanu*), and *'el* ("God"). *Immanu* + *'el* = "God with us." Perhaps more than any other word in the Bible, *Immanuel* represents the essence of the Christian and Christmas message: God has invaded the domain of man and dwelt among us.

Immanuel was prophesied by Isaiah, and the gospel writer Matthew declared Jesus of Nazareth to be the fulfillment of that prophecy. The apostle John best captured the meaning of Immanuel in John 1:14: "And the Word became flesh and dwelt among us, and we beheld His glory." Sadly, many who celebrate Christmas today have never understood the central point of the season: "God with us." God entered the human race in the person of a baby who was the God-Man, Jesus Christ, Savior of the world. To fail to recognize Immanuel at Christmas is to miss the reason for the season.

Many who acknowledge "God with us" have never said "God with me." Don't let this Christmas pass without making sure God is with you in the person of Jesus Christ in your heart.

Now there were in the same country shepherds living out in the fields,
keeping watch over their flock by night.

LUKE 2:8

Nahum Tate was born into the home of an Irish Puritan pastor
in 1652. After studying at Trinity College, Nahum traveled
to London to become a writer and playwright. It required
hard work, but in 1692 he was named the Poet Laureate of
the United Kingdom. Unfortunately, Nahum wasn't good at
handling money. Always tottering on the verge of bankruptcy,
he died in an institution for debtors in 1715.

Yet Nahum Tate left a rich legacy. While studying the Bible
one Christmas, he crafted Luke 2:8-18 into a poem describing
the story of the shepherds watching over their flocks near
Bethlehem. His poem became a carol you've probably sung this
season:

While shepherds watched their flocks by night / All seated on
the ground, / The angel of the Lord came down, / And glory
shone all around.

Just like Tate, the shepherds were among the poorest of
the land, but what a legacy they left. Our leverage and legacy
doesn't depend on silver or gold or fame or fortune, but on the
joy of passing on the greatest message in history: "For there is
born to you this day in the city of David a Savior, who is Christ
the Lord" (Luke 2:11).

"Behold, the virgin shall be with child, and bear a Son, and they shall call His name Immanuel," which is translated, "God with us."
MATTHEW 1:23

Almost forty years ago, a well-known credit card company popularized their slogan: "Don't leave home without it." The company wanted consumers never to be without their credit card. Today, without a slogan, the smartphone has become the indispensable extension of human life and activity. Most people rarely (never?) leave home without their phone. And yet even the phone is not immune to forgetfulness or to being lost. It is possible to go through a day without our phone.

Unlike credit cards, phones, and other modern inventions, Jesus is with us *all the time*. Day or night, He is there. So important is His omnipresence that He was given the name *Immanuel*, which means "God with us." The Bible's most thorough illustration of the ever-presence of God is provided by David in Psalm 139:7-16. He was amazed that wherever he went, God was there. God is inescapable! From the womb throughout the days of our lives, God is with us.

Wherever you go today, know that Christ will never leave you nor forsake you (Hebrews 13:5). He is Immanuel—God with *you*.

Amen. Even so, come, Lord Jesus!
REVELATION 22:20

Revelation 22:20 provides us with the final prayer in the Bible. It's an unusual prayer because the "Amen" comes at the beginning, not the end. The word *Amen* means, "May it so be!" It's a prayer for the return of Christ—Come, Lord Jesus!

Have you been praying for the Second Coming of Christ? Often when we ask for prayer requests, we get a long list of people needing healing, help, or salvation—all of which we should pray about. But God has some prayer requests He wants us to offer too, and the final one is for the return of our Lord to this planet.

But what do the words "Even so" mean? It refers to the phrase immediately preceding the prayer, which is a red-letter quotation from Jesus: "He who testifies these things says, 'Surely I am coming quickly.'" The "Amen" is attached to that statement and links it to the prayer, "Even so, come, Lord Jesus!"

"Even so" is a phrase referring back to the adverb "quickly." We're not taught to merely pray that Jesus will come again, but that He will come again quickly, soon, suddenly.

And one day soon, by the grace of God, He is going to do just that. Try offering this prayer right now and put it on your regular prayer list: *Amen. Even so, come, Lord Jesus!*

DECEMBER 28
God's Purpose for Next Year

To everything there is a season, a time for every purpose under heaven.
ECCLESIASTES 3:1

The longest section of Scripture used as lyrics in a popular (secular) song is Ecclesiastes 3:1-8. Folk artist Pete Seeger used those words in the 1950s as the basis for his song "Turn! Turn! Turn!" The song achieved number-one status when it was recorded by the rock group The Byrds in 1965. Typical of the sixties, it was positioned as an anthem for world peace.

The original author of the lyrics, Israel's King Solomon, wrote the words from a different perspective: the vanity of railing against the vicissitudes of life instead of submitting to the sovereign hand of God (Ecclesiastes 12:13-14). There is a time and a season for everything, Solomon wrote with his limited understanding. We read those words today knowing they describe a fallen world in which not all circumstances are good. We don't accept difficulties fatalistically, but we accept them knowing God is with us. He uses even the hard parts of life to show us His love and conform us to Christ (Romans 8:28-29).

Resolve to find God in every moment of 2020, be the moments easy or hard. Look for God's "purpose under heaven" in every part of your path.

Brethren, I do not count myself to have apprehended; but one thing I do, forgetting those things which are behind and reaching forward to those things which are ahead, I press toward the goal for the prize of the upward call of God in Christ Jesus.

PHILIPPIANS 3:13-14

In movies, whenever a hero or heroine is running from danger and looks behind them, we want to warn them, "Don't look back!" Looking back slows them down. When the year we are leaving behind is filled with regret and failure, it is tempting to ruminate on it.

While there is value in learning from the past, there is danger in allowing failures and regrets to become our focus, or worse yet, to define us. Satan would like nothing more than for us to get caught in the past and forget God's power and love.

Peter moved past denying Christ to become the rock of the Church. Joseph surrendered the betrayal and loss of his family to serve God with passion and purpose. Regardless of what the past has held, turn your eyes to God. Trust His redemptive power for a new beginning.

The Lord will guide you continually, and satisfy your soul in drought, and strengthen your bones; you shall be like a watered garden, and like a spring of water, whose waters do not fail.
ISAIAH 58:11

When we're standing at the brink of an obstacle or challenge, it is difficult to remain optimistic. Sometimes it is not the baggage we carry, but the path ahead that stirs up discouragement in our souls. When we are in a desert experience, the new year may not feel like a new beginning at all.

Regardless of what the new year holds for you, God's companionship will never forsake you. In Scripture God sustains His people through the darkest of times: deserts, betrayal, fire, failure, deep waters, loss, and grief.

God is our greatest asset and deepest hope in the new year. He changes situations and the hearts of people in an instant. When we are stuck and afraid, He offers strength. Begin by asking Him how to pray for the new year, and to open your eyes to His endless possibilities.

DECEMBER 31
A New Year's Verse

At the beginning of the year ... the hand of the Lord was upon me.
EZEKIEL 40:1

Whew! How did we make it through the past year with its challenges, heartaches, blessings, opportunities, and distresses? If the old year worried you, don't take your anxieties into the new one. If the holidays exhausted you, pause long enough to thank God for mercies that never cease.

Think of Ezekiel. At the beginning of the year, when Ezekiel was reeling from news that Jerusalem had fallen to the Babylonians, God touched him. The Lord lifted him up and transported him by revelation into the future. Ezekiel saw what God is preparing for days to come, and the prophet was so overwhelmed it required the rest of his book—Ezekiel 40 – 48—to describe the glories he saw.

God's revealed promises will take us through time and into the future. You can trust Him with the coming year, with all the years of life, and with the endless ages of eternity. Here on the eve of a new year, the hand of God is on us.